BIGGER THAN THE GAME

BIGGER THAN THE GAME

BO, BOZ, THE PUNKY QB, AND
HOW THE '80s CREATED THE MODERN ATHLETE

MICHAEL WEINREB

GOTHAM BOOKS

GOTHAM BOOKS
Published by Penguin Group (USA) Inc.
375 Hudson Street, New York, New York 10014, U.S.A.
Penguin Group (Canada), 90 Eglinton Avenue East, Suite 700, Toronto, Ontario M4P 2Y3,
Canada (a division of Pearson Penguin Canada Inc.) • Penguin Books Ltd, 80 Strand, London
WC2R 0RL, England • Penguin Ireland, 25 St Stephen's Green, Dublin 2, Ireland (a division of
Penguin Books Ltd) • Penguin Group (Australia), 250 Camberwell Road, Camberwell, Victoria
3124, Australia (a division of Pearson Australia Group Pty Ltd) • Penguin Books India Pvt Ltd,
11 Community Centre, Panchsheel Park, New Delhi—110 017, India • Penguin Group (NZ), 67
Apollo Drive, Rosedale, North Shore 0632, New Zealand (a division of Pearson New Zealand
Ltd) • Penguin Books (South Africa) (Pty) Ltd, 24 Sturdee Avenue, Rosebank, Johannesburg
2196, South Africa

Penguin Books Ltd, Registered Offices: 80 Strand, London WC2R 0RL, England

Published by Gotham Books, a member of Penguin Group (USA) Inc.

First printing, August 2010
10 9 8 7 6 5 4 3 2 1

Gotham Books and the skyscraper logo are trademarks of Penguin Group (USA) Inc.

LIBRARY OF CONGRESS CATALOGING-IN-PUBLICATION DATA

Weinreb, Michael.
    Bigger than the game : Bo, Boz, the punky QB, and how the '80s created the modern athlete /
by Michael Weinreb.
        p. cm.
    ISBN 978-1-592-40559-6 (hardcover)
    1. Sports—United States—History—20th century. 2. Athletes—United States. 3. Nineteen
eighties. I. Title.
    GV583.W44 2010
    796.0973'09048—dc22   2010002057

Printed in the United States of America
Set in Minion
Designed by Elke Sigal

Contents

Contents

Prologue

"'When the legend becomes fact, print the legend.' Heard that in this Western I saw one time, down at the Keith's."

"What's that mean?"

"Hell, man, I don't know."

—George Pelecanos, The Sweet Forever

He came screaming into the picture from some faraway place, helmet in hand, a mongrel's mane of spikes and curlicues and rattails glistening in the artificial lights of an aged football stadium. He may have been barking; on television, it was difficult to tell. And while it is true that he did not actually belong on this field at that particular moment, it is also true that he did not abide by traditional rules or social mores. His heroes had never been football players: He saw himself more as a modern-day version of Randle McMurphy from *One Flew Over the Cuckoo's Nest,* as an insurrectionist amid the asylum of organized sports. He drove a white Corvette, he wore an extremely large earring, and he had a standing appointment with a hairstylist. He had taken to calling himself The Boz.

New Year's night, 1986: I was thirteen years old, watching the moment unfold on a nineteen-inch RCA television in a family room in State College, Pennsylvania. It was the second quarter of the Orange Bowl, and the winner between Penn State (my hometown team) and Oklahoma would take home the national championship; there was little understanding or concordance between the sides. And here was The Boz, the most dynamic linebacker in college football, looming and smirking on our screen, celebrating a University of Oklahoma touchdown pass (one that would ultimately win them the game) by smothering his quarterback in a bear hug, thereby guaranteeing himself a few extra seconds of screen time while his teammates boogied in the end zone. He was an inscrutable and terrifying figure dressed up in a crimson jersey, the manifestation of a flamboyant and calculating new-age dogma that I did not yet comprehend.

A few years earlier, Penn State's coach, a Brown graduate named Joseph Vincent Paterno, had classified Oklahoma's Barry Switzer, the son of an Arkansas bootlegger, as among the least honorable men in his profession. Paterno had since apologized and walked back from his remarks, but the contrast between their programs remained obvious: Oklahoma's quarterback, a freshman named Jamelle Holieway, carried a Louis Vuitton purse ("my little clutch bag," he called it) and wore a diamond stud and a gold watch and a gold chain, and had a tattoo on his arm that read JAMMIN'. John Shaffer, Penn State's tin-can quarterback, possessed no such adornments; he was so slow and unremarkable that he had once managed to dislodge his shoulder from its socket while leaping up for a high five. A few days before the game, *The New York Times* reported, The Boz—proper name: Brian Kenneth Bosworth—had passed by Shaffer underneath the Orange Bowl stands, wearing a pair of gold chains over his jersey, wearing sunglasses in a steady drizzle. And Shaffer eyed him from head to toe without moving his head, "not unlike the way hard hats once sized up hippies."

All of this raised questions about whether a college football game could somehow mirror a social divide in the 1980s, about whether we were bearing witness, in the Orange Bowl, to a generational schism, about whether The Boz and his embrace of glamour and status on a football field was a sign of the impending breakdown of modern society, about whether Penn State and their prison-issue uniforms and their square quarterback and their seriousness were the last embodiment of a bygone era. "The Penn State players," wrote John Ed Bradley in *The Washington Post*, "carry on as if on some dire, portentous mission of the soul."

This book was born of the curious contrast displayed on my television screen that evening; the stories contained within are no doubt shaped by the visceral experiences of a teenage boy coming of age in central Pennsylvania in 1986. But I would like to think that this is actually a story about how sports shaped and defined the cultural perceptions of a generation of American youth—of all those kids like me who grew up largely within the mythological confines of our own television screens, gawking at strange creatures like The Boz. It is a story that culminates precisely one year and one day later, on January 2, 1987, when Penn State again played for the national championship against a group of rogues and miscreants from the University of Miami. Each of these games was marketed and packaged as a morality play, and yet, as with most morality plays of the era, the personalities I grew up watching on that nineteen-inch RCA were not as nakedly uncomplicated as the imagery often made them out to be. They were a product of the ideals and innovations and evolutionary leaps of the eighties. They were a testament to the power of marketing, to the growing impact of MTV and ESPN and Hollywood, and to the influence of money upon the games we watched. They arose to stardom at the height of a period of conspicuous consumption, at a time when we became smitten, as a culture, with power and status and the accumulation of wealth, at a time when twenty-four-year-old Wall Street brokers and twenty-two-year-old athletes suddenly made millions of dollars, at a time when ambition and self-interest—and the perpetuation of one's own personal legend, and the generation of dissonant alter egos such as The Boz, and the unprecedented melding of sports and entertainment—no longer seemed mutually exclusive from the concept of forming a winning team. It was an overwhelming time to become a superstar in America; the complications were daunting. Mythmaking was a powerful thing. "I got so famous, so quick, I didn't know how to handle it," Bosworth would confess many years later. "I had created a monster."

What follows, then, is an attempt to examine and explore more deeply the myths and legends of a time that has often been rendered in shallow brushstrokes, in a series of pixels and pastels and power chords and regrettable hairstyles and larger-than-life images. Through the course of 1986, the ideals of the decade tilted upon their axis: A spacecraft vaporized on our television screens, a wildly popular president chose to defy the directives of Congress, and several Wall Street brokers affirmed, with both their words and their deeds, that greed had become a virtue in America. It was a year marred by duplicity and scandal and self-involvement, a year of sudden awakenings, a year when hubris and national pride faded to disillusion, a year of beasts slouching from their cages. "Not since the turbulent sixties," wrote *The Washington Post,* "had so many things gone so stunningly awry."

In sports, a series of conflicts arose—partly manufactured, partly real, all of them amplified within a burgeoning media landscape. In Chicago, a young antihero of a quarterback became stubbornly determined to defy the establishment and make a profit at the same time; in Washington, D.C., a college basketball player became so caught up in material concerns that he lost sight of his own mortality; and in rural Alabama, the greatest athlete to emerge in a generation burnished his legend when he refused to conform to society's expectations for him. It was the dawn of an era of outsized appetites and bold statements, of athletes seeking success on their own terms. It was an age that transformed both the games we watch and the way we watched them; it was an age that served as a dividing line between what had been and what would be.

BIGGER THAN THE GAME

CHAPTER ONE

Ronnie and Jim

In the myths of the eighties, he was the greatest mythmaker of all, and the most striking of his myths was his own life. He was a man who emerged from a family background of pain, privation, and humiliation, living on the margin, who went to California and remade himself and his world. . . . Ronald Reagan invented himself. It might even be argued that he invented an age.

—HAYNES JOHNSON, *Sleepwalking Through History*

I.

Everything goes back to a young man fashioning tall tales of athletic glory.

His name was Ronald Wilson Reagan, and he was a member of the Tau Kappa Epsilon fraternity house at Eureka College in Illinois, and sometimes he would entertain his brothers by broadcasting imaginary football games, employing a broomstick as microphone. He was twenty-one when he graduated, a football letterman, president of the Eureka Boosters Club, an economics major with mediocre grades; he immediately indulged a seemingly hopeless fantasy by looking for a job in Chicago, in the fledgling industry known as radio. But this was 1932, and there *were* no jobs, and the young man was laughed out of several studios, until, the story goes, he was told by one kind woman at an NBC affiliate that his best chance for employment lay out in the sticks. So after missing out on a position managing the sporting-goods department at Montgomery Ward, the young man set forth for Iowa, and he knocked on doors and pleaded for work until he landed his first job at WOC, a radio station in Davenport founded by a chiropractor (the call letters, in fact, stood for World of Chiropractic).

The story goes that the program director, a raspy-voiced Scotsman, took a chance on the young man as a football announcer, after he evoked from memory the play-by-play of the fourth quarter of a Eureka game in which a right guard (also, conveniently, the author of said story) had missed a key block on a linebacker. In the revised version, Ronald Reagan leveled the linebacker, sent him reeling, and nearly killed him. The Scotsman, duly impressed by this ad-lib, offered five dollars plus bus fare for a broadcast of the Iowa-Minnesota homecoming game. The young man did so well that they offered him ten dollars to broadcast each of the remaining three games.

The football season ended. The young man moved on. He searched for something more permanent, but there was nothing else to be found. He went back to WOC as a disc jockey, then moved on to its larger sister station, WHO in Des Moines, where he was promoted to do play-by-play for baseball games he could witness only in his own mind. The information came in over a telegraph wire in Morse code, sketchy details of contests played out by the Chicago Cubs and Chicago White Sox several hundred miles from the studio. Through the sheer force of his ingenuity and charisma, he fashioned a narrative. The young man was tall, and his thick brown hair was parted in the middle and combed back in a pompadour; he radiated an unmistakable confidence. His nickname was Dutch.

It didn't matter if the details weren't entirely accurate. It was the story that mattered. The engineer provided the sound effects, cracking a bat on a piece of wood, raising the volume on a phonograph album of crowd noises. The young man's job was to entertain, to reassure, and to paint a portrait almost entirely of his own making. Sometimes he was forced to base the truth upon nothing at all. One day during a Chicago Cubs game, a telegraph operator named Curly handed him a note: *The wire's gone dead.* For nearly seven minutes, Dutch Reagan improvised, describing in thorough and graphic detail a series of pitches that Dizzy Dean of the Cardinals threw to the Cubs' Billy Jurges. Each was a foul ball. One missed being a home run by a mere foot. One was fouled back into the stands, precipitating a fight between two young boys.

Dean fiddled with the resin bag. He shook off pitches. A redheaded child caught another foul ball. Soon the at-bat was nearing record proportions, seven minutes of false delays, and the young man was getting scared. When the telegraph was finally restored, the operator wrote, *Jurges popped out on the first pitch.*

It became a signature Reagan story, one he repeated perhaps more than any other in his lifetime. He would later say that those four years at WHO, immersed in the mythology of American sports, were some of the most pleasant of his entire life.

He was born in 1911, the son of a shoe salesman from Dixon, Illinois, named John Edward "Jack" Reagan, who was also an alcoholic. As a kid, Ronald Reagan escaped into tales of King Arthur and Tarzan, as well as more contemporary stories like *Frank Merriwell at Yale,* about a multitalented college freshman who engages in innocent mischief, creates a champion crew team, and pitches against Harvard on the varsity baseball team. Many of his first heroes were athletes, like the high school football players in his hometown of Dixon, who came to represent the purity of competition. Reagan went on to become his own idealized version of Frank Merriwell: He played football at Eureka, and continued to play football even after he failed to make the first team during his freshman year. He was a basketball cheerleader, a swimmer, and a lifeguard, and while he made his name in sports, the radio carrying his voice across the flat terrain of the American Midwest, the young man harbored even greater aspirations.

In the mid-1930s, as part of his job at WHO, Reagan began traveling to the Cubs' spring training camp in Southern California. In his mind, he'd always dreamed an impossible dream of Hollywood, and in 1937, with the help of some friends, he took a screen test with Warner Bros. He left Des Moines, moved to Hollywood, and starred in a series of B movies. His fascination with football led him to begin writing a screenplay about Knute Rockne, the legendary Notre Dame coach who died in a plane crash in 1931. A studio beat him to the idea, and Reagan begged for the opportunity to play the team's star, George Gipp, who died three weeks after his final game. He showed the producer a photo of himself in a Eureka football uniform and won the role, and at the film's first test screening, the theater fell silent as Reagan delivered his maudlin and climactic speech: *Someday when things are tough and the breaks are going against the boys, ask them to go in there and win one for the Gipper. I don't know where I'll be, but I'll know about it and I'll be happy.*

It was treacle, but the delivery was so utterly sincere that his audience bought it completely. It didn't matter if it was based in any sort of truth. Reagan was an actor now; he would forever be an actor, playing athletes and cowboys and eventually even an exaggerated version of himself. "I'll never forget one game with Mendota," he would recall of his high school football days in Dixon, and then he would lapse into one of several versions of the story, which changed over the years, depending upon the circumstances and the audience and the message he was attempting to convey. He was so skilled that it took Reagan's biographer Lou Cannon several years to recognize that *every* version of the story was a fake.

It was this unshakable faith in the power of his own mythology that enabled Ronald Reagan to win election as the governor of California in 1966. And eventually, in 1980, in an entirely different era of heroes and the media who covered them, that simple belief earned Reagan the job as the fortieth president of the United States.

He swept into office on an agenda of optimism, promising to cut taxes and to liberate the marketplace from excessive regulation, from the undue burdens of a government and the pervasive sense of pessimism that had, in the previous decades, proved a drag on the American dream. He was the first president to embrace the imagery of television, utilizing his gifts as an actor, modulating his voice and his expression to match the gravity of the moment, harnessing the power of the medium. And yet his visage hearkened back to the America of Frank Merriwell and Dizzy Dean, to the days when sports were a simple pastime, to a time when a lone voice emanating from a radio could carry across the farms and plains of the Midwest.

Over the course of those decades, amid Ronald Reagan's political maturation, as radio gave way to television, "sports exploded before our very eyes," wrote legendary sports columnist Jim Murray. "A new royalty sprang up in our midst. A new ruling class formed. . . . Sports stars became mythic. They occupied the place the knights errant did in Arthurian England. They were larger than life, richer than Croesus. They drew the adulation movie stars did a generation before."

And so there was something to be said, at this moment, for the virtues of nostalgia. There was something to be said for a president who would tell a group of sportscasters that he didn't much care for football anymore, because when he lettered at Eureka, everybody played on both sides of the ball and nobody ever came to the sidelines. It was both the boon and the illusion of the Reagan era. There was comfort in simplicity, in shielding our eyes from the complexities of life in the 1980s, from the fact that television had changed the very framework of the games themselves. Average salaries in all three of the major sports in America increased exponentially between 1980 and 1985 (in baseball: $144,000 to $371,000; in football, $79,000 to $194,000; in basketball, $170,000 to $325,000). More television meant more marketing and more sponsorship opportunities, which meant that money was increasingly involved in decision-making, and when money was involved in decision-making, the pressure to win became enormous, and the pressure to win had a natural tendency to carve holes in the moral landscape. "To each sports scandal, whether it involved recruiting, cheating, or drug use, public response was the same: a collective yawn and a figurative wink," wrote author Haynes Johnson. "If ingesting drugs, steroids, bribing officials, or skirting collegiate rules helped make one's team win, so be it."

By 1984, Ronald Reagan was seventy-three years old, a popular incumbent, running a reelection campaign on a narrative of optimism that one of his advisors referred to in a campaign memo as "mythic America." The opposition complained that Reagan was out of touch, that he delegated responsibilities, that his policies favored the wealthy and privileged, that his lack of complexity and his combativeness would ultimately prove to be his downfall. But the majority of Americans simply *wanted* to believe in themselves again, in one man's notions of a national spiritual cleansing, in the repudiation of the angst and anti-heroes of Vietnam and Watergate. Even amid his failings, Reagan maintained a sympathetic persona: He was so pleasant and ingratiating that most Americans did not even *see* him as a politician. "There is a lesson for us all in Vietnam," he had famously stated several years earlier. "Let us tell those who fought that war that we will never again ask young men to fight and possibly die in a war that our government is afraid to let them win."

With Reagan in office, all we wanted was to feel good again. All we wanted was to *win* again. And so the 1984 Olympics in Los Angeles, though marred by an Eastern Bloc boycott meant to repudiate the American boycott of 1980, became a spectacle of patriotism and kitsch and corporate synergy. Because of the International Olympic Committee's pressing financial issues, these were the first games to be staged and organized and financed by the private sector, and they were officially sponsored by Coca-Cola and Xerox and Levi-Strauss and 7-Eleven. The result was a jingoistic bonanza, the most politicized Olympics since Berlin in 1936, according to author Nicolaus Mills: Chants of *U! S! A!* (also heard at Reagan campaign rallies) were so persistent and grating that, at a volleyball game between America and Brazil, foreign fans began chanting, *B!R!A!* All of it was fueled by the media, so much so that International Olympic Committee president Juan Antonio Samaranch wrote a letter complaining about ABC's unabashedly patriotic coverage of the games. "Oh, what we've done to the Olympics," the journalist Frank Deford wrote in *Sports Illustrated*. "God only knows what the 2.5 billion people around the globe who are watching the games will think of a vain America, so bountiful and strong, with every advantage, including the home court, reveling in the role of Goliath, gracelessly trumpeting its own good fortune while rudely dismissing its guests."

No expense was spared in accomplishing such a feat. Director David Wolper's opening and closing ceremonies in Los Angeles involved an orgy of trumpets, kettledrums, balloons, marching bands, a small battalion of baby-grand pianos belting out Gershwin's *Rhapsody in Blue,* church bells, skywriters, jazzercise dancers, a flock of doves, a man wearing a jet pack, and enough pomp and glitz, according to the *New York Times* columnist Dave Anderson, that it made a Super Bowl half-time show look like a high school play. (A twenty-two-year-old bald eagle named Bomber was supposed to fly over a section of spectators and land on a set of Olympic rings on the field;

he arrived overweight and, following an intense training session in the Los Angeles smog, died of vascular collapse and an acute bacterial infection.) "The American ideal is not just winning; it's going as far as you can go," Reagan told the American athletes. The ceremonies cost six million dollars; the opulence was part of the aesthetic. This was the prime directive of the '84 Olympics: They were a one-sided showcase of American superiority. The host country won eighty-three gold medals. No other country won more than twenty.

Given this prelude, it came as no surprise that the 1984 presidential election was never particularly close. Reagan won 59 percent of the popular vote and 525 of 535 electoral votes from his Democratic opponent, Walter Mondale, despite a disastrous performance at a debate in Louisville that raised concerns over the president's advancing age. It didn't matter: He had won the admiration even of Democrats who disagreed with his policies; three out of five new voters cast votes for him as well. Here was a man who had taken on the biggest role of his life. His swagger, even after all these years, was unmistakable.

II.

Halfway across the country, in the state where Ronald Reagan was born, the local professional football team faced a vexing problem with its quarterback. The problem was that the quarterback didn't know when to shut his damn mouth. He was forever tweaking egos and embracing crudeness and thumbing his nose at authority just because he could, just because was so utterly capable at it. At thirteen, he'd been tossed from his Little League team for stealing the coach's cigarettes, and the fact that his father was the coach didn't aid his cause very much at all. The quarterback was an unrepentant brat, a legitimate pain in the ass, the kind of kid who inserts thumbtacks into the posterior of an overweight classmate during the pledge of allegiance and lights firecrackers during shop class and refuses to apologize for any of it. Police record at age twelve (vandalism at school et cetera), drunk for the first time at thirteen, puking champagne in left field at a Little League picnic, and he hadn't looked back since.

He was twenty-six years old in September 1985, and he hadn't matured much at all. His overarching philosophy of human existence was that he didn't really give a damn what anyone thought; even his parents still pissed him off. His was a remarkable case—somehow he had a Mormon wife and two kids at home and seemed a responsible father, yet he managed to subvert adulthood in every other circumstance. And those whose job it was to steward the quarterback, to attempt to somehow "control" him, were beginning to realize the problem went beyond the quarterback not knowing *when* to shut up. It was that he didn't know *how* to shut up, except maybe when you inserted a can of Budweiser into his gullet. The only question now was whether this meant he was ultimately unsalvageable, or whether somehow his inability to keep his lips locked might, in fact, be his greatest asset.

Since 1982, the quarterback, christened James Robert McMahon Jr., known to friends and enemies alike as Jim (because he did not tolerate formality, in any of its societal guises), had ostensibly been the starting play caller for the motley National Football League outfit known as the Chicago Bears. The Bears, once a proud franchise peopled by hard-nosed legends like Dick Butkus and owned, until his death in 1983, by a legendary and tightfisted former coach named George Halas, had been moribund for years until a surprise run into the 1984 playoffs. Now they had won their first two games in 1985, and in a city where football still took precedence over all other extracurricular activities, a city long known for the futility of its sporting enterprises, that was all it took for fans to start believing that maybe they finally had something here, if only their quarterback could avoid impaling himself on his own hubris.

McMahon had at the moment a purely physical problem; he had checked himself in to Lake Forest Hospital that very week, in mid-September. The problem with employing a quarterback who feared nothing was that he didn't know when to quit, and that meant some rather distasteful meetings with unfriendly men much larger than he, which raised concerns as to whether McMahon would ever be able to stay in one piece for an entire season. He'd missed seven games plus the playoffs in 1984, due to a series of injuries that began with a broken hand and culminated in a lacerated kidney in a vicious game against the Los Angeles Raiders, which short-circuited the Bears' season and nearly ended McMahon's career. This time a compressed disc in McMahon's neck, aggravated during a win over the New England Patriots, had caused neck and back spasms, and he spent three days and two nights in traction. A game against a divisional rival, the Minnesota Vikings, loomed on Thursday night, and McMahon didn't check out of the hospital until Tuesday. The conventional wisdom was that McMahon was finished at least for the week, if not longer, if only because he couldn't practice.

"I mean, if you don't practice, how in the hell can you play?" Mike Ditka would profess. Ditka, a bruising and fearless Hall of Fame tight end who helped lead the Bears to an NFL championship in 1963, became head coach the same year he chose McMahon with the team's number one pick in the 1982 draft. By now he had grown accustomed to McMahon's radical ways, yet Ditka was himself a hothead, and the combination was endlessly combustible. They had more commonalities than differences—McMahon admitted, much later, that he would have enjoyed the younger version of Ditka in his huddle—but the generation gap set them apart. So it had already been an adventure for the past three years, with McMahon playing a spiky-haired Dennis the Menace to Ditka's mustachioed Mr. Wilson.

The more Ditka pushed him to conform to the traditionally conservative norms of the National Football League, the more McMahon rebelled.

And while pro football had harbored its share of rebels through the late 1960s and 1970s, there was something bolder and less refined about McMahon. There was no great countercultural statement here, merely a sense of purposeful contrarianism and defiance that seemed engineered for no greater purpose than to piss off as many people as possible. "He didn't have any particular agenda," said longtime Chicago journalist Rick Telander. "Except *'Fuck you.'*"

III.

In late 1985, outside a movie theater in Boston, a reporter from *Newsweek* magazine conducted an interview with a ten-year-old boy. This primarily involved asking the boy to explain why he admired a fictional boxer from Philadelphia who was, at that moment, the most famous "athlete" in America and who had managed to short-circuit the Cold War entirely on his own, in a span of approximately ninety minutes. "He always *wins*," said the boy, whose name was Robert Fillman. He had just emerged from a showing of *Rocky IV*, in which that boxer, Robert "Rocky" Balboa, had defeated a near-invincible Russian automaton, avenged the death of his friend, won the approval of a hostile Soviet crowd and a Mikhail Gorbachev look-alike, and declared, in perhaps the most implausible moment in an era of entirely implausible Hollywood fantasies, that if he is capable of changing, we are *all* capable of changing.

Rocky IV, released during the Christmas season of 1985, was an immediate and explosive box-office hit. It was also reviled by most intellectuals, including movie critics, who dismissed the movie as "bloated and hollow," "anticommie agitprop," "offensively predictable," and "jingoistically implausible." But those of us who were approximately Robert Fillman's age couldn't have cared less. We clamored to see this movie, and we saw it in groups, virulent packs of adolescents and preteens swarming out of station wagons and charging forth into theaters and cheering and hissing and hurling our popcorn at the screen. *Rocky IV* wound up grossing $32 million in its first five days of release, and nearly $128 million domestically, and the reasons for this were not hard to figure. No movie played more effectively upon the Zeitgeist and upon the rampant sense of Cold War agita that Reagan had fostered through his first five years as president; it was essentially a propaganda film.

Still, something else was happening here. Rocky had been born as an uplifting folk hero in the mid-1970s, but in *Rocky IV* he became something else entirely, a striking incarnation of a new kind of anti-antihero, a John Wayne for the Reagan era. One historian referred to them as "legitimate savages," rugged individualists who operate "outside the laws and strictures of civilization and use violent means to worthy ends." And no one embodied the legitimate savage more ably than Sylvester Stallone.

Stallone had already infuriated millions of thinking Americans earlier that year, with the second installment of his film series featuring John S. Rambo, a Green Beret and revisionist Vietnam veteran who, upon being recruited to return to Vietnam to find a camp full of American prisoners of war, asks, "Sir, do we get to win this time?" One critic called it "loud, stupid, nasty, brutish, and short." Reagan loved it. The movies appealed to the same base emotions as his own public persona. He, too, believed Vietnam was a failure because America's angst had made it so. He was so enamored of the character that he evoked the film several times in speeches, and began referring to himself in a private joke with friends as "Ron-bo."

In *Rocky IV,* no longer was our hero just a mealymouthed longshot heavyweight from the streets who had fought toe-to-toe with the champ (*Rocky*), or a self-made celebrity (*Rocky II, Rocky III*) who embodied the rags-to-riches stories of the past. He was, *Newsweek* concluded, a geopolitical emblem, "as much a part of the symbolic future of Reagan's America as the president himself—a can-do America re-emergent, in his vision, from a can't-do past."

The plot of *Rocky IV* is admittedly a mind-bending brand of camp: After watching his old friend Apollo Creed die in the boxing ring during an exhibition with a state-manufactured Russian killing machine named Ivan Drago, a wealthy and out-of-shape Rocky decides (while driving his sports car in an airy montage) that in order to restore balance, he must fight Drago, despite the never-ending protestations of his pacifist wife. So he travels to Russia, and he grows a beard, and he prepares for the fight amid a mélange of thrumming synth-based period music and scenes that portray Rocky as the solitary underdog, the hardworking and unappreciated American hero—out in the snowy wilderness of what we can only presume is Siberia, where he pushes a horse sled in a blizzard and cleaves wood with a rusty old saw and does pull-ups in a cabin by firelight. "Our fantasy heroes are less mirrors of what we are," *Newsweek* wrote at the time, "than windows into what we might like to be."

At the same time, Drago is portrayed as a technologically superior human cyborg, training at state-of-the-art facilities and taking steroid injections. He is entirely incapable of thinking for himself and takes directions from his wife and a cabal of government handlers who seem bent on winning at all costs. He is all our worst fears about the future come to life. He is an institutional machine. In some ways, he is perhaps the most realistic character in the entire movie.

After fourteen rounds of what syndicated columnist Ellen Goodman called "blood and parody," after a fight so epic that it alters the entire geopolitical landscape, Drago turns on a Russian cabinet minister who exhorts him to win. He begins choking the man. Then, overcome by indignation, Drago recites his own modern manifesto.

"I fight to win," he says. "For *me*."

IV.

A couple of months earlier, Jim McMahon had given himself a hair-cut. Normally, his wife, Nancy, a low-key Mormon girl he met while at Brigham Young University, cut his hair for him, but McMahon wanted something different this time, so he borrowed a pair of clippers from his teammate Willie Gault, and he began hacking at himself. A couple of decades earlier, Ditka did the same thing and wound up with a head like a shag-carpeted bowling ball. But what McMahon wound up with was something much more unruly, a spiky mess of dark tufts, part faux hawk, part bird's nest, which, combined with the omnipresence of his sunglasses, made the quarterback look a little like either the Sex Pistols' Sid Vicious or a homeless person, depending upon one's generational perspective.

The sunglasses were a key element of the McMahon persona, the product of a freak accident that McMahon—intentionally and unintentionally—used to bolster his image. That's how it was with him; his inanities were both entirely calculated and completely un-planned, beginning at the age of six with an unpleasant incident in-volving a toy-gun holster and a fork. McMahon said that the eye had improved over the years, but his vision out of it was 20/200. He strug-gled to see long distances, and his sensitivity to bright lights led him to wear sunglasses in public, lending him instant street cred and en-abling him to bridge the traditionally disparate worlds of sports and rock and roll.

On Tuesday, two days before the Minnesota game, McMahon, hair still in tatters, showed up at practice wearing his sunglasses and a neck roll that one reporter likened to a "small life preserver." He complained that practicing the week before had unnecessarily irri-tated his injuries, and he complained that Ditka was requiring him to practice the next day if he expected to play against the Vikings on Thursday night. Every time McMahon cocked his arm back, a pinching sensation returned, and on top of all the spasms and aches, a turf burn on his right shin had become infected. The quarterback was a mess, as usual, but he insisted that with a couple of days' rest, he'd be fine to play on Thursday.

Still, Ditka couldn't get past the notion of his quarterback being allowed to play without taking a single repetition in practice. The coach felt the pull of previous generations; his coaching hero was Tom Landry, the stoic who had won several Super Bowls with the Dallas Cowboys while seemingly never smiling. Landry was as old-school as old-school got—quiet, controlling, a planner, a stabilizing force, mum's the word. Ditka was a font of energy and anger and rage. Ditka was uncontainable and haphazard. His second year as coach, in 1983, in a loss to the Baltimore Colts, after attempting to drop-kick his headset over a goalpost, he punched a trunk in the locker room and broke his right hand.

He liked to think he had mellowed since then. But even a chilled-out Ditka was like a dormant Vesuvius. The Bears nicknamed him "Sybil," after the Sally Field movie about a girl with a split personality, and nobody drove him to distraction more than his eternally questioning quarterback. Ditka's neurosis that week was heightened by the fact that a Thursday-night road game had not yet become a routine accessory of television. It meant an unusual preparatory routine for NFL teams accustomed to playing games on Sunday afternoons and occasionally on Monday nights. This was being billed as a special edition of ABC's *Monday Night Football,* yet another example of television's ever-increasing sway over the schedule, and when one of the program's newest commentators showed up to interview the Bears' injured quarterback on Tuesday, McMahon chose to sit with him in the bleachers rather than hang around on the sidelines and endure a close-up view of a practice session he felt was entirely irrelevant.

This was *Joe Willie,* after all, and if McMahon had any hero in sports (he didn't care much for spectating), Joe Willie Namath was the one. He knew enough about history to realize that there would have been no Jim McMahon without Joe Willie. In his time, Namath had also flouted convention and disobeyed rules and done his fair share of late-night carousing. And maybe McMahon wasn't a playboy (he was more of a *Hustler* man), but if there was one thing he respected, it was someone who didn't buy in to the conventional wisdom merely because it existed, merely because others said it must be that way.

Yet even Namath wasn't Namath anymore. This was his first and only year on *Monday Night Football,* and it would come to be viewed as a disastrous experiment. The eighties Joe Willie was bland and uninterested in exploring controversy. His purpose for coming to Chicago was to do a story for the half-time show about how McMahon was finally healthy again. "I want to bring out the bright side, the good side," Namath told reporters. "I don't want to dwell on the mistakes."

McMahon viewed every affront to his own sensibilities as a personal attack. Merely by sitting with Namath rather than standing with his teammates, the quarterback was acting out against his coach, and this latest act of deliberate nose-thumbing only made Ditka more furious. On Wednesday, still aggravated, Ditka told the local media that he was going to start Doc Blanchard, who had won the Heisman Trophy in 1945 while at Army, and was currently sixty years old. Then Ditka said that McMahon wouldn't play and that the team's blandly capable backup, Steve Fuller, would start in his place. He insisted that he would not change his mind on the plane ride to Minneapolis, nor during pregame warm-ups, and he didn't particularly care how McMahon reacted to his decision. A furious McMahon refused to answer questions before practice on Wednesday, then said, after watching practice from the sideline, "I'm not going to answer any more stupid questions."

It was typical McMahon: By insulting the media, he simultaneously fed their natural affinity for controversy, thereby bolstering his persona. It was hard to know how much of this was intentional, but in an age when principled rebellion comported with patriotism, it was an effective marketing ploy. McMahon says he had no such agenda and that he protested merely because Ditka's principles seemed legitimately idiotic to him. Maybe in high school it made sense. But a professional quarterback didn't need to practice in order to play. It wasn't that he didn't study the game plan; it was that it all came so *easily* to him. For whatever reason, McMahon was able to read defenses in ways other quarterbacks couldn't, which was how, despite a mottled physique and a mediocre arm, he'd gotten here in the first place.

On Wednesday night, McMahon was lying in his hotel room, icing his swollen leg, when the phone rang. It was one of the assistants; there was a meeting going on downstairs, and Ditka expected his quarterback to be there, dammit, even if he wasn't playing. "I don't care what he's doing," Ditka said. "I expect him to come to all the meetings."

McMahon limped downstairs and took a seat in the meeting room. "You told me I'm not playing," he said. "Why the fuck do I need to sit here?" And now Ditka was pissed, and McMahon was pissed, and everyone else was caught in the middle, which might have seemed unusual except that this was already a team with an epic grounding in dysfunction. Ditka and his defensive coordinator, Buddy Ryan, hated each other so much that they rarely spoke, fostering a rift between the offensive and defensive sides—generally, the defense, already one of the league's best, with Ryan's swarming 46 scheme loosing them to chase and torture opposing quarterbacks, regarded the offense as a bunch of pussies. The conventional wisdom had always been that a team that didn't bond as a family couldn't possibly win a championship. But this Bears team was in the process of shattering conventional wisdom, one timeworn tenet at a time.

The coach of the Minnesota Vikings, Bud Grant, was fifty-eight years old, a born-again Christian who had enlisted in the navy during World War II, one of a brand of longtime NFL coaches, an old-school stoic who valued the Reagan-era surge in patriotism so highly that he criticized ABC for blacking out the national anthem to its television audience before football games and had castigated at least one previous opponent for the team's sloppy demeanor during the anthem. Grant quit in 1983 after seventeen seasons with the Vikings, then returned for one more year in 1985 (he would retire again, for good, at the end of the season). "ABC could be a little more American," Grant said earlier that week, and as he often did, Mike Ditka somehow found a way to take this comment personally. In part, it was because Grant, upon hearing Ditka had been hired as the coach of the Bears after his friend Neill Armstrong was fired, accused Ditka of benefiting from nepotism.

So Ditka, exhausted by the events of the week, infuriated by the antics of his quarterback, demanded in his pregame speech that his players stand at attention during the anthem. "You don't ever want to be upstaged in anything in life," he said. (Oddly, given Grant's pressure, ABC chose to show the national anthem at halftime.) And then the game began, and the Bears could not score any points, and once again, McMahon would not shut his damn mouth. Three field goals on seven possessions, with McMahon flapping his gums in Ditka's face the whole time, a pale green towel draped around his neck.

"Goddammit, Mike, we're gonna lose," he said.

"Shut up," Ditka said.

"Better put me in, Mike," he said.

"Shut up," Ditka said.

"I can play, Mike," he said.

"Shut up!" Ditka said.

"Better put my ass in, Mike, or we're gonna lose," he said.

Ditka didn't want to give. Screw McMahon. He wanted to win with Fuller. McMahon "told me that nothing could keep him from playing in this game tonight," Namath said at the beginning of the broadcast. "He must have forgotten about Coach Mike Ditka." In keeping with the values Landry and others had taught him, Ditka wanted to prove that no one man was larger than the team and that he didn't need any one player in order to win. Mostly, he wanted to prove that he didn't need McMahon. "Shut up!" Ditka said, until he could say it no more.

Finally—and this is true, and both sides swear it is true, as do impartial witnesses—Ditka relented, merely because the quarterback would not shut his mouth. He had told the broadcast crew that he would only play McMahon if a "catastrophe" took place, but with seven minutes, twenty-two seconds remaining in the third quarter, McMahon had accomplished what may have been a first in the history of the National Football League: He had literally filibustered his way into the game. "Maybe a catastrophe is measured by eight points down midway through the third quarter," said the television play-by-play man, Frank Gifford. The Bears trailed 17–9, and while Fuller had not been ineffective, he had not been effective, either, and there was something about McMahon's presence that seemed to change the entire dynamic of the huddle. He was the helmeted personification of the fictional soldier known as Rambo, who had been described by *Newsweek* as "a kind of noble savage who got fed up with a system that reduces men to numbers and who took arms against it with cunning, wit, and skill."

The first play call McMahon received that night was a conservative one, a screen pass designed to go to the fullback, Matt Suhey.

Generally, McMahon couldn't have cared less what the call was. He was convinced that he knew what worked and what didn't more than any coach on that sideline—Ditka had been a *tight end,* for Christ's sake!—and he wasn't about to cower behind some esoteric game plan that had no basis in the reality of the moment. He had been known to audible to plays that weren't even in the game plan, that hadn't been called since training camp, if he felt they might work better than what was coming from the sideline. But this time, grateful just to be playing, after taking a moment to proficiently curse at his teammates, he went with the play he was asked to call. He took the snap from center, and maybe it was the lights, or the sudden burst of adrenaline, or the haze of the painkillers and muscle relaxants he'd been ingesting all week long, but two steps into his drop, McMahon lost his footing, and if it hadn't been for Walter Payton—who'd been nursing some sore ribs all week—throwing a hard shoulder into an onrushing linebacker, McMahon would have gone down right there, and maybe none of this would have ever happened.

Payton had been the backbone of the Bears through that ignominious era of the late 1970s and early 1980s, an unassuming man with prodigious talent and a sterling personal reputation whose great professional burden was that he had never played in a Super Bowl. He tolerated McMahon for the same reason most of his teammates did: because they wanted to win. And they had seen something in their quarterback that Ditka had not yet seen. But he was about to see it, on national television, on the rock-hard turf of the Hubert H. Humphrey Metrodome, with Joe Willie in the booth and Steve Fuller back on the sideline where he belonged.

McMahon stumbled, and then he regained his footing and dropped back to avoid several raging savages in purple jerseys charging at his fragile body, preparing to both insult and injure him with one fatal blow. Before the snap, he'd read the blitz, and he knew that meant man-to-man coverage in the secondary, and that man-to-man coverage against a team with decent linebackers meant a screen pass was pretty much futile. So he cast his eyes downfield, to Willie Gault, who was supposed to cut in but instead had sprinted deep and was now ten yards behind the nearest defender, and what the hell, McMahon just hurled the damn ball as far as he could. It was a typical McMahon ad-lib, a hybrid of school-yard improvisation and instinct and intelligence, both a refutation of his coach's authoritarian wisdom and an undeniably smart read.

"I love it!" Namath shouted as the ball sailed over the entire Minnesota defense.

The result was a seventy-yard touchdown, narrowing the score to 17–16.

On the sideline, Ditka fell into a full-throated holler. He asked McMahon what play he had called. McMahon said he called the screen. Ditka said, "Then why'd you throw it to Willie?"

"Because he was fucking open, Mike," McMahon said.

Right away, the Bears got the ball back, on a turnover in Minnesota territory, and McMahon called a bootleg. The options were simple: Throw short to Payton in the flat, throw a midrange pass to the tight end streaking across the field, or run with the ball. See how the coverage shakes out, and find the open man. But McMahon's simple calculations had led him to recognize another variable. It all depended upon the free safety; if he cheated forward to cover the tight end, a wide receiver, Dennis McKinnon, would be wide open downfield. "I always told Dennis, 'Make sure if that guy leaves, you replace him,'" McMahon said. "Sure enough, I roll out, they jump Walter in the flat, I look for my tight end, and here comes the free safety. I knew Dennis was open, so I held the ball longer and just kept running, running, running."

McMahon rolled to his left and threw across his body, threading the ball between defenders, and McKinnon caught it for another touchdown. The Bears led, 23–17. Two passes, two touchdowns. His third pass of the night, another deep ball to Gault, was dropped—"I hit Willie in the face," McMahon said—and once again, Ditka questioned his wisdom.

"Why the hell did you throw that?" Ditka asked.

"Mike, watch the film tomorrow," McMahon said. "He was ten yards behind the guy."

You could see it happening. You could see the Vikings falling into a panic, the Metrodome quieting, eleven defenders completely flabbergasted by what they'd just witnessed. "They figure this guy's liable to do anything or try anything out there," Namath said on the air.

McMahon did throw another touchdown pass that night, again to McKinnon, and the Bears won 33–24. "It was like one of those old-time Notre Dame movies," Payton said afterward, and while the comeback raised echoes of bygone eras, the man who accomplished them had demonstrated that he was distinctly a product of the age: The unrepentant individualist. The noble savage.

"McMahon," said Gifford, "has been *outrageous*."

The next day, after numbing himself with barley and hops on the plane ride home, McMahon checked back in to the hospital for more rest. About the need to bother with such trivialities as practice, he figured he'd proved his point.

V.

Throughout 1985, amid a cancer scare, amid continued battles with Congress over tax policy, the Reagan aura continued to swell. By November, the stock market had surged to record levels, and one month later, in Geneva, Switzerland, the same man who had once labeled Russia "the Evil Empire" shook hands with Soviet general secretary Mikhail Gorbachev. They spoke for more than fifteen hours. It was the beginning of a slow thaw that would eventually end a decades-long standoff between the most powerful nations in the world.

This—the facilitation of the end of the Cold War—would become Reagan's singular achievement; he managed to simultaneously charm and cajole the Soviets with his rhetoric. And perhaps it could be argued that he was precisely what we needed at this moment, at least in terms of foreign policy—a man who was unafraid to say what he thought, who took risks in boldly calling out Soviet aggression, and who often just didn't know when to shut his mouth. "Reagan said things that everyone knew," said an expert on Russia (and future secretary of state) named Condoleezza Rice, "but no one would dream of saying publicly."

A poll taken just before the Geneva summit measured Reagan's approval rating at 67 percent, its highest level since the assassination attempt against him in 1981, the highest level it would ever reach during his presidency. By then, the Reagan effect domestically was not just political; it was cultural. Deregulation, lower taxes—all of it fostered an attitude of conspicuous consumption in America. In December, the Dow Jones industrial average jumped above 1,500, "one of the most amazing rallies in its history," according to *The New York Times*. "What I want to see above all is that this country remains a country where someone can always get rich," Reagan had said a couple of years earlier, but in certain circles, it was no longer enough *just* to get rich. Wealth became a brand, and no one embodied this more than a New York real-estate mogul with cotton-candy hair who was also the owner of the New Jersey Generals, a member of the fledgling United States Football League.

Donald Trump was not just a billionaire. Donald Trump had his name on office towers and airplanes and cruise ships, money as a conduit to power and influence, money stretched to its limit, money as a manifestation of the American dream. The pursuit of happiness was inextricable from the pursuit of wealth, and it was only a matter of time before the balance would tip, before the moral landscape would feel the effects of such pressures.

Scandals were roiling beneath the surface, both inside and outside of sports: on Wall Street, in the Oval Office, tied to faraway countries and to the inner cities of America, where the focus on opulence masked problems of poverty and unemployment. The mood was euphoric and the mood was unsustainable, but we were, above all, "in a mood for the resurrection of old myths," Haynes Johnson wrote. "In the survival and good luck of Ronald Reagan, [Americans] found what they were seeking." Our president was tough and he was clever and he was charming and he embraced the theatricality of his role—even if it was based, at least in part, on half-truths and false recollections, on a self-generated mythology, on an image reflected through a picture tube into our homes.

CHAPTER TWO

I Am Superman

. . . he and a few others—how many?—three hundred, four hundred, five hundred?—had become precisely that . . . Masters of the Universe. There was . . . no limit whatsoever!

—TOM WOLFE, *The Bonfire of the Vanities*

I.

The self-generated creation myth of one Vincent Edward "Bo" Jackson begins in the summer of '76, with the epic tale of a boy hurtling across a forty-foot-wide ditch filled with dead pigs so as to evade the wrath of a Baptist minister. This was, Bo would later claim, the seminal experience of his youth, and whether the details are entirely accurate hardly matters, because this is Bo Jackson we are talking about, and it is often hard to tell the difference between truth and apocrypha. Either way, it seems a fitting tale of origin for a modern-age superhero.

He was thirteen years old at the time, and his childhood bridged a gap between eras in the Deep South; just five years before Bo leapt that divide in the woods of rural Alabama and almost a decade after James Meredith became the first African-American student at the University of Mississippi, Coach Paul "Bear" Bryant finally integrated the football program at the University of Alabama. According to an aunt, the young Bo bore a striking resemblance to Martin Luther King Jr., though he did not share the reverend's temperament: He was, by his own account, an unapologetic juvenile delinquent. Raised on the outskirts of a little town called Bessemer, sired in a redbrick house on a dirt road by a mother of ten children, he was largely neglected by an absentee father who lived across town and worked in the steel mills. It was not an unusual circumstance, in Bessemer or elsewhere. "We had quite a few kids from broken homes," said Dick Atchison, the football and track coach at nearby McAdory High School.

Between 1970 and 1980, the number of single-parent households nationwide grew exponentially, and that number would keep rising through the first half of the decade. It was an issue that portended a growing political and cultural divide in Reagan's America—conservatives lamenting the rise of "welfare culture" for the breakdown of the family, liberals faulting a president whose father had benefited from the New Deal policies of Franklin Roosevelt, and who now slashed social services and cloaked himself in the philosophy of laissez-faire. Of course, for Bo, politics were of little concern. All he knew about such things was that he grew up poor and fatherless and with a serious chip on his shoulder. Even watching *The Brady Bunch* made him angry.

The Jackson household was short on both money and space, what with all those children roaming around in three little rooms and one outhouse, sometimes with nothing more than grits and margarine to eat (though at least one of his former coaches says Bo often played up his level of poverty, as if stoking a legend). There were nights when Bo slept on the living-room floor, his butt curled up next to the heater. He envied his friends and their possessions, their material wealth. Bo's mother, Florence Bond, worked as a maid at the Ramada Inn and lorded over her household with a dictatorial eye for punishment. She took after her children with broom handles and switches and extension cords, and she would roust them before dawn to take out the garbage and mow the grass by floodlight and wax the floors and scrub the porch, and yet none of it seemed to tame Bo, who just kept getting worse and worse as he approached pubescence.

What made Bo stand out was his physique, which he leveraged to vent his anger and exact his will as the self-proclaimed "John Gotti of my neighborhood." He was merciless; he flung rocks and crab apples and punches with equal accuracy, and at one point, in the midst of a fight over a Ping-Pong paddle, he hit one of his female cousins with a baseball bat and said he would have hit her again if his siblings hadn't stepped in. He'd steal a bike, strip it, toss it into a fire to burn the paint off, spray-paint it, and that same afternoon, ride down the street past the house he'd stolen it from. He would extort his class-mates' money and loan it back to them at interest. From his father, he inherited a speech impediment, a stutter that plagued him through-out childhood, and this only inflamed Bo's anger and defensiveness. After a while, you learned not to mock Bo for the way he talked, or you'd find yourself laid flat on the pavement. Because of his ability to withstand punches to the chest from his older brothers and sisters, because he wrestled children twice his age and ducked no fight and reveled in his own stubbornness, he had been given a nickname, truncated from the Southern shorthand for a wild boar. In time, *Bo-Hog* became *Bo.* "When I was coming up, we didn't have drugs, cocaine, gangs," he said. "We did what country boys did back then—crab-apple fights, wrestling in the dairy lake."

During that summer of '76, at the height of his mischief, young Bo and twenty of his friends, bored to death, wandered away from the local rec center and toward a nearby mountain, where they dis-covered a new pastime: pelting the local minister's hogs with sticks and rocks and bricks until the animals keeled over and died. They killed purely for pleasure. They felled thousands of dollars' worth of animals, and they were taking aim at an especially large specimen that would not keel over, when a gunshot rang out and spoiled their plans. The minister's hired man had found them. They scattered, and Bo did what he did better than anyone in the state of Alabama, then or now: He ran like hell. He was going full speed when he encountered the ditch—a repository for the corpses of the minister's dead swine—and then he soared over it, both literally and metaphorically, from one stage of his life into the next.

It did not take long for Bo to get found out. He had a reputation by then. Shortly after he arrived at home and changed out of his bloody clothes and attempted to hide the evidence, the minister's man—who was also Bo's barber—came by the house and asked him to give up the names of his friends. The way Bo spins his own story, this was the moment when our hero faced a crucial choice: reform himself, or get sent off to reform school by a mother who couldn't take it anymore. Bo, frightened by his brother's horror stories of reform school, spilled his guts, ratted on everybody, and worked odd jobs the remainder of that summer to pay back the money he owed the minister.

At that moment, driven by fear of an uncertain future, Bo chose to channel all of that anger into a purpose, by running toward something rather than away from it. At that moment, by force of will, the hero was transformed.

He was the most talented college football player in America by the fall of 1985. About this, there was no dispute. In fact, there was a growing consensus among those who saw him work out on a regular basis that he was already the best athletic specimen in America, bar none. He had a sculpted body (a gift largely of genetics, since he rarely lifted a weight) and sprinter's speed and natural abilities the likes of which his coaches at Auburn University had never seen before, and doubted they would ever see again. Bo ran track and played baseball too: He hit .401 with seventeen homers in the spring of 1985. In the first night game ever played at Georgia's stadium, in front of three thousand fans, Bo grounded out in his first at-bat, drawing boos from the crowd, who now presumed the Bo of real life could not possibly live up to the hype that had preceded him. The next time up, he hit a ball so hard that it struck a light standard ninety feet in the air. Then he hit two more home runs in his next two at-bats, and when he merely doubled off the top of the wall his final time up, the fans booed him once more. His propensity for dramatics had already made him a national curiosity, as well as a favorite to win the Heisman Trophy, but this was nothing to those who had seen Bo's rise from disgruntled teen to college-age Adonis; he had been doing these kinds of things for years by the time he arrived at Auburn.

He was bigger and stronger and faster than anyone had a right to be, and when he set his mind to something, he just *did it*. He made it through a couple of weeks in Little League baseball before he was moved up to Pony League, and when he was Pony League age, he began playing in a men's semipro league. He played every position—as a ten-year-old catcher, he could throw out runners at second base from his knees—though he hated to pitch because he found it inherently uninteresting. (Once, he began an inning by walking the bases loaded, trying to get himself pulled; when his coach stared him down, Bo chose to strike out the side and walked off the mound.) By his sophomore year at McAdory High School, he had begun to develop the body of a man ten years older, a massive frame like that of his father, A. D. Adams. That spring, Bo finished third in the decathlon and his school won the state championship. The following summer, a twenty-four-year-old named Terry Brasseale interviewed for the job as the baseball coach at McAdory. On his way to the office, he saw a man he assumed was a janitor. The man was shirtless and carrying a shovel, and he was built like no one Brasseale had seen before. "That janitor," Brasseale asked when he arrived at the office, "is he a bodybuilder?"

"That's not a janitor," said the principal. "That's Bo Jackson."

Bo worked a summer job at McAdory, but he was still given to streaks of youthful rebellion. He hated lifting and conditioning, the tedious trappings of the off-season. Brasseale and Atchison, the football coach, threw him off their teams several times, but by Bo's junior year, something happened: That acute sense of awareness kicked in, and Bo began to realize he could make a living this way, that he could remove himself completely from the circumstances of his boyhood, that perhaps by succeeding he could prove something to the classmates who mocked his stutter and the father who had burdened him with it. And once Bo had a mission, a charge, that's when Bo became the Bo of legend. Midway through his junior year, Atchison recalls, "he turned out to be a really good kid." Major-league scouts flocked to his games, and Bo did what he had to do to make himself known, to bolster his future. When a Yankee scout flew in from New York just to watch Bo hit, Brasseale initially refused. He was a young coach, and he was trying to instill discipline, and he was trying not to afford Bo special treatment. It was a dilemma that every one of Bo's coaches eventually caved in on, realizing that Bo was going to be Bo whether he practiced hard or not, and the risk of their treating Bo the same as everyone else was that they would alienate the entire team. What they all came to see, soon enough, was that Bo didn't *need* practice. Bo was a gift from above, and that gift came wrapped in a perfect body.

Practice had just ended, Brasseale told the scout that day, and the scout explained that he'd flown in all the way from New York, and if he could only see Bo hit a few, he'd be on his way. Upon hearing this, Bo stepped into the batting cage and said, "I'll hit two balls."

The first ball he hit smacked hard against the corner of the cage.

The cage began to rattle, up and down, up and down. Then the whole thing collapsed.

"I've seen enough," the scout said.

As a junior at McAdory, Bo won the state decathlon championship without having to run the final event, the mile, which was an ideal situation since Bo loved to run but didn't particularly enjoy running long distances. (Later, when he was at Auburn and attempted to go jogging merely for the sake of his own health, he returned home, called a friend, and said, "People who run are stupid.") He trained for the high hurdles by leaping over folding chairs. He didn't train for the pole vault at all. He high-jumped six feet nine inches and threw the discus 149 feet without spinning his body, because no one had taught him the proper form. His senior year, after a competitor broke the state triple-jump record by four feet, Bo broke that record by nearly two feet on his final attempt. "You think I can make any money in track?" Bo once asked Brasseale, and given the success of Carl Lewis at the Los Angeles Olympics in 1984, maybe Bo could have made it both as an Olympian and as a pitchman. But this was Alabama, after all, and in Alabama, there was football and there was *football,* and everything else came in a distant third. It was at an indoor track meet, in fact, that the coach at Auburn University, Pat Dye, first caught sight of Bo in person. He won every event he entered, and Dye left thinking that perhaps this kid was far better than he looked on film.

Bo's physique, and his obvious physical advantage over any other human he encountered, didn't stop his mother from worrying about the well-being of the eighth of her ten children when it came to extreme contact. She hated the very notion of Bo playing football. "You go to football practice today," she told him one day, "and you don't come home."

Bo went to practice anyway, and his mother locked him out of the house, and Bo slept in an old parked car out in the street. He enjoyed the games, the point of impact, the notion of outrunning eleven other men; he did not enjoy the slow pace, one game per week, the grueling practices and the heat and the unnecessary contact and the incessant screaming from the coaches. His attention span wandered. Several times, he walked out of practice. By the time football season ended, he was ready for track, and when track ended, he was ready for baseball. During phys-ed classes, Bo thrashed all comers at tennis and at table tennis (he was ambidextrous), and one day in the gym, when Bo assumed no one was looking, Brasseale watched him pick up a basketball, leap into the air, and dunk it over his head. He was even the best Pac-Man player in town.

Bo led his baseball team to the county championship game his senior year and hit a pair of towering home runs to left field in his first two at-bats. His third time up, with the left fielder's back up against the fence, Bo hit a short fly ball between the left fielder and the shortstop. *If he hustles,* Brasseale thought, *he'll get a double out of this thing.* Then he looked up and saw Bo rounding third. He scored standing up. It's such an improbable tale that no one believes Brasseale when he retells it, and this is perhaps the most frustrating part of being present at the onset of a legend—none of it seems rational or even plausible.

"We had an outdoor party at a lake after we won the county championship," Brasseale said. "Bo's just out there in water up to his waist. All of sudden, he jumps up, does a back flip out of the water, and lands on his feet. I said to my girlfriend, 'Did you see that?'"

That's how it was with Bo. And it is true that there have always been stories like this, passed on in a telephone game from one generation to the next—about Babe Ruth, about Josh Gibson, about Red Grange, about Marion Motley and Jim Brown and Mickey Mantle—and they seemed apocryphal, almost silly, in their exaggeration. The difference is that we would soon *see* Bo Jackson part the Red Sea on our televisions. He did things that could not be explained or believed or rationalized. Later in his career, when he scaled a wall to catch a fly ball in Kansas City or when he outran an entire National Football League defense on a Monday night in Seattle, even the videotape seemed somehow deceptive, as if it were somehow a photographic manipulation or an optical illusion. Already, he was building himself into a contemporary myth, a Paul Bunyan in cleats. He even seemed to recognize the contours of his own story and how they would play with the masses, and he had an uncanny ability to rise to the gravity of the moment. "It's almost as if he choreographs his whole life," one of his friends would say years later.

It so happened that it was a perfect time for a man like Bo to come along. In this new age of popular hero worship, a man like Bo could make a fortune just for appearing on television and playing someone very much like himself.

II.

The most important innovation in the new age of televised sports seemed, at first, more like a bizarre sartorial experiment: One September evening, approximately sixteen weeks before the onset of the 1980s, two men wearing pink-hued sport jackets and oversize ties materialized from the darkness and prefaced the debut of a radical new cable television outpost. "If you're a fan," proclaimed one of the men, a veteran television anchor named Lee Leonard, "what you'll see in the next minutes, hours, and days may convince you you've gone to sports heaven."

What followed that broadcast, on the fledgling network known as ESPN—the network that, according to *Newsweek,* comprised "cable television's most ambitious new concept"—was most certainly not anything like heaven, unless the Almighty has an awfully peculiar sense of humor. What came on next, if anyone stayed around to watch, was a professional slo-pitch softball game involving a team called the Milwaukee Schlitzes. And what followed that, in the minutes, hours, and days afterward, were broadcasts of greyhound racing and go-kart racing and hurling and tractor pulls and a constant deluge of Australian Rules Football and more Australian Rules Football, so much Australian Rules Football that a high school in Florida actually contacted the network to request the rules so it could start its own team. There was little doubt that a potential audience for such an orgy of sports programming existed. The question was whether they would congregate at some distant location on the cable dial (when most of them didn't even *have* cable yet) in order to watch this mishmash of human activity, some of it heavily disguised as sport. The notion they were banking on was that there were enough people out there—the ones whom Scott Rasmussen, the son of the network founder Bill Rasmussen, had labeled "sports junkies"—who had been waiting all their lives for something like this to come along.

That first night on the air, ESPN (short for Entertainment and Sports Programming Network) beamed itself to two million potential viewers from a half-finished studio in a little Connecticut town called Bristol, where a parcel of land across from the city landfill could be acquired on the cheap. The headquarters bustled with overworked producers and largely anonymous anchors and still lacked indoor plumbing. If the venture wasn't doomed to immediate failure, it was hard to imagine that something so far outside the mainstream would ever find a place in the big time, given the decades-long hegemony of the major television networks over the prime sporting events in America. There were believers—Getty Oil acquired 85 percent of the stock, and Anheuser-Busch (naturally) signed the first advertising deal, at $1.4 million—but all of this was a high-stakes gamble, a blind stab at the future.

Of course, there had never been a time since the advent of television when the fortunes of the medium and the fortunes of organized sport in America were not intertwined. But it had always been the networks—ABC, NBC, and CBS—that brought these moments into our homes, from the 1944 NBC broadcast of the Willy Pep–Chalky White featherweight championship bout on the brand-new *Gillette Cavalcade of Sports,* on through the postwar baseball and boxing broadcasts of the forties and fifties and on toward the merger of the American Football League and National Football League and the advent of the Super Bowl. By 1970, the networks were paying $50 million to broadcast the NFL, and $2 million for the NBA, and another $18 million for Major League Baseball, and into the 1980s, those numbers kept rising. In 1985, the figures had risen to $450 million, $45 million, and $160 million respectively. By that time, what had begun in a half-finished studio in Bristol had not altered merely the business of television and the business of sports. It had altered the culture itself.

It was force of personality that boosted ESPN from marginal curiosity into social arbiter. In the summer of 1980, during one of the station's "Sports Recaps," a young anchor named Chris Berman, while reading baseball scores, referred to John Mayberry as "John Mayberry, R.F.D." It was sometime after two-thirty in the morning, and Berman figured no one was watching; that was the beauty of those early days, of this new and fragmented media world. Berman's was a shtick born entirely of the circumstances—*It didn't matter,* he thought—and the producer giggled in his ear, and the cameraman laughed so hard that the picture shook, and hence one of the network's defining traditions was born. Soon there were hundreds of nicknames (Oddibe "Young Again" McDowell, Dave "Parallel" Parker, Joaquín "The Dog" Andújar), and Berman, with his megaphone of a voice and Fred Flintstone visage, rode the wave to become one of the faces of the network, a rising star, a broadcaster who wasn't "like anybody who ever lived," according to Nick Canepa of *The San Diego Union-Tribune:*

> Everybody's supposed to have a gimmick.
> But that's hardly true.
> Everybody doesn't have one.
> That's why people across America see so many clones, so many TV sports anchormen who sit there night after night reading scores and showing us their bridgework. Then, when their three minutes are up, they turn to the news anchorperson, who gushes something like: "That Marcus Allen is quite a right fielder, isn't he, Biff?"
> Fortunately for us all, not everyone is like that. . . . Chris Berman isn't like that. . . .

But it wasn't just Berman, and it wasn't just the program that Berman appeared on—which would come to be known as *SportsCenter,* a daily recap of the day in sports, a series of highlights and wisecracks that quickly grew into ESPN's signature program. It was the *energy* at ESPN that drew us to it and kept us there. Most notably, there was the whirlwind of manic energy and ceaseless wind power known as Richard "Dick" Vitale, a former coach originally hired at $150 per game to provide color commentary on ESPN's copious coverage of college basketball, which was one of the few sports that proved both affordable and available to a channel still regarded as a third-world outpost. From the start, Vitale was a spout of immoderation and gregariousness, virtually impossible to shut off, his bald head gleaming beneath the lights. At one point, a viewer complained in a letter that Vitale resembled the motormouthed talker in the Federal Express commercials who spoke ceaselessly at 78 rpm; Vitale took it as a compliment. Every night, he streamed silliness and saliva and manufactured lingo and initials: W's and L's and PTPers and M&Mers and TOs, so much that it induced motion sickness in *Sports Illustrated*'s William Taaffe, who wrote, "Whereas [Howard] Cosell can appeal to the intellect, Vitale only assaults the senses. . . . He's essentially an entertainer. Not that an analyst can't entertain, it's simply that the balance must tilt toward analysis."

But that was the appeal of Vitale, and of Berman, and that was the appeal of ESPN itself. As the name promised, it melded sports with entertainment in ways that were both bracing and discomfiting— its very existence fomented the cultishness of our sports fandom, in the same way another contemporary cable pioneer, MTV, embraced the cultishness of rock and roll. Each channel validated the obsessions of our youth; and if there were entire networks dedicated to such trivialities, we presumed, certainly there must be *others* like us. By the mid-1980s, ESPN and its steady stream of highlight reels had begun to change not only the way we viewed athletes, but also the way athletes viewed themselves. "The guy's great!" the Padres' Tony Gwynn told Canepa when asked about Berman, and it was only a matter of time before athletes began *asking* for nicknames and endeavoring for a place within the *SportsCenter* highlights, a spot amid the nightly conversation. And it was only a matter of time before we bought in to all of it, before we came to expect the gimmicks and the aggrandizement as part of the games themselves. We understood that the stodgy ethic of previous decades, the notion of sports being guided by militaristic principles, of the team's achievements blotting out all traces of individualism, had already withered away. ESPN just gave the modern age its voice.

At the same time, a major shoe company, at least partially inspired by the ethic of ESPN, began creating and manufacturing promotional posters in which athletes somehow personified the nicknames they'd been given—the most famous was of the San Antonio Spurs' George Gervin sitting on a massive block of ice. (Nickname: "The Iceman.") "We had all these ways to target insiders who followed the game enough to know what we were talking about," says Mike Caster, who worked in the marketing department at Nike, Inc.

All of this was happening even as ESPN bled money for the first several years of its existence, even as it attempted to make its name by force-feeding its subscribers a steady diet of yacht racing and Irish cycling and placed its faith in a contract with the upstart United States Football League. All it needed, really, was time to grow and an appropriate benefactor to foster that growth. In 1982, the network's losses totaled forty million dollars, and Getty considered liquidating, so Bill Grimes, ESPN's new president, made a calculated gamble in order to save the entire enterprise—he went to the cable companies and asked them to pay for the right to carry ESPN. This was a jarring shift for a system that had, until then, worked the other way around, with ESPN paying the cable companies five cents for every subscriber, and it did not go over particularly well at first—when Grimes brought it to the attention of Cablevision's Charles Dolan, he was reportedly thrown out of Dolan's office. But after a protracted push-and-pull, it was adopted in January 1983, and it solidified the financial stature of the company. In April 1984, when ABC bought an 85 percent interest in ESPN (largely to keep it out of the hands of Ted Turner's own burgeoning cable enterprise), there was a sense that a corner had been turned. The time was right: Deregulation under Reagan was a boon for a rapidly expanding cable industry, "the largest unregulated monopoly in the country," one observer told *The Christian Science Monitor*.

By the end of 1985, ESPN was in nearly thirty-seven million homes, and it turned a profit for the first time, presaging a future where moderation no longer seemed prudent, a future where *everyone* would have a gimmick, be it a nickname or a pair of shiny Technicolor shoes.

III.

The first pair of shoes were hastily designed red-and-black monstrosities, infused with a small and largely useless pocket of air, audacious and impractical and utterly prescient in their garishness. In the brief and occasionally sordid history of the industry known as sports marketing, there is a before and after, and those sneakers mark the demarcation between the archaic and the contemporary, between black-and-white and living color. They debuted in the fall of 1984 on the feet of a rookie guard for the NBA's Chicago Bulls, and they burst through the monochrome and largely white-canvas tradition of NBA footwear manufactured by shoe giants like Converse, who paid Larry Bird and Magic Johnson approximately seventy thousand dollars per year to wear their shoes. It was nothing new, the notion of athletes getting paid to promote a certain brand of shoe. But an athlete promoting *these* shoes, for *this* kind of money—that was what got people's attention.

The shoes so perplexed the management of the National Basketball Association that the league threatened to fine the wearer—Michael Jordan, twenty-two, originally of Wilmington, North Carolina—if he took the court in them, because they didn't match the red-and-white color scheme of the Chicago Bulls. Jordan wore them anyway, in his second game as a pro, and Nike paid his thousand-dollar fine, then ran ads touting the subversiveness of their product: "On September 15, Nike created a revolutionary new basketball shoe. On October 18, the NBA threw them out of the game. Fortunately, the NBA can't keep *you* from wearing them. Air Jordans. For Nike."

It was the counterculture gone to market; it would become a defining advertising trend in the age of the socially acceptable antihero, amid the rise of the teenage wasteland known as MTV. *We don't need people to tell us what to do; we should wear what we want to wear* (the irony being that Nike was telling us *exactly* what to wear). Which was funny, because there was absolutely nothing countercultural about Jor-

dan himself: When first shown sketches of Nike's red-and-black prototype, he said he couldn't wear them because "those are the devil's
colors." The NBA's commissioner, David Stern, quietly approved Nike's
use of the ad—he found it amusing—and Jordan switched to a red-
and-white shoe to comply with NBA regulations. But the image was
what mattered. It was the sort of publicity coup Nike, Inc., had aimed
for as it struggled to redefine itself amid the changing recreational culture of the mid-1980s, as it cut many of its endorsement contracts in
order to focus on certain athletes, and on Jordan in particular. They
believed in him because their people believed in him, because their
scout, a man named Sonny Vaccaro, had promised he would stake his
career on Jordan's success.

Nike, Inc., based in Portland, Oregon, and founded in the 1960s
by former University of Oregon runner Philip Knight, had positioned
itself as the very embodiment of entrepreneurial free-spiritedness, an
institution whose employees saw it as more of a religion than a corporation. Their people were brash and arrogant and insanely competitive, a reflection of their founder. The company had thrived amid
the rise of the national jogging craze, its earnings rising at an average
annual rate of nearly 100 percent between 1978 and 1983. But now
Nike found itself rudderless, following the sudden death of jogging's
highest-profile promoter, Jim Fixx, who collapsed and suffered a
massive coronary in the summer of '84. Running shoes had given
way to aerobics shoes and jazzercise shoes, to the increasingly sophisticated fitness routines of Jane Fonda and the cultural elite, and Reebok had beaten Nike to that market. Reebok's shoes were soft and
white, and Reebok's shoes were selling to the masses, and what was
Nike anymore except a lagging running-shoe company seeking an
identity, the rebel gone to pasture?

In February 1985, Nike would report a $2.1 million quarterly
loss; they were scaling back, laying off workers, and they had mortgaged their future and their identity on the body of a single young

man out of the University of North Carolina who defied the traditional demographics of an athletic-gear pitchman in several predominant ways. Most notably, two things: He played basketball, and he was black.

In the past, both had been red flags, and neither portended mass appeal. The presumptions of the 1950s still held true on Madison Avenue—team athletes couldn't market themselves like, say, tennis players, and black athletes did not have the ability to break through to the suburban white market or to appeal to great swaths of rural America. Late in 1984, *Fortune* magazine ridiculed the company for signing Jordan to a $2.5 million contract; it seemed like a desperate move by a desperate company that had lost its way. Asked by *Fortune* whether he might sell his share of the company, Knight said "we wouldn't necessarily turn anything down."

And yet the executives at Nike, along with Jordan's agent, David Falk, saw something in Jordan. They saw a path to reach an untapped market, a conduit to urban youth, and to the rebirth of the company itself. Sneaker contracts were becoming an increasingly relevant factor in professional basketball—Falk's own client, James Worthy, had recently signed an eight-year, $1.2 million deal with New Balance, raising the ante on the numbers—but Jordan's pact was a breakthrough because Falk and the management at Nike envisioned the transformation of Jordan into something more than merely a basketball player. They saw a way to reinvent the team-sport athlete as the centerpiece of a campaign, as a commercial icon. They envisioned Michael Jordan—soft-spoken, determined, and gifted with rare abilities and an electric smile—as a brand whose television appeal would carry over the masses.

All three parties needed one another; the relationship would be symbiotic, for Falk, for Jordan, for Nike itself. Jordan's mere presence seemed to energize the creative minds at Nike, veterans of the company like Rob Strasser and Peter Moore, who saw Jordan as a palette on which to experiment with their own radical ideas. Nike didn't only design shoes specifically for Jordan. They designed an entire clothing line: sweatpants, T-shirts, tank tops, all of these things that no one could have imagined a young basketball player—a young *black* basketball player—would have the ability to sell. Just as important, they fast-tracked it all, forming their own group outside the corporate bureaucracy so as to hurry their products to market, caution be damned. "I did think the black-and-red shoes were too far out there," said Mike Caster, the first marketing manager for the Air Jordan line. "But I was just used to sneakers that were white. Those guys were brilliant. They were some of the best creative people I've ever worked with."

What they recognized—both by accident and by design—was that times had changed. There was something nonthreatening about Jordan, about that smile, about his fantastical leaping ability, and it did not take much of a spark in this age of twenty-four-hour sports networks, amid the rise of a generation that was far too young to recall the struggles of the civil-rights movement, for his appeal to bridge the chasm between the inner city and the suburbs. "If Michael Jordan, he of the brilliant smile, was not burdened by race," wrote author David Halberstam, "why should you be burdened by it either?"

IV.

In 1982, during Bo Jackson's freshman year at Auburn, there were 18,401 students enrolled at Auburn University; 446 of those students, or 2 percent, were black. On July 11 of that same year, the United States of America brought suit against the state of Alabama and most of its four-year colleges, questioning whether the state with a black population of 25.6 percent "operated a racially dual system of higher education, and if so whether the vestiges of the dual system have now been eliminated." The trial carried on for more than two years, and arguments ended in the summer of 1985, the summer before Bo Jackson's senior season at Auburn, when the same boy who had leapt that ditch and nearly fallen into a future as a juvenile delinquent faced another crucial decision about his future.

Bo had seemingly never been fettered by the lingering racial divides of the South. His senior year at McAdory, a white teammate, Steve Mann, the quarterback, was voted the best male athlete in the class, and this created a divide, blacks on one side, whites on the other (Bessemer was about 70–30, white to black). The principal called a meeting of the senior class in the library, words flew back and forth, and eventually, Bo stood up to speak. He claimed he didn't care much about winning awards. At this point he had discovered a path to take him beyond Bessemer, if only he behaved himself. Said Bo: "I'm here to get an education, to graduate, and to get the hell out of here." He said that his classmates were welcome to stay and argue and fight it out, but that he was going back to class. And he stood up and left. In this manner, the situation was defused.

By then, this new and reformed Bo had a vision, a goal. He was already imagining ways to increase his value in the marketplace. When the New York Yankees drafted Bo in the second round of the 1982 draft and offered him $250,000 to sign with them, he turned them down—and when a pair of Yankee representatives showed up at the doorstep of the house in Bessemer, Bo had his mother turn them away without speaking to them. How could he miss the money when he'd never had it in the first place? He'd go to college, he thought, and he'd play two or three sports, and then he'd pick one and do it for a living. If it were anyone else, it could be dismissed as a teenage flight of fancy, but this was Bo, and nothing was a flight of fancy with a kid who could kick forty-yard field goals and high-jump six feet nine inches and set a state record in the long jump.

The football recruiting letters arrived at the house in Bessemer in droves, and the phone rang so often that they left it off the hook. Still,

Bo was seen more as an "athlete" than as a pure football player, and he was not even the highest-rated running back in the state (that was Alan Evans, from a town called Enterprise). When Bo went to visit Paul "Bear" Bryant at the University of Alabama, the coach hinted that he might use Jackson on defense, and that he wouldn't play much as a freshman or a sophomore, because this *was* Alabama, and everyone paid their dues.

At Auburn, Pat Dye, a former assistant under Bryant who until recently had been coach at Wyoming, had no such reservations. Dye was hired in 1981 to energize a program that hadn't beaten its in-state rival since 1972. This was the Bear's state, and Dye needed all the help he could get to close the gap, and he went hard after both Evans and Jackson, who was being pursued by an Auburn assistant named Bobby Wallace. It was Wallace who reported back to Dye that he'd found "a big strong kid that could run fast," and it wasn't until Dye saw him in person that he realized what he'd found—a genetic freak, a once-in-a-lifetime athlete with the ability to change the fundamental nature of the Auburn-Alabama rivalry. Eventually, Dye signed Alan Evans as well; by 1984, hopelessly stranded behind Jackson on the depth chart, Evans transferred to the University of Tennessee at Chattanooga.

The choice of Auburn fit with Bo's tendency toward contrarianism. It wasn't the obvious destination for a young man who grew up in Alabama in the era of the Bear, but it was *Bo's* choice, and he would make the Bear regret even the implication that Bo might not be good enough to play offense, or that he wasn't good enough to play right away. He arrived at Auburn possessed of nothing more than his clothes and a color television his father had bought for him.[1] And it

---

1. There were rumors—vehemently denied by Bo—that Auburn boosters bought his mother a chain of 7-Eleven stores and Bo himself a forty-thousand-dollar sports car; among Alabama fans, in an era of recruiting improprieties, this became a simple way to explain the snub.

didn't take long for word to spread about his multifaceted abilities. In his first scrimmage, he plowed over a defensive tackle, the team captain, for a touchdown. That season, sharing carries in the wishbone with two other tailbacks, Bo ran for more than 800 yards, including 123 in the season opener against Wake Forest, and drew immediate comparisons to Herschel Walker, a similarly sculpted tailback who played at the University of Georgia.

Walker had been a folk hero himself, a self-made success who grew up in a blue-collar household, the son of factory workers who had met while picking cotton. As a freshman in 1980, Walker led Georgia to the national championship. He built his body through interminable sessions of push-ups and sit-ups, and though the comparisons seemed apropos within the moment, what people could not see at the time is that Herschel Walker was not really like Bo at all. One of his pro-football teammates would later say that Walker "couldn't dribble a basketball. I mean, he literally couldn't bounce the ball twice in a row."

Bo did not have such problems; he was strength, he was power, he was speed, he was all of the above. He is still the only human known to have thrown a ball high enough that it bounced off the overhanging scoreboard at the Louisiana Superdome, and he did it without warming up. In the spring of 1983, Bo became the SEC's first three-sport letterman in more than twenty years, and his time of 6.18 in the sixty-yard dash made him the only freshman to qualify for the NCAA final (he was later timed at 4.175 in the forty-yard dash). To Dye, there was fast, and then there was *Bo Jackson Fast;* as often as defenders tried to adjust their angles of pursuit to keep Bo contained, Bo would simply outrun the angles, defying the geometry of the game itself.

And yet he almost didn't make it through that first fall at Auburn. At one point, he got into an altercation with an assistant football coach who chastised him for fixing his pants during a drill. What was the *point?* What good did practice do, anyway, as long you showed up on game day? *Who cares?* Bo said. (Throughout the progression of the next couple of decades, as this question became a common mantra among the hierarchy of superstars, Bo may have been the only one for whom it possessed validity.) That was the moment when the Auburn staff, like Bo's high school coaches before him, realized that this one was simply not cut out for practice. "My approach to it," Dye said, "was that you don't take something as special as this and ruin it."

Freed from the iron grip of his mother, Bo had trouble adjusting to college. He still stuttered badly. He feared speaking to the media. He spent most of his free time in his dorm room, listening to gospel music, and playing video games at the arcade on College Street. He was so homesick that the week before the Alabama game, he spent five hours at the Greyhound bus terminal, contemplating whether he should just go back to Bessemer and fall into his old life. Eventually, Bobby Wallace, the assistant who had recruited him, came back and picked him up, and the next day, he was called into Dye's office, this teenager with the preternatural body and the wandering psyche, and the coach fell into a lecture and a plea that went something like this: *Bo, do you realize what you mean to this football team? Your presence on this football team gives Auburn people hope. I don't know how to put it any different than that. I can't take the pressure away. Football is way more important in Alabama than maybe it should be, but that's a fact of life down here. You've got to deal with it on your own terms.*

With that, Bo found his direction again, and in the final seconds of the game against Alabama, with the ball resting eighteen inches short of the goal line and Auburn trailing by six points and facing a fourth down, Bo took a handoff and leapt high into the air with a single bound, just as he had done years earlier, just as he would do time and time again in his career, stretching his body over the goal line and delivering Auburn to its first victory over Alabama since 1972.

At that moment, something changed, both for Bo and for the

institution he represented. "Bo Jackson did not play in a vacuum, but in an atmosphere of great questioning and problems for the university," wrote David Rosenblatt, a political science professor, in a paper examining Bo's impact on Auburn. He wasn't an activist, but he didn't have to be—he was the greatest football player the state had ever seen, and in a state where football *was* the culture, that was enough. In the midst of a slow and painful transition at Auburn, as a black student group—one of the first of its kind at a school where blacks were woefully underrepresented—protested the staging of an "Old South" parade by a campus fraternity, as questions arose in the courts as to whether the universities in Alabama still showed "vestiges of segregation," here was a young man who stood as the exemplar of change, who seemed burdened neither by the limits of his race nor the limits of the human body itself.

So it was that in the summer of '85, Bo Jackson faced another watershed decision about his future: Would it be baseball or football? The newspapers, local and national, spent much of the summer and fall speculating; Bo himself was noncommittal. He liked baseball better during baseball season; he liked football better during football season. "I wish I could do both," he told one reporter. "At least, I'd like to try it to see if I liked it. But there's always going to be somebody to say, 'No, you can't do it.'"

At some point, Bo would have to choose. This was the unanimous sentiment of every talent evaluator and every journalist and even Bo's own coaches; it was unimaginable that, in this complex and specialized era, even an athlete as uncanny as this one could accomplish the feat of playing two professional sports at the same time. Everyone assumed Bo would choose football because contract offers would be huge and would pour in from both the National Football League and the United States Football League, and how could Bo resist the money and the prestige when it came at him with such force? All the while, Bo seemed to revel in the slow growth of his legend above and beyond the state of Alabama. He toyed with the national reporters who came to interview him that summer. He told them about the unruly child he used to be. He told them about the pigs and the ditch, and he told them he'd make a decision about his future on his own terms. ("I'll get ten pieces of paper, write *football* or *baseball* on 'em, and throw 'em in a hat," he told *People* magazine.) If there was one thing Bo did not abide, it was presumptuousness about his motives. You told him he couldn't do something, and Bo only wanted to do it that much more.

That fall, Dye shifted his entire offense from a wishbone to an I-formation in order to showcase Bo's talents. In the first six games of the season, Bo averaged more than two hundred yards rushing per game. The one exception: when Bo pulled himself from an early-season game against Tennessee with a strained knee. Auburn lost, 38–20. Five weeks later, in a loss to Florida, Bo pulled himself again in the second quarter with a bruised thigh. He returned for two plays in the fourth quarter, gained nothing much at all, and vanished from the scene once more. "I knew if he got hurt, he would pull himself from the game," one Florida player said. Auburn lost 14–10, prompting a harsh rebuke from the columnist for the *Birmingham Post-Herald*, Paul Finebaum, who began his Monday column like this:

> AUBURN—There are some things in life that people take for granted. Death and taxes. Heat in the summer, cold in the winter.
>
> Now, there's a new one—Bo Jackson pulling a disappearing act in critical football games.

Soon after, *Sports Illustrated* put a little-known running back, Joe Dudek, from Plymouth State in New Hampshire, on the cover and insisted that Dudek deserved the Heisman more than Bo because Bo had pulled himself from a pair of crucial contests. "In big games, Bo grabs more bench time than Sandra Day O'Connor," wrote *SI*'s Rick Reilly, and then went on to compare Bo unfavorably to Herschel Walker.

All of this talk about a lack of toughness angered Bo, but it also exposed the paradox of his persona. In a way, the criticism had a certain amount of validity, in that Bo did not see his challenges in the way others saw their challenges, in that Bo *was* considering his future as much as he considered the moment. "I can't go out and get hurt to the point that I can't run no fucking more," he later told his biographer, Dick Schaap. Bo had tried to play hurt when he was younger, and it only made things worse. So he pulled himself from those games because it equated with his own notion of common sense. Certainly, Bo wanted to win football games, and Bo expected to win football games, but as had always been the case, what got to him more than the adoration and expectations of fans and journalists were the challenges that struck him as personal affronts, as if somehow he were being patently disrespected.

Mostly, Bo liked to run, and Bo especially liked to run people over. He did not seem caught up in the growing perception of contemporary athletics as a win-at-all-costs proposition. He viewed his gifts as a ticket out of Bessemer; he viewed his image, his growing legend, as a way of elevating his value in the marketplace. It wasn't that he didn't care about winning and losing—Bo's fear of failure was acute, as evidenced a year earlier, when he misheard a play call and ran the wrong way during a crucial goal-line play in a 17–15 loss to Alabama—but he accepted that both had a place, and he certainly didn't care about vague and subjective recognitions like the Heisman Trophy. Until people began saying he didn't deserve it. "He didn't get a thrill out of being in the limelight or winning the Heisman as much as he did you telling him, 'You can't jump over that fence like that,'"

Dye said. "When somebody told him he couldn't do it, he got a kick out of doing it."

So when the criticism came that fall, then Bo began to think that maybe he did have something to prove after all. It was in moments like this that Bo became the force that captured the national imagination.

In the week after the loss to Florida, with his thigh still aching, Bo ran for 121 yards and scored two touchdowns in a win over Georgia, and the week after that, Bo ran for 142 yards in a last-second loss to Alabama. With three minutes remaining in that game, ABC analyst Frank Broyles made a surprise announcement, one that changed the narrative completely. He said he had received a call from Dye the day before, and Dye had shared a secret with him. "He said that Bo Jackson broke two ribs against Georgia," Broyles told the viewers. "He asked me not to use it for sympathy or any other thing, but if I wanted to, I could use it during the ball game at the right time."

Even Broyles's own broadcasting partner, Keith Jackson, was completely unaware of the news; the force of it shattered the conventional wisdom about Bo and burnished his aura as a superhuman, as a font of possibility, capable of anything at any time, whenever he felt like doing it. As confirmation, a *Birmingham News* reporter managed to track down the X rays of Bo's ribs: One was broken completely through, the other cracked. There was a reason *The Atlanta Journal-Constitution* shot photos of Bo bursting out of a phone booth wearing a Superman outfit. So great were his accomplishments that we began to believe he could do anything with that body, whenever and however he felt like it, if only he deemed such actions gallant and necessary.

On December 7, on the same day a United States district judge issued an order demanding that Auburn "submit to the court . . . a plan to eliminate all vestiges of the dual system of higher education in Alabama," Bo Jackson was awarded the Heisman Trophy in New

York City. In Auburn, at the intersection that divides town and campus known as Toomer's Corner, they danced in the streets and rolled the trees with toilet paper.

A few weeks earlier, a Nike executive named Bill Kellar, in search of the face for a new prototype of shoe called a cross-trainer, had flown down South to watch Jackson play football. Already, the school's equipment manager had assured Kellar that Bo could throw a pass one hundred yards. This seemed patently ridiculous, given that most professional quarterbacks couldn't throw it that far, and Kellar said so, and then he came by practice as the team was warming up the next day, and saw it with his own eyes, a football soaring from one end of the field to the other. Upon returning, he recommended to his superiors that they sign this miracle man to a contract as soon as possible.

V.

In February 1985, two months before the first Air Jordan shoe was to be released in eight test markets (retail: $64.95), Michael Jordan competed in the slam-dunk contest during the NBA's All-Star Weekend in Indianapolis. The dunk contest was, at that time, an event in search of a higher purpose, and the NBA's attempts to infuse it with color—including a new "dunking song" called "High Rise," with such lyrical flourishes as "the taste of dunk is sweet"—seemed thoroughly absurd even to the modern progenitor of the dunk. "It's silly," said Julius Erving, who had been the runner-up the year before. The 1984 winner, Larry Nance, had called himself "dunked out," lamenting that the league was using the dunk for a show. Another of the NBA's young stars, a rotund young man out of Auburn named Charles Barkley, had withdrawn, citing homesickness. But Jordan was there, and he was already being touted as the future of the NBA, and the people at Nike saw this as an opportunity: They provided

Jordan with an outfit to match his shoes (the original black-and-red model), in an attempt to drive up demand for the line of clothing that would bear Jordan's name. Instead of wearing his Bulls warm-ups, Jordan swathed himself in Nike, a company whose products he'd admittedly had little taste for before he signed with them. He wore tiger-striped pants and a loose tank top over a T-shirt, and there was something about it that did not go over well. No one had ever seen anything like it before, and even after Jordan lost to Dominique Wilkins in the finals, his appearance raised the question: *Who does this guy think he is?*

Most notably, it bred resentment among Jordan's All-Star teammates, who conspired to freeze him out of the scoring during the game itself—he had one dunk and missed seven of his other eight shots. They spread rumors about Jordan's aloofness and his presumptuousness and questioned whether he had snubbed Detroit Pistons guard Isiah Thomas while riding with him in an elevator, and while it all seemed ridiculous and petty within the moment—Dr. Charles Tucker, an advisor to Thomas and Magic Johnson, said Jordan had an "attitude problem"—the relationship between Thomas and Jordan would be fraught with animosity for years afterward. And Jordan himself would begin to view his purpose differently.

"I feel like I can trust people," he told the *Chicago Tribune* shortly after the All-Star game, following a forty-nine-point performance in a win over Thomas and the Pistons. "I've always operated that way, everywhere I've been. But I think from now on my actions will be a little different when I meet new people."

We would learn, in this moment, a few important things about a man who would soon become the most famous athlete in the world, whose rise to prominence would prefigure, and briefly coincide with, that of Bo Jackson. We would learn that Michael Jordan did not forgive easily, and we would learn that Jordan, when challenged, was capable of virtually anything. At the same time, Jordan was dealing with the signature dilemma of this new age: He was attempting to reconcile his actual persona with his celebrity persona, with the brand he was about to become, with the commercials that choreographed his image. He was as much an actor as an athlete.

Within a year, revenue from the Air Jordan shoe would top a hundred million dollars ("It's become our Cabbage Patch doll," one spokesman said), and Nike was on the verge of regaining its preeminence in the market. *Sports is bigger than entertainment,* Phil Knight would imply a few years later. The era had found its defining models; the very perception of an athlete, of the ethic he appealed to, of how he was packaged and marketed and presented and placed on a television screen, was about to change. This was the eighties, and the shoes made the man as much as, if not more than, the man had ever made the shoes.

Greenwood, South Carolina

It's true, what she says about the graves. I went to see them not long after I heard Lonise Bias tell an incredible story to a group of South Carolina high school students: that while witnessing the burial of her son Jay, she looked down and realized she was standing on the grave of her eldest son, Leonard. I assumed that it was a rhetorical flourish, a metaphor crafted for effect by a guest speaker who was getting paid to whack some sobriety into a roomful of spaced-out pubescents with self-image issues. But then I drove to the cemetery, in a Maryland suburb of Washington, D.C., called Suitland, and I trudged up a hill and found the markers, a couple of rectangles blotched with age, stamped into the dirt and rocks and tufts of grass. And it is true—there is perhaps a foot of space between her boys. They are, quite literally, resting side by side.

The graves, tucked together like this, are a stark testimony to the complexity of Lonise Bias's grief. It is virtually impossible to comprehend the hellish depths she has plumbed in the decades since they were interred, and it is equally difficult to see how she emerged with such palpable vigor and determination and self-assurance. This can also make her come across as kind of a strange lady, especially to a roomful of twenty-first-century teenagers; instead of crushing her spirit, unspeakable family tragedy has stripped her of the angst and self-doubt that paralyzes much of her audience. She opens her speeches by telling people that she does not particularly care what they think of her, which then permits her to bellow phrases like "I AM THE LEGACY THAT WAS LEFT BEHIND!" and "I CAME THROUGH TO SHOW YOU THE WAY!" and somehow make them sound authoritative rather than bombastic.

"I've been termed as being ABNORMALLY ENTHUSIASTIC," she often says. "But I am full of passion BECAUSE I BELIEVE IN YOU. I am standing here to TELL YOU that you CAN MAKE IT."

I went to see her on a Monday morning. She was sweating under the spotlights on the stage of a high school auditorium in a quiet corner of South Carolina. The assembly was mandatory. And it didn't matter that no one in this room knew who she was anymore, or who her sons were, or where they'd come from, or why her story meant anything at all. It didn't matter that she was hired blind by a teacher who had read Lonise Bias's biography on the Web site of a speakers' bureau and thought it appropriate for a schoolwide assembly, and it didn't matter when she momentarily forgot where she was and referred to the students of Greenwood High School as the students of Green*ville*. It didn't matter, because it was hard *not* to listen when a woman with this kind of overbearing presence WAS TALKING RIGHT AT YOU.

She had always possessed a robust set of vocal cords. When she was in elementary school and the faculty needed a child to speak loud enough for a large group to hear, they chose her. She grew up tall and imposing, with a natural-born gravity; after her speech at Greenwood, more than one student said Lonise Bias reminded them of her mother. Mrs. Bias had always thought she would teach someday, but she'd imagined it would be in Sunday school, not in a place like this, a public school several hundred miles from the suburban Maryland county where her past two decades had often played out like a soap opera.

She was working as a customer-service manager at a bank on that day in June when her eldest son's death became a national headline, when he became something more than just a tall young man who could handle a spherical object with precision, when he somehow became a totem for all the excesses and social injustices of the 1980s. Here, though, is what's weirdest of all about Lonise Bias: She, of all people, does not believe the events of that day were unjust. In fact, she believes the events of that day were unavoidable. She has never allowed herself to project into the future or to examine the possibilities, the endless permutations of what-ifs that guide the discussion of her son whenever his name arises in the ceaseless cycle of arguments about alternate realities in sports. For her, there was *only* this future. For her, there was *only* this possibility. In the days after her son died, Mrs. Bias's public demeanor was so stoic and unflinching that she says she received letters from people declaring her a phony. Even now, she admits that among the other emotions her son's death brought on, it brought relief.

Not long after Len's death, she made a life-changing appearance on a Christian television program, *The 700 Club*. She described the premonitions she'd been having, and the dreams, and the inexplicable emotional breakdowns, and the visions she assumed were coming directly from above, all imbuing her with a heavy and inextricable feeling that her son was not meant to play professional basketball. One day, she said, she had been reading her Bible and she paused to consider a portrait of her son, an oil painting of Leonard in a Maryland uniform that hung on the wall of the family's living room in the suburb of Landover. And that was when she swore a voice called out to her. And she swore the voice said, "He'll never play pro."

She didn't want to believe it. She knew how absurd this sounded, especially at a time when her son was being touted as one of the great talents of his generation, a future millionaire, a success story in a city and a nation plagued by the failure of its African-American youth. She refused to speak to anyone about what she thought she heard, and she attempted to assure herself that the voices were imagined. But the feelings would not subside. She heard these warnings when she stared at that portrait, or when she spoke to her son on the phone.

Her son who, in his senior season at the University of Maryland, was generally regarded as the best college basketball player in America, a can't-miss talent with absurd hang time. Her son who was drafted with the number two pick by the World Champion Boston Celtics on June 17, 1986. Her son who would be described in an autopsy report two days later as a "well-developed young Black male," six feet seven, 221½ pounds, otherwise fit and healthy and well-liked and clean, with the exception of the copious amount of cocaine in his system.

"I can remember speaking to this woman once before Len died, and she had said, 'Things are going to be so wonderful for you all,'" Lonise Bias recalled years later. "And I remember telling her this very clearly. I said, 'It looks like I can go over to that table and pick up whatever's on that table. It *looks* like I can do it, but there can be something that can stop me from doing it.' So I guess what I'm saying is, while everyone else was cheering, I was still waiting to see if it was going to happen, because—"

For a moment, she was somewhere else, her gaze fixed on a table a few feet from where she sat in her suburban Maryland office—the walls adorned with photographs of her posing next to presidents and congressmen as a motivational speaker of some renown, as a proud foot soldier in the interminable war on drugs.

A generation has passed, and clouds of doubt and shame and confusion linger, and no one wants to talk very much about the long-term meaning of Len Bias—it is as if those who knew him would rather bury their regret—except for Lonise Bias, who cannot *stop* talking about it. All because, several years before her sons would come to lie side by side in two narrow plots of land, and several months before her life became altered by grief, the mother had a vision of her eldest son as a martyr.

I do not know if Len Bias was a martyr or a hero, or whether in death, as Lonise Bias often says, he has brought life. I do not know if, as Jesse Jackson claimed in eulogizing Bias—likening him to Martin Luther King Jr., Mozart, Gandhi, and Jesus—that the Lord "sometimes uses our best people to get our attention."

I do not know if Len Bias died for any reason at all, divine or otherwise, beyond the fact that he ingested a massive amount of 88 percent pure cocaine in a brief period of time, short-circuiting the electrical impulses to his heart muscle.

I do not know if, as many claim, the Boston Celtics would have extended the 1980s Bird-McHale-Parish dynasty by several seasons if Len Bias had lived, and I do not know if he was the catalyst for another decades-long New England curse, and I do not know if he would have been better/as good as/in the same stratosphere as Michael Jordan if he had lived to play in the National Basketball Association. We can argue these esoteric hypotheticals all we like, but at some point, I believe the true answers to such questions became irrelevant, obscured by the mythology that he has engendered.

I do know that death—especially sudden and premature death—

has a way of obscuring many truths (see: Dean, James; Cobain, Kurt; et al.).

I do know that the public narrative was deceptively simple: Len Bias had just experienced the most euphoric moment of his life, and he had an unquestionably bright future, and he had chosen to experiment with illicit substances for the first time—perhaps, some errant rumors went, even with crack cocaine—and in a freak occurrence of bad karma, his heart had stopped.

I do know that I was thirteen years old at the time, a teenager, just like the hundreds of adolescents Lonise Bias shared her prophecy with that day in South Carolina more than two decades after the fact. And while I cannot speak for the children of Greenwood, South Carolina, I can say that back then the mystifying circumstances of Bias's death succeeded in scaring the hell out of me, and thousands of pubescent and prepubescent youths just like me, in ways that all the fears triggered by nuclear buildup and exploding spacecraft and deadly viruses couldn't. We didn't quite know how to take it, or what it meant in the grand scheme of things; some of us had trouble understanding why it had hit us so hard in the first place. But there was something about this one—about an athlete dying young—that cut through the filter of adult society.

At a high school basketball camp in southern Pennsylvania, several boys, including one who asked Bias to sign the back of a torn envelope during an appearance at the camp a year earlier, sat stunned in the gym. In Maine, a young boy began clipping articles about Bias for a scrapbook, for reasons he still couldn't quite articulate as an adult. At a small college in North Carolina, a student sat in the car and listened to a local disc jockey cut off the music and deliver the news, his voice cracking. The student did not move for a long time, until he realized he was already late for class.

Something changed that morning, although it had actually been changing for years, as the games evolved from a pastime into a business, as they increasingly became the canvas on which the nation's moral dilemmas and social divides were played out. This moment just brought it to our immediate attention. So it was that on the morning Len Bias lay dying in a Maryland hospital bed as a team of doctors attempted to undo an irrevocable mistake, as the mythology took hold, we could no longer escape the fact that the modern age of American sports was upon us.

CHAPTER THREE

Glamour Profession

You are not the kind of guy who would be at a place like this at this time of the morning.

—Jay McInerney, *Bright Lights, Big City*

I.

Even as she fought back premonitions of her son's inevitable demise, Lonise Bias began to manufacture her own set of truths about the circumstances. Her child did not *do* cocaine. Her child was *moral*. Her child was *righteous*. One Sunday, he asked his Maryland teammates to accompany him to a church in Washington, D.C.; then he approached the altar by himself and said he had been born again. After his death, Lonise Bias found her son's Bible, the names of his teammates written inside the front cover. *This* was the Leonard she knew—not the Leonard who fetishized the lifestyle of the professional athlete, not the Leonard who hung posters of Porsches and Lamborghinis in his dorm room next to a life-sized poster of himself that was the most popular promotional item on campus (Caption: I'm Bias. Maryland #1); not the Leonard one reporter referred to as "the surliest, the most uncooperative of all the players . . . one of the biggest jerks I've ever dealt with." When he made the brief trip from

the Maryland campus to his home in Landover, Lonise Bias continued to admonish her son, as his fame swelled, not to lose sight of
himself. *The Lord has given you a beautiful gift,* Lonise would say.
*You're a great player, and you're on television, but remember it came
from the Lord.*

Her child, she insists, was not enticed by the trappings of celebrity, nor was he tripped up by the complications of his own burgeoning fame. Hadn't he *chosen* to remain at Maryland to complete his
senior season and get his degree instead of jumping straight to the
NBA after his junior year (when, it should be noted, he probably
would have been a mid-to-late first-round draft selection rather than
a lottery pick)? In public, even around most of the friends who
thought they knew him well, he was apparently so committed to his
health and his image that he wouldn't even touch a beer; once, when
Maryland coach Lefty Driesell took a call from someone who had
seen Bias carrying a six-pack on campus, it turned out he'd been carrying a six-pack of root beer.

Even now, Lonise Bias remains convinced of her child's relative
innocence on the night in question. She wonders often whether
Leonard made an unintentional error, whether he was horribly naïve,
whether perhaps he drank the cocaine by mistake, whether perhaps
he was even poisoned by someone with a grudge against a young
African-American man with a promising and lucrative future. Otherwise, it does not make sense; the dichotomy, she feels, between the
Leonard of that night and the Leonard she knew is too great to be
reconciled. And she has held to this conviction despite all of the evidence to the contrary, despite even the sworn testimony of a Maryland teammate who testified in a courtroom that at some point late
in the year 1985, not long after his twenty-second birthday, Leonard
Bias had introduced *him* to cocaine.

II.

It had all sounded so glamorous when it first came back around: In 1973, in a *Time* magazine story headlined "Tyrannical King Coke," a drug dealer in Boston hailed cocaine as a miracle drug, as the equivalent of the Almighty blowing life into your nostrils. Decades later, the story reads like a bad parody. It opens at a party on the East Side of Manhattan, where the hostess presents her guests a "glass jar filled with white powder" as a token of friendship. Here it was, a new turn-on to carry us out of the 1960s and into the regrettable cultural indulgences of the '70s. Here was a drug with Hollywood cachet among both blacks (*Superfly*) and whites (*Easy Rider*); here was an expensive high that screamed of status and wealth and success. "Smoking pot has become commonplace, even passé," *Time* wrote, "and some people look for new thrills."

In 1977, a *Newsweek* story compared cocaine to Dom Perignon and beluga caviar, and quoted Jimmy Carter's drug czar, who claimed that "there's not a great deal of evidence of major health consequences from the use of cocaine." (He was operating largely under the assumption that the drug was so prohibitively expensive, most Americans couldn't *afford* to get addicted.) In the summer of '81, on the cover of *Time:* A photo of a martini glass filled with white powder. Headline: "High on Cocaine: A Drug with Status and Menace." Still, cocaine was seen by its proponents as a frivolous party enhancement, "a supremely beguiling and relatively risk-free drug—at least so its devotees innocently claim. Although in very small and occasional doses it is no more harmful than equally moderate doses of alcohol or marijuana, and infinitely less so than heroin, it has its dark and destructive side." Cocaine, said one executive, made him feel like a new man; the only problem was that the first thing this new man wanted was another line.

Despite that underlying sense of peril, there was something undeniably *modern* and of-the-moment about cocaine that continued to fuel its popularity—it was a drug that sped everything up, a drug that fueled one's self-image in an increasingly complex and mechanized society. And so why wouldn't it spill over into sports, into perhaps the largest base of suddenly wealthy young individuals in the history of this country? Here were scores of traveling entertainers, many under the age of twenty-five, making hundreds of thousands of dollars a year, with nothing better to do on a Tuesday night in the big city than dabble in the local nightlife. Here were the newest of the nouveaux riches, their salaries ballooning as free agency and endorsement contracts opened more doors; and here was a drug that appealed to upwardly mobile professionals of all sorts. "It wasn't just the professional athlete," said Micheal "Sugar" Ray Richardson, who by the early 1980s had become a reluctant connoisseur of the drug. "It was doctors and politicians. It was in the society. But anything you do out of moderation, it gets expensive. And if you've got an addiction, you're *going* to do it excessively. That's the problem."

Slowly, cocaine was finding a way to democratize. For the first time in memory, a "hard" drug had pervaded suburban America, white-collar America. And why not? It didn't *seem* particularly hard. It was an easy high. But this was merely the newest cultural incarnation of a substance—derived from the leaves of a plant known as *Erythroxylon coca* and imported from South America, where it had once been revered by Peruvian Incas (*herbs which make one run,* they called them)—that had a long and venerable history of humans' underestimating its effects on the body. Its effects were cumulative. It sneaked up on you. "Absolutely no craving for further use of cocaine appears after the first, or repeated, taking of the drug," wrote Sigmund Freud, and in the late nineteenth century, cocaine was used as the primary ingredient in a new category of over-the-counter medicinals and tonics: ointments, sprays, and eventually a soft drink known as Coca-Cola. In 1877, a Canadian doctor gave coca leaves to the members of a Toronto lacrosse club before a match and reported that it sustained them throughout the game. It was generally dismissed as a harmless stimulant until the turn of the century, when America developed a population of opiate and cocaine addicts that numbered more than 250,000. In 1914, the Harrison Narcotics Act rendered a number of drugs illegal under federal law, and by the early 1930s, cocaine abuse had basically vanished as a public health issue.

And then, ever so gradually, it trickled back into the national consciousness, in part due to its potential as a performance-enhancing drug for athletes. In a 1954 story about a high school coach in Ashland, Ohio, who gave his athletes "pep-up pills" before games, *Sports Illustrated* asked: "Where should athletes draw the line, if any, between tea and cocaine?" In 1960, in an *SI* editorial: "Individuals and teams should rely on skill and practice rather than on Benzedrine and cocaine."

But then came the sixties, and by the end of the decade team doctors admitted that they administered all sorts of quasi-legal substances: Dexamyl, Dexedrine, Seconal, Tuinal, Nembutal, Triavil, Tofranil, Valium—"the excessive and secretive use of drugs is likely to become a major athletic scandal, one that will shake public confidence in many sports just as the gambling scandal [of the 1950s] tarnished the reputation of basketball," one doctor said. He was speaking of the use of drugs to enhance performance, but at some point, the lines became blurred. What was the difference, really, between an amphetamine plucked from a bowl in the training room and a bump of cocaine? "Pregame medication is a fact of NFL life," said Thomas "Hollywood" Henderson, a linebacker who was drafted by the Dallas Cowboys in 1975, snorted cocaine from a spray inhaler during the Super Bowl in 1979, began freebasing in 1980, and soon after became the first pro football player to go public with a cocaine addiction. Drugs were part of the culture, both inside the locker room and outside of it. As long as you showed up for work/practice the next day, what was the harm in it?

In 1982, John Belushi died after being injected with a combination of heroin and cocaine known as a speedball; it was largely dismissed as a manifestation of Hollywood excess. But by 1985, all these isolated incidents had begun to form a pattern—almost six million Americans were believed to be regular users of cocaine, up 38 percent from 1982. "Early in use, all of the positive things about cocaine are true," one researcher told *The New York Times.* "As use continues, all the negative things become true."

III.

Now the confessions were beginning to emerge, from athletes who became cornered in dire and desperate circumstances, from athletes in search of penance and second chances. Years of slow-building addiction had begun to take a toll; the drug *Time* had pictured as a harmless diversion of the rich and fabulous was now becoming a serious habit. In 1982, Don Reese, a six-feet-six, 280-pound defensive lineman, told *Sports Illustrated* that he had been taking cocaine since 1974, that it was pushed on players, sometimes from the very edges of the practice field, and that he was thirty thousand dollars in debt because of his habit. He named names, including that of All-Pro Chuck Muncie. He told of drug dealers hanging around on the sideline; he told of "tooting" in training camp with his teammates in Miami, which by the early 1980s had become the violent epicenter of the cocaine trade, the major players machine-gunning each other at shopping malls.

Reese's article was a broad indictment of a sport rife with cocaine use—the most candid drug exposé to date—and in its wake came a flood of sordid tales that had been welling up in football locker rooms for the better part of a decade. In Denver, the club had initiated drug-testing on its own to gain control of the problem; in Cleveland, running back Charles White was reported to be in rehab; in New Orleans, George Rogers, the league's leading rusher in 1981, was named as a cocaine user; in San Diego, Muncie was banned from training camp until he completed drug treatment; in Miami, former Dolphins running back Mercury Morris was sentenced to prison for cocaine trafficking; in *The New York Daily News,* a report emerged that *50 percent* of active players used cocaine recreationally. In 1983, NFL commissioner Pete Rozelle suspended four players for the first four games of the season because they'd testified in court that they had bought cocaine. To the general public, this made no sense. Athletes had a grand tradition as barflies, but drinking was legal; what had led them to *this?* "Football players who partied, now with weed and coke instead of beer and whiskey," wrote author and former NFL player Michael Oriard, "were no longer doing the All-American thing."

And perhaps that was the allure. Perhaps it is not difficult to understand why the All-American would embrace the illicit, why he would rebel against authority and conformity, why he would insist on doing things his own way. In the fall of 1985, as his senior year began, Len Bias started hanging out at a club called Chapter III in Southeast Washington with a friend named Brian Tribble, who had once played on Maryland's junior varsity basketball team and who would later be imprisoned on drug charges. It was a friendship Bias largely kept quiet; it was a friendship even his own mother knew next to nothing about until after her son's death. When Bias hung around with good people, said his high school basketball coach, Bob Wagner, he could be good as any one of them. "If you put him with bums," Wagner said, "he'd be the best bum."

In September 1985, a five-feet-ten, 265-pound chef named Curtis Strong, who specialized in barbecued chicken wings and the acquisition of cocaine for professional athletes, stood trial on the eighth floor of the Pittsburgh Federal Building, in a seedy downtown neighborhood near the bus depot and several pornography shops. The negative reality of cocaine had begun to take hold, along with the first hints of a societal fatigue. Two decades of an evolving drug culture had exacted a toll; the number of eighteen-to-twenty-five-year-olds who admitted to trying cocaine rose from 13 percent in 1976 to 27 percent in 1982. By 1985, the headlines on the newsweeklies had turned dark and tragic, linking the drug trade to terrorism and tyrannical South American dictators. In *Newsweek:* "Cocaine: The Evil Empire."

Amid this atmosphere, the trial of Curtis Strong became a bizarre spectacle, an example of just how ingrained drugs had become in the day-to-day lives of professional athletes; and Sugar Ray Richardson was right—it wasn't *just* athletes—they had always stood as the exemplars, as role models, for America's youth. None of that seemed to matter much anymore. Viewed up close, they were as flawed and vulnerable as the rest of us. *Your idols have feet of clay,* Judge Gustave Diamond would inform the jury.

It made for a bizarre and voyeuristic show. Strong's defense attorney, Adam Renfroe Jr., emerged as a brash emcee, more than willing to embrace the drama of the moment if it could exonerate Curtis Strong. In this case, he said, his client was not actually the one on trial. His client was merely the facilitator. It was *baseball* that was being judged here, and it was baseball that had shirked its societal duties. "It is these high-priced superstars, these junkies, these hero-criminals, who should be on trial—they are the ones who are guilty," said Renfroe, a compact African-American man who came to court in hand-tailored suits. At one point, he joked that he could see a sexual attraction between the prosecutor, J. Alan Johnson, and a female juror. He spoke more in sermons than in questions. He complained that "the rich and powerful can get away with anything"; in retrospect, it seems unsurprising that Renfroe would later admit to his own sixteen-year cocaine addiction.

Federal prosecutors portrayed Strong (nickname: "Chef Curt") as a traveling salesman who dealt in cocaine. The real problem, they insisted, was not the users but the dealers. Dale Berra of the Pittsburgh Pirates testified that Strong had sold him a gram of cocaine for a hundred dollars in his room at the Franklin Plaza Hotel back in 1982. But in the end, Strong's actions mattered little to the public; it was the testimony of Berra and six other major-league players that pierced the game's aura. In the wood-paneled courtroom, granted immunity from prosecution, major-league baseball players spoke of drug buys and drug users and the drug culture of America's pastime. Names were named. Reputations were sullied. Lonnie Smith, an outfielder, came to the park so strung out one day in 1983 that he couldn't play; he spoke of cocaine sent through the mail and packaged in girlie magazines. He spoke of feeling "a little invincible" and of "hearing hallucinations." Keith Hernandez, an All-Star first baseman, admitted that he regularly woke up shaking, his nose bleeding. In the middle of the 1980 season, after a three-month binge, he realized he'd lost ten pounds. He flushed a gram down the toilet; it took him three years, he said, to quit completely. Rod Scurry, a relief pitcher for the Pittsburgh Pirates, came into a game with the bases loaded and was so burnt out that he walked both hitters he faced.

Strong was one of seven small-time dealers indicted. Among the others were a freelance photographer, a professional gambler, a heating repairman, a disc jockey, and an accountant. Not all were major players in the drug trade, but they were drawn in by the allure of proximity to professional athletes. The photographer, Dale Shiffman, was a longtime friend of Kevin Koch, who played the Pirate Parrot, the team mascot. Eventually, Koch, cooperating with authorities, wore a wire, and Shiffman was sentenced to twelve years in prison (he was released after twenty-two months). Everyone was giving up everyone else to save their own careers, orgiastic indulgences collapsing upon themselves. Berra named twenty different players in his 143 pages of testimony to a grand jury. By early 1985, players were being flown into Pittsburgh to testify, some of them All-Stars, like Tim Raines of the Montreal Expos, who claimed to have spent more than forty thousand dollars on cocaine in 1982 and who carried a vial in his hip pocket and slid headfirst while running the bases to avoid breaking it. On the last day of Strong's trial, another Pirates player, John Milner, implicated *Willie Mays* in the use of liquid amphetamines. Cocaine, Hernandez said, was "the devil on this earth"; he estimated that 40 percent of major-league players were using it in 1980, the year after he was named the National League's Most Valuable Player.

The judge, Gustave Diamond, sentenced Renfroe to thirty days in prison for contempt of court. Strong was found guilty on eleven counts. When it was over, Diamond turned to the jury and declared that major-league baseball players "have learned of the evils of fooling around with drugs in a way that no advertising campaign could have accomplished."

It didn't matter that most of the drug use had taken place at a time when even the experts couldn't entirely agree on the extent of the detrimental effects of cocaine, when it was still seen by the culture at large as a benign stimulant, as a party enhancement, and when it was tacitly being sanctioned (and used) by many of the same lawyers and judges and prosecutors and politicians who were now working against it. "We have abandoned our old-fashioned values," one philosopher told *Time* in 1981, amid the magazine's exploration of the cocaine phenomenon. The seventies, *Time* speculated, had produced an existential vacuum in America, and now, in Reagan's America, with a president intent on restoring the soul of capitalism, the backlash was inevitable. "Drugs are bad," Reagan said, "and we're going after them." And what represented more clearly the abandonment of old-fashioned values than overpaid ballplayers dirtying their noses for no reason other than their own personal amusement?

"Just because they have a lot of money doesn't make them better than anyone else, to do something illegal," said one juror, a surgical nurse.

"I can't really relate to these people making what they make and making what I make," said another, a self-employed tile setter.

"I thought they were jerks for taking cocaine," said the foreman, Betty Clay, a private nurse.

In 1984, the first lady of the United States—like her husband, a former actor—visited an elementary school in Longfellow, California, and in answering a question from a fourth-grader about what to do if his friends press him to smoke marijuana, answered, "Just say no." Hence a generational mantra was born, a cultural bludgeon that discarded the subtleties of the drug war in favor of certitude, the good-versus-evil mentality that had served the Reagans well both in Hollywood and in Washington. *Just Say No.* How easy it sounded, especially to those of us who grew up in the remote safety of the suburbs, largely shielded even from the *opportunity* to say no. How easy it sounded, given the surfeit of cautionary tales, given the public flogging that served as punishment in a case like this one.

The players who testified agreed to donate 10 percent of their salaries to drug programs in order to avoid yearlong suspensions; baseball's commissioner, Peter Ueberroth, having failed to implement mandatory drug testing due to protestations from the league's players' association, declared that "baseball's drug problem is over" and that he believed "baseball is going to be the first sport to be free of drugs. The players have had enough of it."

Said a juror, pun seemingly unintended: "I think it might give baseball a bad name, but it'll blow over."

Life did go on, but the image of a cocaine user—that glamorous picture, born in the 1970s, of cocaine as the natural extension of champagne and caviar, of cocaine as heaven manifest on earth, of cocaine as a balm for the army of upwardly mobile capitalists in Reagan's America—had now been overshadowed by the confessions and the trials, by tales of heartbreak and woe, by that now-ubiquitous government-mandated slogan: *Just Say No*. It was about to get much starker. In November 1985, *The New York Times* ran a front-page story with this lead: "A new form of cocaine is for sale on the streets of New York, alarming law-enforcement officials and rehabilitation experts because of its tendency to accelerate abuse of the drug, particularly among adolescents. The substance, known as crack..."

You can imagine where it went from there. You can imagine the frenzy that ensued, the panicked exhortations of law-enforcement officials who said they'd never seen anything like it, who described the ugliness of the crack houses in the Tremont section of the Bronx, who forecast an epidemic and described the drug as "instantaneously addictive." Here it was, a horror plaguing the inner cities of America; immediately, the perception of a cocaine user shifted from the parlors of the Upper East Side to the ghettoes of the Bronx, from white to black, from rich to poor.

It was not a new concept, the notion of freebasing, of altering the properties of cocaine to render it smokable: As the price of the drug fell throughout the 1970s, it became more common, an easy fix for the user in search of a more intense high. By the end of the decade, head shops were selling special kits with the instructions and the solvents for cooking up. The high was short and intense; it made your ears ring, and then it made you want more. It also ended careers: Coy Bacon, one of the best pass rushers in the NFL in the 1970s, opened his door in Washington, D.C., one morning in 1986, in the throes of an addiction that had been spiraling ever since he had freebased during a postgame celebration six years earlier, and was shot in the chest by someone he believed to be a drug dealer (he survived).

The first time Thomas "Hollywood" Henderson fell hard into freebasing, it was 1980, and he was trying to salvage his career as a linebacker with the Houston Oilers, having been cut by both the Dallas Cowboys and the San Francisco 49ers because of his cocaine habit. (In June of that year, Richard Pryor, in the midst of a five-day freebasing binge, accidentally set himself on fire.) Henderson arrived at his friend's house at one in the afternoon, started basing, and didn't leave until nearly ten the next morning. It had a *hum* to it, Henderson said. It was as if his whole body had either come alive or died altogether, though he wasn't sure which anymore.

Eventually, wise entrepreneurs figured out a way to prepare smokable cocaine without forcing their customers to cook it up themselves. In South Central Los Angeles, at the beginning it was known as Ready Rock; twelve days before the *Times* ran its front-page story, it first referred to this new iteration of cocaine as "crack." It "sounded like a new drug altogether," Dominic Streatfeild wrote. "It was dangerous. Its name sounded Bad. The drug story of the century started to roll."

IV.

Amid this sudden and apoplectic frenzy, at a party two days after Christmas in 1985, Sugar Ray Richardson disappeared for the last time in his NBA career.

It had happened several times before. Two years earlier, Richardson slipped out of a hotel room near the campus of Princeton University virtually unnoticed even by his own roommate. The bed was still made from the day before; his shoes were still lined up neatly next to the wall. That night, Richardson would later confess, he blew off the routine and tedium of NBA training camp, checked in to another hotel, and used cocaine with a few friends. At that point, he had already been to two different rehab centers, and neither seemed to curb his longings for the drug—and perhaps more importantly, for a sense of acceptance that continually eluded him. He was only twenty-nine years old at the time, a promising young guard with a silky playground presence who had emerged from the ghettoes of Denver and the University of Montana to become a star with both the New York Knicks and his current team, the New Jersey Nets. And yet he felt depressed and unwanted; like Bo Jackson, he fought a persistent stutter, but unlike Bo, he did not possess an internal confidence and a sense of self-possession that enabled him to dismiss the trappings of the age. Maybe, he thought, he'd be better off as a truck driver.

His was an upbringing wrapped in self-consciousness: The son of a hospital cook, Richardson moved from Lubbock, Texas, to a low-income Denver neighborhood at the age of six. His mother, Luddie Mae Hicks, described him as a "momma's child"; if she was sick, he would sit on the bed with her until she felt better. He attended Manual High, a basketball power in Denver, and went on to the University of Montana, where he was one of about a dozen blacks among a student body of seven thousand. His command of English grammar was limited. In one essay, later acquired by *Sports Illustrated*'s Bill Brubaker, Richardson wrote: *I think that white people our more understanding then blacks, because they no how to talk to each other.*

At the age of twenty, in the summer of 1975, he married his high school sweetheart. Two years later, she gave birth to their daughter, and after averaging 24.2 points his senior season, Richardson was drafted by the Knicks. His first contract was for four years and $909,000; asked about his nickname, Sugar, he responded, fighting back his stutter, "Because I'm kind of sweet on the court." Even before he signed, he'd attempted to buy a Rolls-Royce, then returned it a few weeks later after the Knicks coach, Willis Reed, balked at his ostentatiousness ("a victim of the times and of himself," Reed would later say of Richardson). But Micheal Ray couldn't help it. He *liked* to party. He *liked* the clubs. Sometimes he'd wake up his roommate, Mike Glenn, in the middle of the night and insist Glenn accompany him to the disco. He liked to drive his cars—Porsches, BMWs, Jaguars—careening wildly around Manhattan, frightening even the cabdrivers, telling Glenn, "You've got to drive like this. If you don't, you won't get nowhere." He borrowed fifteen hundred dollars from his first agent to make a down payment on a Datsun 280Z. It was not uncommon to see his Mercedes 450SL (the word *Sugar* engraved in gold on the stickshift) parked outside of Studio 54 or near the infamous swinger's club known as Plato's Retreat. Given the lifestyle, cocaine was a natural fit. By 1983, Micheal Ray had burned through six agents, sixteen cars, and a wife, the detritus of a promising career piling up around him.

Four days after Richardson's training-camp binge began, as the Nets walked through practices without their best player, Sugar called a friend named Charles Grantham, who was also executive vice president of the NBA Players Association. He told him, "I don't think basketball is for me." Grantham urged Richardson to meet with representatives from the Life Extension Institute, a counseling service the league had contracted with in 1981 in an unprecedented effort to help its players deal with personal problems. The deal with Life Extension had been reached not long after the *Los Angeles Times* reported that 75 percent of NBA players used cocaine. Clearly, Micheal Ray Richardson was not the only one—it was a *teammate*, after all, who had introduced him to coke in the first place—but he seemed especially flummoxed by his problem and by the personal vulnerability that the drug eventually exposed. Liked by everyone, protected by no one, Richardson failed to keep four different appointments with Life Extension officials, was nearly released by the Nets, and finally checked in to yet another rehab program, this one at Manhattan's Regent Hospital, on October 14. Whose responsibility was it, Grantham later wondered, to educate Micheal Ray about so many different things?

He was as dynamic as he had ever been when he returned to basketball, averaging 20.6 points as the Nets upset Philadelphia in the first round of the playoffs that spring, and winning the NBA's Comeback Player of the Year award. In February 1985, at the same All-Star game where Michael Jordan was shunned for the audacity of his clothing, Richardson made an appearance too. It was proof that cocaine did not have to melt everything it touched, that perhaps Sugar had overcome his anxieties, that perhaps he had finally shed his naïveté. "I'll be playing basketball until, you know, until the day they kick me out," he told *Sports Illustrated,* a quote that reads, years later, almost as a subconscious prophesy.

By the final days of 1985, Richardson had become the linchpin of a resurgent franchise; he told his story in a drug prevention film shown to other players. The Nets were 19–12 and had won nine of their last ten games. It was Richardson's team. He was the point guard. He was the catalyst. On December 27, the Nets held a Christmas party at George's Restaurant in Moonachie—a *nice* party, according to the Nets rookie coach, Dave Wohl, who congratulated Richardson on his play and on his newfound happiness. "It was what he wanted," Wohl said. "He wanted respect."

Richardson was in a good mood. He danced with a bookkeeper. He danced with a secretary. The club gave out ski jackets, and then Richardson and two of his teammates left for the Sheraton Hotel in Hasbrouck Heights, arriving at a team hangout known as the Sports Bar. Richardson danced some more, he signed autographs, and then, according to the bartender, he left with a girl he'd met for a party in Fort Lee.

And then he was gone for good.

He did not come home that morning. He did not show up at practice the next day. One of the teammates who accompanied him to the Sports Bar, Daryl Dawkins, lamented the fact that he'd left Sugar alone. Richardson was back on the precipice, and his teammates knew it; when he called in a few days later, he told a team official he'd been hiding out at a girl's house in a nearby town. Another disappearance, another binge, another stint in rehab: Now Richardson was nearing the end. The National Basketball Association's policy, set a couple of years earlier, dictated that a third positive test meant a ban from the league for at least two years, and more likely for life. Richardson already had two positive tests, and in February '86, the day after Sugar was arrested at one A.M. for attempting to break in to the home of his now-estranged wife, he failed another test. He would never play another game in the NBA. In the tabloids the next day, boldfaced headlines marked the demise of Richardson's career:

SUGAR FOULS OUT!
BANNED FOR LIFE!

Eventually, he would move to Europe and become a star in an international league; eventually, he would kick his habit and find a new wife. Eventually, Micheal Ray Richardson would patch a life back together, and he would even express his appreciation for NBA commissioner David Stern's decision to ban him from the league, perhaps sparing him a worse fate, perhaps even sparing him the fate of one Leonard Bias. But not before Richardson became a prominent example of how the modern age, with its glittering distractions, could chew up the vulnerable and spit them out in pieces. *One of the nicest guys I've ever met,* said his teammate Buck Williams, and it made you wonder—what if that was the problem? What if Micheal Ray was simply *too nice* to comprehend where he was headed?

"Here's a kid who, right out of college, was chased by agents, probably offered large sums of money by them, is approached by people with drugs to give him and really just finds himself in a different world," said Charles Grantham, who toward the end had become Richardson's agent. "This isn't an excuse. Micheal Ray did this to himself. But when you look at it, I see a lot of potential Micheal Ray Richardsons out there. Not just in the pros now, but guys in college and high school."

V.

It was a confusing time, as well, for the best college basketball player in America, the beginning of a senior season filled with obligations that he did not necessarily have much interest in fulfilling. This accounted for Len Bias's knee-jerk surliness with certain reporters. On more than one occasion, he told an interviewer that he was never quite comfortable with the attention he received. He had other interests; he was a talented artist who drew cartoons and caricatures and architectural renderings and spoke of becoming an interior designer if basketball did not work out—recently, he said, he had drawn a cartoon of a pair of hands reaching through the clouds to slam-dunk a basketball.

But how could basketball *not* work out? How could he not look at himself in the mirror, or in that oil painting on the wall of his mother's house, or at that life-sized poster of himself, and see anything but a sure thing? The kid who came out of Northwestern High School as a gawky and petulant teenager—who had been cut from the junior high team in the eighth grade, who had his share of on-court tantrums, whose grades had slipped his senior year when he agonized over his choice of colleges—was now an All-American with long arms and a soft baseline jump shot, and he was showing up for practice in a floor-length leather coat with an ermine collar.

He had a keen grasp of the iconography of fame and wealth in the 1980s. Ostentation was a trend, on Wall Street and in Washington, and the privileged few drove Porsches and Lamborghinis and dressed in sharp suits and gold chains and floor-length leather coats (how Bias could afford such things became yet another outstanding question in the wake of his death). Bias was a preseason All-American, the Atlantic Coast Conference Player of the Year as a junior, averaging 19 points per game. "Len Bias has a chance to become one of the best players ever to play his position," one NBA scout said. "He's replaced Newton's theory of gravity with Michael Jordan's theory of gravity—which is that there is none. He just climbs up there and hangs."

He *knew* he was going to be rich; he bet a friend a thousand dollars that he'd be the top pick in the NBA draft the following spring. He was the biggest man in the most high-profile sport on campus. It was only a matter of time now before he came out on the other side, before he sloughed off his modest upbringing in a middle-class household, before he became one of them.

Vulnerability and invulnerability: In the same city, the flip sides of Len Bias's psyche—not to mention the psychological dichotomy of cocaine itself—played out side by side. Sugar Ray Richardson was gone, out of the NBA, his confidence shattered, his career a wreck. And Lawrence Taylor was—well, he was *Lawrence Taylor*. Nothing could change him, because he saw no reason to change. Here was a man who could handle anything, an athlete who embodied the id of the decade, who seemingly lived his life by Ronald Reagan's 1980 inaugural declaration that the era of self-doubt had ended. As a child in Williamsburg, Virginia, Taylor's father had told him that he would have to be twice as good as the white man to achieve equality. And he was at least twice as good on the football field as any man around him, regardless of color. He was also utterly fearless. He would take on any dare. In college at North Carolina, as his reputation grew, he fostered it by scaling six-story buildings, by cruising bars in search of a fight, by knocking out car windows, by taking a bite of a glass and chewing it, just to see the reaction he could get. He drank a case of beer in a single night; he conned his professors and hung out at pool halls instead of showing up for class. Because he was a football player, he got away with all of it.

Talent gave him license, as well as a nickname that also served as a de facto alter ego: *L.T.* By 1985, as an outside linebacker for the New York Giants, he had succeeded not just in mastering his position but in revolutionizing it. He was a perennial All-Pro, an elusive pass rusher who ruined game plans by disrupting the offensive flow and managing to strike fear into large men who did not scare easily; he so freaked out Ron Jaworski that the Philadelphia quarterback, unable to locate L.T.'s uniform number on a particular play, wound up calling a time-out—L.T. wasn't even on the field. On November 18, during an otherwise routine *Monday Night Football* game, L.T. charged in on quarterback Joe Theismann of the Washington Redskins and wrestled him to the ground with such ferocity that Theismann's leg popped and then shattered. It was a gruesome tableau that immediately became the real-life standard for gratuitous violence, not to mention the most famous and replayed injury in sports history. "Sometimes," Taylor would later say, "I couldn't control what would happen when I made contact."

But he did not see the need to control himself. He was a *football player*, wasn't he? Nobody blamed him for his overzealousness, for his ferocity. Even Joe Theismann quickly forgave him, and a few plays later, after six men helped load Theismann into an ambulance, Taylor celebrated a fumble recovery as if he'd forgotten all about what he'd just done. It was all part of the game; these things happened on a football field. Taylor was intelligent enough to realize that he *needed* to be this way in order to satisfy both his own self-image and the perceptions of others, and in order to feed that hungry alter ego, because L.T. was a furious and unforgiving force of nature.

He first tried cocaine during his rookie season: "What I remember is instant euphoria," he said. Often he stayed out all night, partying in many of the same places as Micheal Ray Richardson—at Studio 54, at the China Club (where he befriended a talented and troubled young boxer named Mike Tyson), at the Hasbrouck Heights Sheraton, from which Sugar would eventually disappear—and yet when he showed up at practice or at a game the next day, he still was a step quicker than everyone else.

In 1983, he leveraged an offer from Donald Trump, then owner of the United States Football League's New Jersey Generals, into a $6.25 million, seven-year contract from the Giants. He was now the highest-paid defensive player in NFL history; his signature became a piece of jewelry, a diamond "L.T." chandelier that dangled from his ear like a warning beacon: *Don't fuck with this man.* He drove a gold Mercedes and blew through tollbooths at full speed. He befriended the manager of a boisterous New Jersey strip club called The Bench, who was later sentenced to three years for receiving stolen property. He wrote a check for sixteen thousand dollars in fines to cover for the fact that he'd skipped an entire off-season of weight-training sessions. Like Bo Jackson, he was driven by his own defiant energy; but whereas Bo was more guarded, more focused on the big picture of his career, L.T. was always rushing toward instant gratification. He did not give a damn about his endorsement value, nor about the approbation of Middle America. He did not buy in to the antiquated notion of athletes as role models. He fueled himself through his lifestyle, staying up all night and buying cocaine at a house on 133rd Street in Harlem and taking over-the-counter speed to stay awake and shotgunning Scope to jolt himself to life on Sunday mornings. Sometimes he paid a ball boy to lie under the covers during bed check at the hotel the night before a game. "When somebody calls me crazy

I take it as a compliment," he said. "I've always felt there was more to arithmetic than two plus two."

Midway through the 1985 season, Taylor discovered freebasing. He still clung to the misguided notion that he could somehow control his urges, even though he had cultivated a persona that was based entirely in lack of self-control. He rolled his cocaine into a Salem cigarette; his paranoia grew worse, to the point that his wife would find him wandering in the woods outside of their four-hundred-thousand-dollar New Jersey home in the middle of winter, seeking out people he imagined were staring in his window. He had failed a drug test before the 1985 season and had refused any help from the Giants; instead, he began devising ways to beat the tests, borrowing his teammates' urine, squeezing it from a Visine bottle into a cup when the time came. Rumors began to spread, leaking into the media, and Taylor went to rehab for the first time in March 1986, the details kept quiet to spare him embarrassment. He played golf as part of his therapy, but he remained the same L.T., flamboyant and defiant.

"Cocaine was illegal, that was true," he later said. "I wasn't *supposed* to be doing it, there was this and that campaign against it, every politician, police chief, and Nancy Reagan were against it—but hell, with a guy like me, that almost made it more attractive. Tell me no and I'll argue and fight you—just to be different."

VI.

On Valentine's Day 1986, as Howard Cosell reported on his radio show that Lawrence Taylor was a "sick man" on his way to a drug rehabilitation program, as the Giants issued no-comments and vague denials, Charles "Lefty" Driesell, the coach at the University of Maryland, suspended three of his players, Jeff Baxter, John Johnson, and Leonard Bias, for violating curfew after a victory at North Carolina State. When they arrived back at the team hotel not long before dawn,

Driesell confronted them by asking if they'd been doing drugs. Bias rushed his coach, furious, raving about unfair presumptions regarding black athletes. His teammates had to restrain him.

And yet, according to another teammate's sworn testimony after his death, and according to the recounting of friends decades after the fact, Bias was already using cocaine by then, if only on a recreational level. Driesell had even tested him once, as he sometimes did to his players if he felt their efforts were lacking (Bias passed), and here was another of the ironies of Len Bias's final months on earth: At the time, Maryland was one of the few programs in the country that employed any sort of drug testing, but the system was haphazard and selective, in part because the university feared a legal challenge from the American Civil Liberties Union—Driesell himself later called it "a joke." None of this deterred Bias. It was not the All-American thing to do, but what did that matter? "Sometimes you do things you wouldn't do just because you can," said one of his teammates. "There's nobody watching, so you say I'll do it now just to spite them."

The warnings, the increasingly negative headlines, the clarion call of Just Say No: None of that seemed to apply to him, because he was Len Bias, and at that moment, he was more than just a little invincible. He felt like he could defy gravity, like he could climb up into the clouds and hang on for as long as he wanted.

CHAPTER FOUR

We're Not Here
to Start No Trouble

You know what hurts me the most? I hate what you all stand for. I hate your values, your morals, your blindness. But I love you. I love you all very much. . . .

—From the TV series *Dynasty*

I.

Something was happening in Chicago that fall, something weird and dynamic and compelling, the origins of which could be traced back to the Thursday night in Minnesota when a woozy and petulant Jim McMahon nagged his way into a football game. It wasn't just that the Bears were winning week after week after week (though, considering their fans had endured two decades of routine futility, that was strange enough). It was that the Bears were winning with such naked audacity; it was that they actually appeared to be *reveling* in their own very public dysfunction. In the same city where a morning-show host named Oprah Winfrey was in the process of refashioning the tabloid talk show into a syndicated group-therapy session, the Bears were quickly becoming an affirmation of the new American ideal: a motley group of individualists who embraced capitalism and celebrity, who embodied nothing so much as immoderation and self-regard.

One week after McMahon's back-to-back touchdown passes helped them defeat Minnesota, the Bears fell behind Washington 10–0, then proceeded to roll up forty-five consecutive points in the second half. Another win over Tampa Bay on the first weekend in October raised their record to 5-0. Three weeks later, Michael Jordan, the young basketball star upon whom both the Chicago Bulls and Nike, Inc., had mortgaged their futures, went up for a layup against the Golden State Warriors and came down with a broken foot. He would miss the remainder of the regular season, but perhaps it was for the best, because there was only so much room on the sports page, and the Bears were about to monopolize nearly all of it for the next several months.

On October 13, the Bears played the San Francisco 49ers, the defending Super Bowl champions, the team that had humiliated them 23–0 in the NFC Championship the year before. Chicago had endured that game without McMahon, whose season had ended a few weeks earlier when he lacerated his kidney in that violent win over the Raiders, but now they had their quarterback again, and their coach harbored an almost juvenile obsession with revenge, and this singular preoccupation birthed one of the oddest celebrity sensations of the decade.

The 49ers were led by Bill Walsh, a gray-haired intellectual whose offensive innovations emphasized finesse and short passing and who had already been credited with revolutionizing the sport. And the Bears? Their coach was *Mike Ditka,* a foulmouthed and mustachioed and gum-spitting former tight end from Aliquippa, Pennsylvania, who stalked the sideline like Sergeant Slaughter from the G.I. Joe comic books. Ditka, who, like his quarterback, magnified every perceived slight into an obsession. Ditka, who could not stop thinking about the bitter end of that NFC Championship game the year before, when Walsh had chosen to insert a 280-pound lineman named Guy McIntyre into the backfield to block for his running backs, just for laughs (he called it the "Angus" formation). Ditka had spent much of the spring formulating his response, choosing to draft a three-hundred-and-*something*-pound weather balloon out of Clemson University with the team's first-round pick. The young man was William Perry, a defensive lineman, and at a time when 280-pounders were still considered behemoths, Perry's girth was off the charts. Ditka compared him to Gene "Big Daddy" Lipscomb, the six-feet-six giant who had become an All-Pro for the Colts before dying of a heroin overdose at age thirty-one. "His belly did not roll out of his pants," *Sports Illustrated*'s William Nack wrote of Lipscomb. "He was hard and trim, and the fastest interior lineman in the league."

Of Perry, none of these things could be said. He was a much better athlete than he appeared to be, but he was a risk, and Ditka admitted as much. Immediately upon his arrival in Chicago, Perry became a walking fat joke. He was a shy kid with a gap-toothed grin who had grown up in a small town in South Carolina, and he took it in stride, embracing the mythology of his girth, even embracing several nicknames—the most prominent of which was The Refrigerator, coined after a college friend watched this very large man attempt to board a very small elevator. On the day he was drafted, he said, "I was big, even when I was little." Said Ditka: "I'm very excited . . . I don't think we'll ever forget this." And then the coach couldn't resist—he made his own joke, about Perry looking good in a Bears uniform . . . or two uniforms, whatever it took.

Ditka's defensive coordinator, Buddy Ryan, did not find this funny at all. Ryan was stout and curmudgeonly and had little patience for frivolity within the confines of the game. He was a native of a tiny town in Oklahoma who had served in the Korean War and had devised a fierce blitz-heavy (and often risky) defensive scheme known as the "46." "Buddy liked playing the prison warden," said Chet Coppock, a longtime Chicago broadcaster.

When Perry showed up two weeks late for training camp after a holdout (weighing somewhere in the vicinity of 330 pounds), when he sweated out thirteen pounds on his second day of practice and then collapsed from muscle cramps, Ryan felt he had seen enough. There was already a burgeoning tension between Ditka and Ryan; both seemed to revel in conflict. That afternoon, Ryan called Perry "a wasted draft choice and a waste of money," then went on a local radio show and said, "He's an overweight kid and a helluva nice kid. But you know, I got twin boys at home who are nice kids, and I don't want 'em playing for me."

Perry's weight peaked in college at approximately 390. His mother, Inez, a school dietician, was five-eleven, 230. His father, a housepainter, was five-nine, 240. Perry was the tenth of twelve children, weighed 13½ pounds at birth, matured to 250 pounds as a sixth-grader, wore double-wide trousers in high school, ate cereal out of mixing bowls, learned to bake his own cakes in junior high school, devoured buckets of Kentucky Fried Chicken for lunch, and drank Coors Light (two cases at a time, the story went) because the cans crushed easily. He considered beer "diet food" because he could sweat it out the next day at practice; this was one example of Fridge Logic, an endearing combination of naïveté and Southern folk wisdom. His teammates called him Biscuit; they also called him Mudslide. He stood six feet two inches tall, had a twenty-three-inch neck and a forty-eight-inch waist, wore a size-61 sport coat, and could dunk a basketball from a standing jump. All of this convinced Ditka that if Ryan wasn't going to use him on defense, then Ditka could use him on offense—that, in fact, The Fridge would serve as the ultimate fuck-you to Walsh and his intellectual sensibilities.

The Bears were the better team this time around. They led San Francisco 26–10 by the time Ditka sent The Refrigerator into the huddle, with little more than a minute remaining in the game. *Gimme da ball,* The Fridge said. Chicago had possession near midfield, and twice in a row, Perry took a handoff and plunged into the center of the line, gaining two yards each time by sheer force of momentum. "That's like a sumo guy," one of the network announcers said, except Perry wasn't quite so elegant. He seemed confused by what to do after the ball actually wound up in his hands; he dropped to the grass like a wounded buffalo. But then, the execution didn't particularly matter at this point. It was obvious that this was Ditka's revenge, a coarse rejoinder to Walsh, the man who had been labeled an offensive genius, the man who had won a Super Bowl by coordinating his offense in almost balletic fashion. Here were the Chicago Bears winning by utilizing the ancient formula of smashing their opponents in the face. "Neanderthal football," New York Giants coach Bill Parcells would call it, and what could be more utterly prehistoric than propelling a massive body headlong into a pile in order to drive an oblong spheroid several inches forward?

It all fed into a perception that Ditka encouraged, that his team somehow epitomized the working-class spirit of Chicago itself. Later in the season, Ditka referred to his team as "Grabowskis," as the embodiment of Chicago's ethnic blue-collar ethos. It was typical of Ditka, who thrived in the role of underdog, of the furious outsider, but had managed to gather a team that now burst headlong into celebrity. For all his bluster, he was coming to understand the cosmetics of the era, and the rise of the individual persona in team sports. This team had issues—*Ditka* had issues—but who really cared, if those issues made them better?

On the flight home from San Francisco, Ditka celebrated by drinking a bottle of white wine. Then he drank another. "If a lot is two bottles," he later said, "then I had more than a lot." Two miles from O'Hare Airport, on Interstate 294, Ditka was pulled over by a police officer. He refused a Breathalyzer test, became abusive, according to the police officer, and was handcuffed and charged with driving under the influence. He issued an apology, quit drinking for a few months, and moved on, the Neanderthal coach now contriving a master plan for a season that grew weirder by the moment.

Eight days later, the Bears played a home game on a Monday night against their longtime archrival, the Green Bay Packers. They were 6–0 for the first time in forty-three years, for the first time since Sid Luckman had been their quarterback. It was a cool night, and the game was broadcast by Frank Gifford, O. J. Simpson, and Joe Willie Namath, the same ABC crew who had worked the Thursday-night miracle in Minnesota. (Gifford opened the broadcast by congratulating Simpson and his wife, Nicole, on the birth of their child.) The Bears fell behind 7–0, both teams repeatedly turning the ball over, and then in the second quarter, after fullback Matt Suhey landed two yards short of the goal line, Ditka sent Perry in to the backfield to block for Walter Payton. The ball was snapped, McMahon handed off to Payton, and Perry charged into the line and into a 224-pound linebacker named George Cumby, who was driven so far backward that he dropped out of camera range. Payton scored, and on their next possession, with the ball perched near the goal line, with the crowd now anticipating such novel brutality, Ditka sent Perry in again. He lined up in front of Payton, behind lineman Keith Van Horne.

Gifford: "He'll be the lead blocker—*they give him the football!*"

In he went, stumbling and falling and landing on the opposite side of the goal line, then leaping up and spiking the football in a sloppy expression of glee—perhaps the purest, most joyous touchdown celebration in NFL history—and then he dashed back to the sideline as quickly as a man nicknamed after a household appliance could possibly scamper. And when, later in the second quarter, he provided another lead block for Payton, when he once again drove poor George Cumby (an All-American at Oklahoma) onto his back and Payton scored and sheer delight spread from coast to coast, Gifford proclaimed, "We are watching a folk hero being made! They will write *songs* about William Perry!"

It was true. Never before had we seen a celebrity quite like The Fridge; his proportions were captivating. For years, we had been jogging and aerobicizing and drinking Tab and joining health clubs and fetishizing body image. And now here was The Fridge, the *literal* physical manifestation of the Reagan Revolution, fat and happy and reveling in his own simplicity, and what more could we ask for as Americans than a hero like this? "Through a guy like The Refrigerator," a political consultant told the *Chicago Tribune,* "we can fantasize what we would do in our fat bodies."

At approximately seven the next morning, the phone began to ring in the Bears offices, and in the office of Perry's agent, Jim Steiner. There were ten or twelve offers every hour. He went on Letterman, on Carson, on *Today,* on all three network news shows. *People* magazine described how Perry "waddled into training camp . . . [looking] less like a lineman than a tub of linguini." (His wife, Sherry, a meticulous caretaker of her husband's reputation, insisted to the magazine that reports he had "wolfed four slices of watermelon during a training camp lunch" were highly exaggerated.) Three dentists called to offer complimentary cosmetic surgery on the gap between Perry's front teeth. General Electric, Frigidaire, and Whirlpool all wanted him for product endorsements, along with several airlines, investment banking firms, car companies, and shoe manufacturers . . . and, of course, McDonald's, the Chicago-based fast-food purveyor where Perry had reportedly eaten fifty-five dollars' worth of food in one sitting. Those McDonald's ads, featuring Perry and several of his teammates, were up within weeks, and within a year, Perry had done advertisements for Diet Coke, Wilson game jerseys, a brand of thermal underwear, NutraSweet, bacon, commercial refrigeration, Pontiac, paper towels, hair care products, and Kraft macaroni and cheese. His sudden emergence into the public consciousness "border[ed] on the burlesque," one psychologist warned the *Chicago Tribune*. "The reason Fridge was doing what he was doing, as some saw it," wrote the *Tribune*'s John Mullin, "was because he was some sort of freak."

And that was *exactly* the point: For Steiner, it was about an agent and his client grabbing all they could until the moment dissipated, until the novelty was gone, until the parody had itself drifted into parody. Preserving dignity was not their primary concern; for The Fridge, all this scrutiny of his eating habits was like a strange dream, anyway. He'd take the money whenever it came, however it came. He had grown up with nothing, and suddenly he had everything.

After the Green Bay game, Pete Rozelle, the NFL commissioner, called The Fridge "a bonanza" for the league—an escapist fantasy at a time when the league desperately needed a distraction from reality, from the strife brought on by the cocaine abuse and players' strikes and legal battles of the early eighties. "He was American excess at its most excessive," one British newspaper reporter would recall decades later, and it's true: The Fridge *was* a freak, but he was *our* freak. Only in America.

II.

Don Pierson arrived in Chicago in the late 1960s, at a time when football itself, staid and straitlaced, stood at a cultural disconnect from the street-level radicalism of the era ("a full-blown expression of America's corporate and military ethos," a historian wrote of the game at that point). There had always been subversives in professional football, those who lived outside the tacit rules, hard drinkers and hard livers: Bobby Layne, the Detroit Lions quarterback, was renowned for his drunken escapades, and Max McGee, the Green Bay Packers receiver, famously caught the first touchdown pass in Super Bowl history while nursing a hangover. But the dominant personality of the era was Vince Lombardi in Green Bay, who preached of sacrifice and self-denial, who was considered a vice-presidential candidate by Richard Nixon (at least until researchers discovered Lombardi was actually a law-and-order Democrat). And until Joe Willie Namath swaggered onto the scene in 1968, wearing white shoes and guaranteeing victory and reveling in his sexual conquests, those kinds of stories were largely either unreported or kept off the record. In Chicago, Pierson recalls, most people didn't care enough about pro football to notice.

Pierson grew up in northeast Ohio and attended Ohio State University, and when he was hired as a young writer at the *Tribune*, college football—and the Big Ten specifically—remained the newspaper's first priority. The Bears had won an NFL championship in 1963 under longtime coach George Halas (with Ditka as their tight end), but by 1969—two years after Halas retired—they were 1–13, and despite the presence of a pair of Hall of Fame talents in linebacker Dick Butkus and running back Gale Sayers, they wouldn't win a playoff game for another two decades.

Pierson became the Bears beat writer in 1972. He was the first person assigned by the *Tribune* to track the Bears on a daily basis. The coverage had always been purposefully casual; no one bothered to attend training camp every day, and the sports editors of the various local newspapers wound up covering the games themselves. Television was generally regarded as a nuisance. Abe Gibron, the five-feet-eleven, 250-pound eating machine who took over the Bears in 1972, was so disdainful of the presence of microphones and tape recorders at his press conferences that he used to swear into them before their owners snatched them away. At times, Gibron conducted his press conferences while sitting on the toilet; other times, he raised a shot of whiskey and said that everything that came after he drank it was to be considered off the record. Gibron was fired after losing thirty games in three seasons, and the Bears continued to struggle throughout the 1970s and on into the 1980s, and Don Pierson continued to cover the franchise, even as the atmosphere surrounding his beat changed completely. By the end of the decade, there was no keeping the cameras out, because the cameras largely paid for everything.

In 1977, the NFL signed a $576 million television contract, which meant that for the first time, the league would earn more from the rights to telecast their games than from ticket sales. By 1982, the number was $2.1 billion, and then, just when it seemed this league could not possibly grow any faster, pro football lost its way. In the summer of '82, a few months after the United States Football League signed television contracts with ABC and ESPN to begin a rival league the following spring, Don Reese's cocaine revelations appeared in *Sports Illustrated*.

That fall, NFL players went on strike for fifty-seven days, blighting Ditka's first season as the Bears' head coach and McMahon's rookie season as quarterback. Owner Al Davis's brazen move of his Oakland Raiders to Los Angeles freed Robert Irsay to move the Colts from Baltimore to Indianapolis in 1984. It wasn't that the NFL didn't matter anymore—"At no time during the decade was the NFL's standing as America's most popular sport seriously challenged," wrote author Michael MacCambridge—but there was a heaviness lying over the whole endeavor, and commissioner Pete Rozelle understood that as well as anyone. Even if it wasn't true, all this bad news made the league *seem* a lot less fun than it used to be. In 1983, veteran *Sports Illustrated* football writer Paul Zimmerman called for a "Turmoil Page, near the sports section but not part of it" to cover everything not directly related to the games themselves, which he also derided for their reliance upon "corporate football," and for the lack of nicknames on defense. "I think there was some truth to the feeling that it was sort of a No Fun League," Pierson said. "I know Rozelle wasn't having any fun."

And so into this void stepped the '85 Bears, inviting distractions, thriving on dissent, and pointing the way for the NFL to embrace the accompanying turmoil. On the field, they were something of a throwback, led by defense—a defense with multiple nicknames and odd personalities that extended well beyond their 350-pound rookie lineman-turned-fullback. At every locker, it seemed, Pierson could find a story. Now there were beat reporters from every newspaper, and television cameras crowding the locker room, and no one in Chicago could get enough of it. What would Ditka say next? What would McMahon *do* next? Did Ditka and Ryan *really* hate each other? When would The Fridge throw a *pass*? "We were children of the sixties, and we were all about self-expression and freedom, and we were the adults of that era," said Hub Arkush, a local sportscaster and writer. "And some of the goofy players started to do or say things guys seven or eight years ago wouldn't even think of getting away with."

This was what Zimmerman did not yet understand: The Turmoil Page *was* the sports page; the two elements were inextricable. At a moment when athletes were only beginning to comprehend the importance of manipulating their own image—of controlling the message, of viewing themselves as a product, of embracing a marketable persona—the Bears sold themselves on drama and personality. They were the NFL's first running soap opera, and the story itself meant as much to the league's fortunes as anything the Bears would accomplish on the field.

Despite the breathless hype over The Fridge, despite the obvious fact that the Bears' abundantly talented defense dictated the tempo, despite the ongoing cold war between Ditka and Ryan, McMahon remained the chief protagonist, the screwball-in-chief. The quarterback regarded himself as an antihero, as yet another kindred spirit with Randle McMurphy from *One Flew Over the Cuckoo's Nest*. After the Minnesota game, this became obvious: With McMahon, the Bears were a spectacular football team that thrived on subversion; without him, they were often a discombobulated and unsightly mess, a radical movement lacking a central agitator. "I like to think that I helped bring their personalities out," he said of his teammates. "When I first came here, I could see maybe that some of the guys were a little tight, a little too afraid to let themselves go. But there's no reason why you can't be a little crazy . . . and still play good football."

He was the first quarterback since Namath who possessed the ability and the authority and the charisma to truly challenge the system; he was, wrote *Rolling Stone*'s David Breskin, "from that first generation of post-Nam high-school jocks who grew up playing stoned and rocking hard, who said *later* to all that Knute Rockne crap—let's have fun and kick some ass." He had always been ahead of the curve: Already, in his early twenties, he had managed to thrill and blaspheme the proponents of a major American religion.

III.

He was six years old when he quite literally stuck a fork in his own eye. He had been playing a movie cowboy, and he was trying to untie a tangled lace on his gun holster, and the fork slipped and took up temporary residence in his right eye, nearly severing the retina. He removed the fork, washed it, sat at the table, and waited for his mother to notice.

At the hospital, the doctors operated, then tied him to the bed for a week so he wouldn't scratch at it. He wore an eye patch for six months, and though his vision improved slowly over time, his sensitivity to light remained—hence, the dark glasses. In San Jose, where Jim McMahon's family had moved shortly after his birth, he claimed to derive a certain amount of joy from torturing his classmates, at least in part because his classmates did the same to him. His parents had grown up in blue-collar towns—father an Irish Catholic in Jersey City, mother a Mormon in Fresno—and they met while on duty at the 5th Army Machine Records Unit in Chicago. They were brash and self-assured: "If you don't feel you're the best," his mother, Roberta, once said, "no one else will believe in you."

Jim Senior did not tolerate timidity. One day when his son came home with a face bruised by a local bully, Jim Senior told him, "You come home crying to me tomorrow, and I'm gonna be the one that hits you in the nose." And so McMahon took care of the bully and became something of a hellion himself, smoking cigarettes, throwing firecrackers in class, poking classmates with straight pins, and getting suspended from school in the seventh grade for hitting back at a teacher. ("She slapped me," McMahon would recall years later. "So I punched her out.") Sometimes he'd sit in a tree and throw prunes at passing cars. His parents took him to a psychologist, who diagnosed him as hyperactive. Mostly, he had a problem with authority. When his mother (who tied Jim and his brother to separate table legs when they were young, in order to prevent fights) told him he had to wear a belt and tuck in his shirt when he went to elementary school, he'd pull off his belt and untuck his tails before he was even out of sight. He swore at teachers and referees alike.

By the ninth grade, he was still knock-kneed and thin and had trouble seeing out of that right eye, but he had developed a hell of an arm. He started for the freshman team at Andrew Hill High School in San Jose, then became only the second sophomore in thirty years to start on the varsity team. He was revered for his cockiness, for his willingness to do things his elders insisted he couldn't do, sometimes to the point of self-abuse: During one game, he dislocated his shoulder and had it popped it back into place, leading to ongoing problems with the joint.

Soon after that season, his father took over a paper-products franchise in Ogden, Utah, and moved the family to the suburb of Roy, in the breadbasket of Mormon country. It was the mid-1970s, and professional football was a burgeoning enterprise, and Jim Senior already had grandiose plans; he already envisioned his son as an

NFL quarterback in the mold of Fran Tarkenton, and Jim Junior did nothing to dispute this notion—by the age of ten, he could throw a football fifty yards, and by the time he got to college, he could throw it eighty yards. He showed up in town a few days before football camp began in Roy, a junior trailing a certain measure of hype from his days in California. Fred Thompson, who was the baseball coach at Roy and the defensive coordinator on the football team, knew enough to realize that a prospect's legend was often amplified simply by crossing state lines, but this was not one of those situations; McMahon's coach at Andrew Hill, Jack Germaine, admitted that he cried when he found out his quarterback was leaving town.

Thompson was out of town for that first week of practice. When he called in to speak to the head coach, Ernie Jacklin, he heard this: "We've got a new starting quarterback." McMahon had started with the third team, leading them to several touchdowns against the first-team defense; soon enough, the two seniors ahead of him had been shifted to defense. Up until then, like most of the schools in their region—like most of the high schools in the state, like most of the high schools in the country—Roy relied upon a rush-heavy wishbone offense. This was because most kids could not throw the ball the way McMahon could, because they did not possess McMahon's innate understanding of schemes and patterns. Even in the NFL, the notion of a prolific passing game was still a radical idea fostered only by a few teams; on the high school level, it was largely a pipe dream. But it all came easily to McMahon. Roy went 11–1 that season before losing in the state semifinals; then they shifted from the wishbone to an I-formation and went 8–2 his senior year, with McMahon calling nearly all of the plays.

At school, he mostly kept to himself. He grew close to an English teacher named Eleanor Olson, discussing with her the travails of a knight errant named Don Quixote. He played three sports, until one day, fed up with the disciplinary methods of the basketball coach, he slammed the ball on the floor and stormed off the court (his first loves were football and baseball—he envisioned playing both in college). In school at Roy, immersed in a muted suburban culture, in a straitlaced Mormon community, he toned down his overt defiance. But he remained supremely confident, the iconoclast in dark glasses. He was also the punter on the football team, and on at least one occasion, with his team trailing late in the game, he refused to obey Jacklin's direction to punt the ball and called a play instead. A punt, he figured, was as good as a concession, and McMahon refused to concede. Eventually, his team drove downfield and won the game.

Among his classmates, his reputation was almost surreptitious. It was a quiet cool. "The first time I ever tasted alcohol happened to be with him," says one of his high school teammates. "His old man chewed him out." At an away basketball game, some fans of the opposing team slipped him a six-pack of beer for the bus ride home, and McMahon gladly accepted it.

Still, his friends and his coaches and his teachers recall him being somewhat subdued, an outsider dropped into a world where he didn't belong. Which is what made it so perplexing that, of all the schools where McMahon could have chosen to matriculate, he chose the one with the strictest rules of all. "At BYU," says his friend Pat Hanley. "*That's* where the whole image really started."

He chose Brigham Young in part because it was one of the few schools that would allow him to play both football and baseball. He also chose Brigham Young because his size—he was only six feet tall, diminutive for a quarterback—had disqualified him from being recruited by his first choice, Notre Dame. And he chose Brigham Young because it was one of the few schools in the country that had embraced the passing game under a coach named LaVell Edwards, who had begun his career running the single-wing at a Salt Lake City high school, then coached defense at BYU throughout the 1960s. When he took over the program in 1971, he refocused the school's recruiting efforts on quarterbacks and receivers, and was grooming a pair of NFL quarterbacks in Marc Wilson and Gifford Nielsen, who were ahead of McMahon on the depth chart when he arrived. To McMahon, BYU seemed as good a path to the NFL as any he could imagine. Here was a program that did not shy away from throwing the football, and let us not mince words: This was McMahon's primary objective in choosing a college, as well as his father's. "My son's going to school to play football," Jim Senior told one of the school's lead recruiters. "I don't want him to take all those religion classes."

So McMahon never made much of a secret of his disdain, and while there were others like him—non-Mormons made up as much as 40 percent of the football team at BYU, a school founded and overseen by the Mormon church—they had managed to keep a low profile, to at least *pretend* that they abided by the school's draconian honor code, to stop and pause for the national anthem when it played through the campus loudspeakers twice a day.

> As a matter of personal commitment, students, faculty, and staff of Brigham Young University . . . seek to demonstrate in daily living on and off campus those moral virtues encompassed in the gospel of Jesus Christ, and will:

- Be honest
- Observe Dress and Grooming Standards
- Obey the law and all campus policies
- Participate regularly in church services
- Live a chaste and virtuous life
- Use clean language
- Respect others

- Abstain from alcoholic beverages, tobacco, tea, coffee, and substance abuse
- Encourage others in their commitment to comply with the Honor Code

The honor code laid out the values of the Mormon church, but to McMahon, it seemed an unnecessary intrusion on his own personal space, an attempt by an institution to instill its values upon him—the values of a bygone generation that seemed entirely disconnected from contemporary experience.

> Hairstyles should be clean and neat, avoiding extreme styles or colors, and trimmed above the collar leaving the ear uncovered. Consumption of alcohol, in any form, is inappropriate and a breach of the Honor Code. BYU faculty, staff, and students should avoid swearing in speech and writing; coarse expressions derived from profanity; displaying of pictures, posters, and other forms of expressions which are crude or suggestive; and expressions that depend upon allusions to crudity for effect.

("You couldn't even beat off!" he marveled.)

For a young man who had grown up relishing a certain profane heresy, who enjoyed the postgame salves of both beer and tobacco, this was not merely a needless hassle; this almost became an *opportunity* to prove that he could subvert their rules and still achieve his goals. (When his high school teacher Eleanor Olson informed him that he'd have to take a class on the Book of Mormon while at BYU, McMahon replied, "That's all right. I like fiction.") The trouble began, McMahon believed, when someone saw him drinking a beer on the golf course one day. But the trouble *had* to begin somehow, and it kept getting worse as his football career burgeoned, after he gave up the notion of playing baseball because of injury concerns. Soon, he was getting in trouble for being seen at parties that he hadn't even attended. Often, he would drive his Plymouth Duster back to Ogden and hang out at Weber State on the weekends, with his brother, Mike, and his friend Pat Hanley; there, one of the best-known athletes in Utah could be assured of anonymity. "Every Monday LaVell would call me into this office," McMahon says. "And he'd say, 'I got twenty more calls this weekend that you were at this party here, here, and here, and I knew you couldn't be in all those places at once.' And I'd say, 'Where were those parties at, LaVell?' 'Here in Provo.' And I'd say, 'I don't know who has it out for me, but I've never spent a fucking weekend in Provo.' I said, 'I'm only here for Saturdays.'"

He arrived in Provo the fall of 1977, playing behind both Wilson and Nielsen. The next year, when Wilson got hurt, he swept into action, starting six of the last seven games of the season, but then he redshirted when Wilson (who was supposed to be the next "Mormon superman," according to McMahon) returned to action in 1979. McMahon considered transferring; a burgeoning friendship with the team doctor, Brent Pratley, gave him enough reason to stay. They had met on the sidelines during McMahon's freshman year. Pratley asked him what position he played; McMahon said he played quarterback, then pronounced Wilson inept and said that he should be playing instead.

Eventually, Pratley convinced McMahon he should stay at BYU because he could win a Heisman Trophy while playing in the school's intricate and pass-heavy offense. McMahon chose to stay, in large part "to shove it to these people," but a year of inactivity caught up to him. In 1980, he missed the mile run at the start of camp because he'd attended a hellacious party the night before. BYU lost its first game, to New Mexico, and McMahon completed only eleven of twenty-five passes. But he soon came around, and the Cougars won eleven straight after that. The numbers McMahon put up were absurd and wholly unprecedented: In four midseason games, he threw for a total of 1,821 yards, an NCAA record; in one game—albeit against Texas–El Paso—he threw for 384 yards in the *first half.* Some teams rushed ten men to get after McMahon; another team played with eleven pass defenders. Nevada–Las Vegas was flagged for roughing the quarterback on three consecutive plays. None of it worked. Offensive coordinator Doug Scovil's schemes were indicative of a new order in college football, and McMahon, with his photographic memory (like a sixth sense, Edwards once said), was the optimal quarterback. "Until recently, football was a game of run-run-pass-punt," wrote Bob Oates in the *Los Angeles Times.* "This year, it's turning into pass-pass-pass.... This has been the most remarkable passing year ever in college football."

It wasn't just McMahon: At tiny Portland State, a coach named Darrell "Mouse" Davis had originated a new offense utilizing four wide receivers on every play, and he was demolishing teams by scores of 93–7 and 105–0. The NFL had changed its rules to encourage more passing, to foster more excitement; now the colleges were taking it on as well. The numbers Oates cites—of consistent three-hundred-yard passes, of Purdue's Mark Hermann throwing for more than nine thousand career yards—seem comparatively lame by twenty-first-century standards. Over four dozen quarterbacks would eclipse Hermann's and McMahon's numbers over the next three decades, including one at Hawaii who would nearly double them. But at the time, statistics like these were indicative of the revolution within the game itself, football's inevitable concessions to progress. "Passing, like anything else, is mostly believing you can," Mouse Davis told the *Times* (and here, again, was the essence of McMahon). "In the last few years a large number of coaches have come to believe that more good things than bad occur when you put the ball in the air. They used to think the opposite.... The passing era in college football has just begun."

Said legendary coach George Allen, playing the curmudgeon: "They should also change the name. They should call it passball. . . . The touchdowns have been cheapened and so have the records."

McMahon finished his junior season with 4,571 yards and forty-seven touchdown passes, setting a total of twenty-seven NCAA records. And when BYU faced Southern Methodist University in the Holiday Bowl, he proved himself a transcendent figure, capable of performing minor miracles when called upon. Over a matter of several minutes, he became the living proof of the superiority of the new passing game.

BYU trailed 38–19 in the fourth quarter when McMahon's improbable comeback act began. It commenced, as could be expected, with a characteristic act of petulance. On a fourth down, Edwards sent in the punt team. McMahon, as he had done in high school, refused to acknowledge the order. He converted the first down and led his team to a touchdown. SMU was led by running backs Eric Dickerson and Craig James, who formed one of the great backfields in the history of college football, and James scored on the ensuing possession to make it 45–25 with 3:57 remaining. McMahon spearheaded a quick touchdown drive, BYU recovered an onside kick and scored in four plays and cut the lead to 45–39 on a two-point conversion with 1:58 remaining. SMU recovered the ensuing onside kick. The Mustangs punted with 18 seconds left, and BYU blocked it and took over at the SMU forty-one.

After two incomplete passes, McMahon called what was known as the "Save-the-Game Play": Essentially, he would throw it up into the middle of the end zone and hope a defender would get called for pass interference. The ball went up, and tight end Clay Brown and defensive back Wes Hopkins both came down with it; under college rules, mutual receptions are rewarded to the offense. Touchdown. BYU kicked the extra point and won the game. McMahon became a folk hero among a segment of the population who still didn't know quite what to make of him, a Heisman Trophy candidate heading into his senior season. And yet on campus, he still felt unfairly persecuted, branded an outsider, his car ticketed for minor violations by vengeful campus police. He was put on probation for chewing tobacco and drinking beer in his room; he was barred from taking tests because the back of his hair touched his collar.

Of course, he brought a certain amount of this trouble upon himself. On a trip to Hawaii his junior year, he arrived back at his hotel room late at night. Buoyed by drink, he ventured out to the balcony, lowered himself onto the ledge, and swung his body downward, onto the balcony below. He knocked on the door. No one was home, so he climbed back up from the twenty-third floor to the twenty-fourth floor. Only the next morning did he grasp the ramifications of what he'd done. "You're crazy," said his roommate, Dan Plater (nickname: Pluto). Said McMahon: "I couldn't argue with him."

When he began dating a Mormon girl, Nancy Daines, the scrutiny only heightened. He used to send Nancy out to buy beer and tobacco for him. On the Friday before the first game of his senior season, Hanley came to stay with McMahon in Provo, in an off-campus apartment. McMahon was staring out the window, at a car in the parking lot; he told Hanley it was a campus cop who had been stationed outside to ensure that Nancy did not sleep over that night. It all seemed so ridiculous—a twenty-two-year-old man under surveillance by a glorified rent-a-cop—and by the time of his senior season, McMahon began pointing this out to the members of the national media who came to Provo to interview him.

They came to Provo because he was setting records—because he was a contender for the Heisman Trophy, and because, in an era of rampant hypocrisy in college athletics, McMahon's admission that he did not much care for his own school, that he was using the Mormon church as a stepping-stone, seemed refreshingly honest. At least representatives of both parties were willing to admit that this was a marriage of convenience, rather than an attempt to adhere to the outdated ideal of amateurism. "The school got what it wanted, "wrote one columnist, "and now McMahon is going to do the same." At colleges like Southern Methodist, boosters were running amok, and the entire football program was plagued by rampant corruption that would heighten over the course of the decade; at BYU, the lone iconoclast was McMahon, who was more than willing to admit, by this point, that he was in Provo only to play football. "I would like to be remembered here as a good player and a good person. But I don't see that happening," he told a reporter in December of his senior season, after another prodigious campaign, after he set records for career passing efficiency and total offense, after he set the NCAA record for most NCAA records set with fifty-five despite a knee injury against Colorado that ruined his chances at the Heisman. (As he limped off the field during that game, with BYU ahead and the Colorado fans jeering him and cheering his departure, McMahon pointed at the scoreboard. If it was not a particularly magnanimous thing to do—if it was not in keeping with the principles of the Latter-day Saints— McMahon did not particularly care. He had already done it several years earlier during BYU's 56–6 win over Utah, thereby originating— at least according to some accounts—a now time-honored taunt: *Scoreboard.*)

"I don't have a lot of fond memories of school," he said in December. "In fact, I hate school. Once I graduate and get to the NFL, I won't be coming back here. . . . People resent the fact that I'm not Mormon and don't want to be. They want everybody to be part of the religion or else they don't like you. They are envious of the fact that I'm not Mormon and I can still play football so well."

McMahon dropped out after the season, without finishing his final semester at BYU. In a letter to the editor of the *Los Angeles Times,* a pair of BYU fans wrote that they had once been fascinated by McMahon's achievements; now they couldn't care less.

No doubt McMahon would have told them—in words that most likely would not have adhered to the school's honor code—that the feeling was entirely mutual. He had used BYU, and BYU had used him; as we entered a decade marked by its emphasis upon opportunism and self-reliance, what was more nakedly utilitarian than a tacit agreement like this one? "Jim is a taker," said Olson, his high school teacher. "He puts his needs above those of others, and his needs were to go to a school that would get him where he wanted to get."

He got there when he was drafted by the Bears in April 1982. Free at last, he took a limousine to the practice facility and stepped out to greet the media, wearing jeans and flip-flops, holding a Budweiser in his hand; he addressed the team's general manager, a man in his mid-sixties, as "kid." A few weeks later, he married Nancy Daines, the Mormon girl he'd stolen away from BYU. The service was held at a nondenominational church.

IV.

By December 1985, they had become media personalities and luncheon speakers and automobile pitchmen and guest newspaper columnists. The communications staff could not keep up; every week, it seemed, they were advancing the relationship between athletes and marketers. "You might say they even *created* sports marketing," said Ken Valdiserri, the team's communications director. Meanwhile, the Bears locker room was astir with tension, with silly little disputes, with what the writer Rick Telander referred to as "creative dissonance" between offense and defense. "There were daily scuffles in practice," said lineman Kurt Becker.

Their wins became performance art: In the midst of a vicious 44–0 blowout of the Dallas Cowboys, two defensive players, Dave Duerson and Otis Wilson, began woofing at each other—*I think they're barking like dogs down here,* said CBS sideline reporter Irv

Cross—and inspired a regrettably long-lasting cultural trend. Taking their lead from McMahon and Ditka, everyone had a persona, and the media embraced it completely: Dan Hampton and Steve McMichael were the badass lunatics on the defensive line; Wilson was a preening linebacker "with an ego as big as Mount Everest—but it was an ego that *charmed you*," said broadcaster Chet Coppock (later in the season, a persistent rumor spread about the Everest-like physical dimensions of Wilson's manhood). The offensive linemen—whom McMahon considered his closest friends on the team,[2] out of utility and a certain commonality of spirit—also had a promotional poster; entitled *Black and Blues Brothers*, it was sponsored by local Chevrolet dealers and featured the entire line posed in sunglasses and hats, dressed up like Jake and Elwood. It was so popular that people began test-driving cars just so they could get a free copy. A backup tight end, Tim Wrightman, was one of more than a dozen players with his own radio show; Keith Van Horne did his from a waterbed every morning. Ditka had ads running on three channels. Gary Fencik, the defensive back, modeled hair mousse. Even Payton, the subdued veteran at the eye of this storm, did a Diet Coke commercial. Ditka made $350,000 doing a radio show and a television show every week, and egos collided, breeding resentment over endorsement deals and media exposure. Just trying to manage and maintain the complexities amounted to a near-impossible task for Valdiserri and his front-office colleagues. (Following the season, NFL teams began melding their marketing and communications staffs in order to take advantage of this oncoming financial bonanza.)

And despite all of this—perhaps *because* of all this—they kept on winning. They beat Minnesota again, and they beat Green Bay again, The Fridge faking out the Packers' George Cumby this time, nimbly

---

2. "Jim's a smart guy," Becker said. "If you're a quarterback, the first guys you're gonna make friends with are the offensive line—it was the first time, at least in my experience, that a quarterback actually appreciated our labor."

juking and catching a touchdown pass, Ditka's toy continuing to elevate himself to new and unprecedented levels of pop-cultural stardom. The next day, The Fridge appeared on David Letterman's show. He was charging five thousand dollars an hour for autograph sessions. In one day, McMahon went from *Good Morning America* to *Oprah* to a luncheon; he had dozens of speaking requests from organizations near and far. "The public must want to hear me talk," he told Bob Verdi of the *Chicago Tribune,* voice dripping with sarcasm, "because I'm very cerebral."

In fact, McMahon's approach to the game itself *was* cerebral. But the public fascination with this team was based on its outward coarseness, on the sense that they were genuinely arrogant and unconcerned. "If bland Boys of Autumn like Dan Marino and John Elway are setting the tone for an entire generation of signal callers, the word has not yet reached McMahon, who tends to rely on the kind of news sources that have a monthly centerfold," *Newsweek* wrote. The fact that McMahon really did peruse skin magazines in the locker room (he posted a photo of an unidentified female breast in his locker, next to pictures of his children), the fact that he really drank beer and chewed tobacco and banged helmets with his offensive linemen and said he daydreamed of becoming an offensive lineman—all that contributed to his reputation as our own permutation of Joe Willie Namath.

He had the antiestablishment routine down pat by now. If nothing else, Brigham Young had prepared him for this. He knew who his friends were; he coddled his offensive linemen, treating them to dinner, moving all the furniture out of his room during training camp in the sleepy town of Platteville, Wisconsin, renaming it "the Beer Garden," and inviting his linemen to drink with him. If he had them on his side, he figured, he could take on the rest of the world. By the heart of the '85 season, in the wake of the Minnesota miracle, it seemed to have caught on: One teammate said the Bears were now "psychologically hooked" on McMahon.

And yet he remained supremely divisive. He considered his only accomplice among the Chicago media to be Verdi, the longtime *Tribune* columnist; he dismissed the other reporters as tools of management, mouthpieces for Ditka and his cronies. "He shit all over the media," said one media member. "A psychobabbling jerk," Chet Coppock called him, and questioned whether McMahon "sought in the press the father he wanted to coddle him."

Perhaps there was a certain amount of truth in that: In 1985, as his fame swelled, McMahon's relationship with his father deteriorated. He would later write about it in his autobiography, released the following fall: about what he perceived to be his parents' resentment of his marriage (according to his friend Pat Hanley, McMahon's father asked his son's first agent to give him a prenuptial agreement), about the way his parents seemed to view him as the ungrateful son who had purposefully distanced himself from home, about the way his father once asked for the Bears tie off the neck of the team's chairman of the board, Ed McCaskey. That, in McMahon's mind, was the wrong kind of boldness; his father lacked the sophistication and savvy that permitted his son to get away with what he did. There was a rift in the family, and it lasted for nearly a decade. During that time, they hardly spoke at all—in later years, when his parents came to Chicago to visit, they never even saw their son; instead, they stayed with Hanley, who took them to a pub with McMahon memorabilia on the wall so Jim Senior could bask in his son's success.

Beyond the Freudian psychology, McMahon also toyed with the media because it raised his standing among his teammates, and he did it because he could see already that this rebellious stance coincided with a cultural moment. (If they wanted to compare him to a punk rocker merely because of his ridiculous haircut—even though he hardly owned any tapes or records—well, so be it.) For all his physical courage, McMahon was inherently lazy. He dreamed of a life in which he would never have to work an actual job, a life where he could play golf in his bare feet all day long and drink beer and not concern himself with much of anything. He had exerted himself one time, to get in shape before the 1984 season, and when he lacerated his kidney at the end of that year, he told Hanley he would never bother with such things again, as if the sin of conditioning had led to the worst injury of his career: a hit from a Raider that wrapped McMahon's kidney around his rib, lacerating it and leaving him pissing bright red blood.

Anyway, it was an optimal time to be a celebrity, and to get rich quick in America; in December, the Dow Jones was rising so fast that no one seemed able to explain precisely what was going on with it. Such was the aura of McMahon, who carried to work an executive briefcase with a sandwich, a bag of potato chips, and a Hostess fruit pie, and who showed up at practice one day throwing passes left-handed, until Ditka had the temerity to ask, *What the fuck is going on here?*

V.

It was a fair question. No one seemed to have much perspective on this thing anymore. Fans were waiting in line in twenty-below wind chills just to catch a glimpse of a wide receiver at a local tavern. "I'd seen it individually, but never collectively," said Chet Coppock, the broadcaster. "That club just had a choke hold on the American public." And then came the biggest explosion yet, in the form of a cacophonous song that began playing on local radio stations. It was yet another self-promotional tool, this one dreamed up by a local record producer and presented in idea form to the dandyish Bears wide receiver, Willie Gault, who was already looking to make a name for himself in show business. The tune was a rewrite of an *Amos 'n' Andy* spoof three Nashville songwriters had penned; it was called "The Super Bowl Shuffle." There were verses from ten Bears, including Payton (*Well, they call me Sweetness and I like to dance / Runnin' the ball* is like makin' romance), from The Fridge (*I'm the rookie / I may be large, but I'm no dumb cookie*), and from McMahon (*I'm the punky QB known as McMahon / When I hit the turf, I've got no plan*), who had managed to injure his trick shoulder again and sat out nearly a month in midseason as the Bears, buoyed by their own astonishing pop-cultural momentum, continued to win without him. Even on the sideline, McMahon made news—he showed up for the Cowboys game in a pair of worn-out jeans, attire that the *Sun-Times'* Ray Sons wrote "might have made Boy George blush."

Upon its release, the song was a mere footnote in the newspapers. And yet it sold immediately. The record ($4.99) was swept off the shelves of local drugstores by eager fans in search of Christmas gifts, the proceeds supposedly to be used to salve needy Chicagoans. But this was not the end of it. As we approached 1986, as The Fridge made a cameo appearance on Bob Hope's Christmas special, as it became clear that the music video was now the dominant form of media among America's youth, the authors of "The Super Bowl Shuffle" realized that it would behoove them to enhance their product with visuals. Those of us who comprised the target audience of the cultural juggernaut known as MTV were of a generation easily seduced by video, by imagery and identity and ornithological hairstyles; and so the creators planned a video shoot for the day after the Bears came back from a *Monday Night* game against Miami.

That week, McMahon, still recovering from the tendinitis in his shoulder, sprained his ankle. According to the quarterback: "I missed one day and Ditka says I'm not playing on Sunday." The hype in Miami was tremendous. There was a sense that this was the last, best chance for someone to knock off the Bears, for someone to temper their rampant arrogance—and for someone to preserve the 1972 Dolphins' place in history as the NFL's lone undefeated team. It was the highest-rated *Monday Night Football* game of all time; The Fridge's new McDonald's commercial debuted at halftime. By Sunday, McMahon insisted his ankle was fine. Ditka, recalling the way this whole odd sequence of events had begun, told him, "We're not going to have another Minnesota."

McMahon: "What do you mean we're not going to have another Minnesota, Mike? You don't want to win?"

Ditka went with his backup, Steve Fuller. Rather than relying on Payton, he called passes on the first nine plays of the game, as if he were once again trying to prove he did not need McMahon. The Dolphins scored on their first two possessions, the Bears got nothing, and by the time McMahon came into the game, with six minutes left, the only suspense that remained was whether Payton would set an NFL record by rushing for a hundred yards in his eighth consecutive game (he did, by ignoring Ditka's insistence on passing and continually audibling to running plays). The final score was 38–24. The Bears were no longer undefeated. McMahon didn't much concern himself with it. His ego was not easily bruised; his team was in the playoffs, and this was what mattered, anyway. He would not miss another game that season, and his team would not lose again.

The next day, at a theater in downtown Chicago, against the advice of Ditka and several teammates who refused to participate, the Bears recorded the video version of "The Super Bowl Shuffle," men in jerseys and football pants wearing dark glasses and silly hats, pretending to play instruments and swaying to a syncopated beat against a blue background. Of the principals who had recorded the original rap, only McMahon and Payton held back from attending, because of concerns about the audacity of the gesture and the question of how much of the proceeds were actually going to charity.[3] But a short time later, their worries assuaged, Payton and McMahon stood on a racquetball court at Halas Hall and performed their parts, their

---

3. Soon after, the Illinois attorney general's office got involved, insisting that the record's producer, Don Meyers, donate 75 percent of the proceeds to worthy causes, as dictated by state law concerning charitable organizations. The parties eventually reached a settlement.

images superimposed into what would become a best-selling single, a breakthrough music video, an almost unfathomable Grammy nominee (Best Rhythm & Blues Vocal Performance—Duo or Group), and a full-on embrace of American excess at its most excessive.

Summit, New Jersey

He was a quarterback once, broad-shouldered and blandly handsome. Today he lives a quiet life in a sprawling manifestation of the American dream: an enormous stucco house on a tree-lined cul-de-sac in a tony New Jersey suburb. He has a wife and four children and a den with a wet bar and a pool table, all of which came about because he has spent the bulk of his adult life quietly and methodically building a fortune across the river, amid the sharp elbows and cheap-shot artists on Wall Street.

He was a quarterback once, and I remember him quite well, even if certain people who watched him play back then—and even many of the opposing players who chased him down—can no longer remember his name. "I do think he would have a hard time playing big-time college football today," one official told me.

"Their quarterback?" said an opposing linebacker. "I don't remember their quarterback."

He was a quarterback once, and he had his moments, both proud and ignominious. In 1984, during the first start of his collegiate career, he completed three consecutive passes. And being who he was—knowing *what* he was—this excited him, and he attempted to engage in a showy and contemporary and entirely uncharacteristic celebration with one of his wide receivers: He leapt up for a high five. And somehow, in doing so, he managed to dislocate his shoulder.

John Shaffer: The name, like the way he played the game, is eminently forgettable. When he graduated from Penn State as an academic All-American in the spring of 1987, he possessed a championship ring and a reputation as a solid citizen who had absolutely no legitimate shot of making it as a starting quarterback in the National Football League. He went to training camp with the Dallas Cowboys as an undrafted free agent. By the end of August, he did something that others could never muster the courage to do: He *asked* to be cut. He had a degree in finance, with an internship waiting at Merrill Lynch. He had another life to start.

Maybe, he says now, he could have hung around for a couple of years, and maybe he could have slipped onto a roster as someone's second or third option, and maybe he could have spent that time aspiring to be something he'd probably never be. But that was the thing about John Shaffer: He had few pretensions. He knew exactly what he was. He was one of those quarterbacks whose job was not to alter the course of the game but simply not to render it FUBAR—a quarterback of the type that, even in the 1980s, was teetering on the brink of extinction.

How imperfect was he? Let us count the flaws: John Shaffer was not fleet of foot, and he did not have a prodigious arm, and he was not an imposing physical presence. When reporters questioned him about the high-five incident, he implored them to tell his coach, Joe Paterno, that he'd been run over by a six-feet-six, 260-pound lineman. He was good-natured but straight; nothing to see here, really.

So it went for him. In the age of natural-born lunatics like Mc-Mahon, of strong-armed robotic assassins like Elway and Marino, he was one of the last of a breed: the signal caller as a cipher, as generic as a tin can. He fit snugly into the system of his conservative coach, whose team wore plain uniforms that were often likened to prison garb, and whose reputation was such that when a manufacturer produced golf balls with Paterno's face printed on them, the unofficial tagline became that they would run up the middle three out of every four times. Shaffer's statistics in 1985 were undeniably mediocre: He completed 45 percent of his passes, threw more interceptions than touchdowns, and went seven-of-twenty-three and four-of-ten against mediocre teams like Pitt and Rutgers. But beneath all of this, there was a certain grace in his orthodoxy. He did not try to achieve anything irrational or absurd because he knew he was not capable of accomplishing such things, and if he had not been aware of it before, certainly the embarrassment of a botched high five had convinced him of this. "I really trusted the authority of our coaches," John Shaffer said. "I felt like if we listened to them, we'd always be successful."

And this is how John Shaffer won football games. Everywhere he went, he won consistently, almost mystically, as if guided by some supreme authority. In junior high school, he did not lose a game. In high school, at Cincinnati powerhouse Moeller, he did not lose a game. And in his first eleven starts of the 1985 season, as the quarterback of a Penn State offense that was alternately described as *unspectacular* and *inconsistent*, John Shaffer ran his streak to fifty-four in a row—up until the last game of that year, until the evening on January 1, 1986, in Miami, until the first of two games in the course of 366 days that would herald the dawning of a new era. "In the fifties, coaches may have made the difference," said the coach of his Orange Bowl opponent, Oklahoma's Barry Switzer. "But you don't outcoach anymore. Players win now."

This was said after Shaffer's win streak had been extinguished by Oklahoma, after Shaffer had forced passes into double and triple coverage and had been outplayed by his opposite, a flashy young quarterback named Jamelle Holieway, who executed the rush-heavy wishbone offense to perfection and carried a gold pinkie ring in his

Louis Vuitton handbag. On that night, John Shaffer came face-to-face with Switzer's prophetic logic about the future of football, in the person of The Boz, the linebacker who wore the sunglasses and the gold chains and dyed his hair strange colors—whose entire act was based in his *distrust* of authority. This one game was the lone, glaring failure of John Shaffer's career, the one time when his adherence to traditionalism betrayed him. "It's just too bad," he said of himself, "that the performance of one person can have so much to do with the outcome of the game."

He was a quarterback once, and he was astute enough to know what this meant for him: The game had changed, just as the culture had changed. Everything was getting louder. And so John Shaffer spent that off-season laboring harder than he ever had before, making one last attempt to stave off obsolescence, all while realizing that perhaps he'd been born thirty years too late.

CHAPTER FIVE

Matches to a Fire

*So what if Libyan planes were staring down America over
the Gulf of Sidra? . . . Did you hear that McMahon swung by
his heels through all those brasseries in the rafters at the Old
Absinthe House and then vomited on Frank Sinatra?*

—CURRY KIRKPATRICK, *Sports Illustrated*

I.

The New Year dawned, rich with symbolism: From Russia, Mikhail
Gorbachev addressed the people of the United States and proclaimed
that 1986 could serve as the beginning of an age of peace that would
last well into the twenty-first century. From Washington, in a speech
broadcast on Soviet television, Reagan offered a similar salutation.
Even the jangling uneasiness of decades of Cold War politics seemed
couched in hope (television anchors were quick to assuage any concerns that these dual presidential broadcasts, at one P.M. Eastern time,
would cut in to the New Year's Day college bowl games). The president's power was greater than it had ever been: In December, without
any disclosure to Congress, he signed an intelligence finding that retro-
actively authorized several shipments of arms to Iran in exchange for
hostages. For now, it remained a secret, as did the back-alley dealings
and insider-trading scandals that would soon blow up on Wall Street.

For now, it was full speed ahead. The year 1986, Reagan told a gathering of leading conservatives, would be the "breakpoint," and then he warned them of complacency in the face of what seemed like unambiguous victory for their ideals.

"We have a hundred and ten million people, roughly, that are employed; the highest percentage of the potential working pool ever in our history is employed," Reagan said at a January press conference, in defense of his economic policies, in defense of tax cuts and shrinking government. "The stock market today set a new high again, all-time high." Later, he laughed off a question about whether the Rambo and Rocky movies might be distorting public perceptions of the Soviet Union, about whether the Hollywood mythology could possibly impact real life.

In Chicago, the Bears prepared for a playoff game against the Giants by retreating to work out in Suwanee, Georgia, away from the home crowds who had already begun mythologizing them, who had lined up to gawk while they shopped for Christmas gifts at Marshall Field's. Jim McMahon assured reporters that he planned to spend New Year's Eve studying film in his hotel room. "I might have a beer," he said, "but we're here to work." He may have even been serious, but it didn't matter—by now, his reputation had preceded him. His response was greeted with laughter.

Two weeks earlier, Joseph Vincent Paterno had turned fifty-nine years old. Born and raised in Brooklyn, he attended Brown University, then took an assistant coaching job at the Pennsylvania State University in 1950. He was named head coach in 1966, presiding over a power-house football program set amid the cow towns in the geographic center of the state, four hours from everywhere. Soon after, speaking with Philadelphia sportswriter Bill Conlin, Paterno laid out a lofty notion, a template for a program he imagined would balance the demands of both big-time athletics and academia in ways that, even in the late 1960s, seemed increasingly untenable: "I'm thinking in terms of a grand experiment. . . . Everybody assumes if you have a great football team, there have to be sacrifices in the area of [academic] standards. People tell me it can't be done without sacrificing academic standards. They tell me I'm daydreaming. . . . I don't want my players just tied to a football program."

If it seemed a pipe dream then, imagine how it looked in 1985, when college sports had long since graduated into the realm of big business. To his critics, Paterno came across as smug and self-righteous, a nerd in thick spectacles set loose in the locker room, quoting Virgil and espousing outdated ideals. He was, to them, a man in denial of the new realities, of the material world of adolescent football stars. Even the way he dressed—in cheap-looking sport jackets and ties, and pants hoisted so high he appeared to be anticipating the return of the Johnstown Flood—seemed a rebuke to the increasingly casual varsity-jacket-and-sweater attire of his peers. Earlier in the decade, shortly after winning the school's first national championship, he had been accused of racism for supporting Proposition 48, the tightened admissions policy that would go into effect later in 1986 and would largely affect black athletes with low admissions-test scores. "Joe Paterno assaulted all blacks," the president of Grambling State University said. "He does not know anything about black athletes." Around the same time, one of his former players, Lenny Moore, accused Paterno of racial insensitivity, and even though he later recanted, the perception lingered—that perhaps the coach had lost touch, that perhaps he could no longer relate to the contemporary athlete.

The previous two years had been among the worst seasons of Paterno's career. After a 6–5 finish in 1984, the coach called his players "a bunch of babies." He questioned their ethic; he reevaluated his own methods. He started getting letters from fans. "The general tone was the fact that there are a lot of fast, young coaches out there, you better get into high gear, that kind of thing," Paterno said. He was as stubborn as any of his colleagues; he believed in adaptation, but not in moral capitulation. He told his team they could either adapt with him and dedicate themselves year-round to a game that now demanded such a commitment in order to win, or they could walk away. Either way, he would not hold it against them. He would also honor their scholarships. Two players took him up on his offer; the rest stayed.

Said Shaffer: "In the dark days, there was a lot of 'me, me, me.'"

Paterno did not stand for such things. He made clear that he deplored this shift away from authoritarianism. He feared the havoc the era of the individual might wreak upon the game. In 1979, asked about retirement at a Friday-evening gathering with sportswriters, he said, "What . . . and leave coaching to the [Barry] Switzers and [Jackie] Sherrills?" He later said he'd presumed the comments were off the record; in fact, he became friends with Switzer (Sherrill, the coach of Penn State's longtime rival Pittsburgh, was another story altogether), and all week leading up to the Orange Bowl, he'd apologized and downplayed his own words, insisting he'd spoken out of turn. But even if the rift between Switzer and Paterno wasn't personal, it was philosophical, as Paterno would admit when he agreed to write the foreword to Switzer's autobiography several years later:

> Barry and I have different, contrary conceptions as to what college football should be, what position it should occupy in university life and in education of the people who play at Division IA schools. . . . This is an important book because it shows a side of big-time college football that, to be frank with you, I naïvely didn't really believe existed.

And yet there it was, right in front of him on New Year's night, in the person of Switzer himself—the gregarious son of an Arkansas bootlegger who had risen from poverty, who didn't have electricity until junior high, whose mother had committed suicide while her son sat nearby in another room, and whose father died in a car accident a decade later. Switzer could be both a charmer and a charlatan, able to maintain relationships even as his recruiting practices at Oklahoma raised questions about his character. He had once been charged with obtaining inside information on a $97,900 stock deal based on information he'd overheard at a track meet (the SEC filed a case against him, but it was dismissed for lack of evidence). He brought home national championships in his second and third seasons as coach and had since "struck up feuds with everybody from Darrell Royal to the state of Utah," according to *Sports Illustrated*'s Rick Reilly. "He was the outlaw unbound. He was roguish, braggish, boorish. He spoke fast, drew fast, partied fast."

By late 1985, following a divorce, Switzer claimed to have to toned it down, in part because he was forced to by the school's administration after three four-loss seasons in the early part of the decade. ("As a winner, Switzer was tolerable to many," wrote *The Daily Oklahoman*. "As a loser, perhaps it is time for him to move on.") He had learned to expose less of his undisciplined side to the media. But this team remained a reflection of its coach. They lived *loose*. Switzer didn't pester them about their lifestyles, about their haircuts, about their clutch purses, about the sweatbands and towels that bore their names and numbers. He allowed them to express themselves and, in so doing, facilitated the creation of a monster, his most braggish and boorish media creation to date, the savvy 240-pound linebacker known as The Boz.

II.

Brian Bosworth had come to the University of Oklahoma from the town of Irving, Texas, a bulked-up linebacker who boasted to have learned in high school a method of projectile vomiting in his opponents' faces. He was lured out of the state by the promise of publicity, which he claims was the only enticement Switzer offered him on his recruiting trip. It worked: By the fall of 1985, he was swimming in publicity, much of it his own doing, much of it based purely on visuals, on a deliberately perplexing haircut that cried out for attention. The hair was, Bosworth said, a statement of rage, but it was also a strategic decision, for The Boz was perhaps the most self-aware of all these media creations sprouting up in locker rooms across America, an academic All-American with a grade-point average well above 3.0.

Like McMahon, Bosworth had come of age in a drab and conservative suburb in the post-Vietnam 1970s, during what he referred to as "the most boring decade of the twentieth century." With McMahon, stardom seemed to develop organically, arising from a punk aesthetic that was meant to make you wonder if he gave a damn about *anything;* with Bosworth, rebellion was about the embrace of glamour and status. He drove a white Corvette, paid for, in part, by the largesse of a local businessman. And his hair—oh, *the hair!*—was carefully styled every week, spiked on top and cut and dyed into strips on the side, a rat tail crawling along the back of his neck. The hair became a signature—even his hairstylist became a minor celebrity.

Bosworth had a natural gift for taste making: When he cut off the bottom of his jersey on a hot day, his teammates started doing it too. At a party sophomore year, after too many beers, he asked one of his teammates to pierce his ear, without alcohol or anesthetic. He pronounced himself the first white player on his team to don an earring at a moment when men with jewelry did not exactly equate with masculinity; eventually, he found an earring in the shape of his uniform number, 44.

Most of all, The Boz specialized in running his mouth. In 1984, as a redshirt freshman, he declared his hatred for the University of Texas and all things related to it, including the school's burnt-orange color scheme, which he likened to the bile he regurgitated after binging at all-you-can-eat buffet meals before high school games. From then on, he became a mouthpiece for all the rage and trash talk and anger that his teammates were reticent to express for fear that their coaches would not approve of their pregame bluster. His alternate nickname was "Bulletin Board."

Switzer let it all pass because of his admiration for Bosworth's abilities. On the field, The Boz was crazed and craven and big and fast, swearing and screaming and barking and spitting and braying at the moon, able to "balance on that line that separates crazed aggression and rational thought," *The New York Times* wrote. Scouts compared him to a fleeter version of Dick Butkus. Unlike most of his teammates, Bosworth pulled good grades without really trying, though he insisted to anyone who questioned him about it that he hated going to school. He also told them that his aim on the football field was to injure people and to pick fights, and that his Doberman pinscher was afraid of *him*. He admitted to *Sports Illustrated* that he would sometimes hang random parts inside the doors of cars while working a summer job in 1985 on the General Motors assembly line in Oklahoma City, so the cars would inexplicably rattle and their owners would have to completely disassemble them in order to find the source (following a minor controversy in the automotive press, his coach later insisted Bosworth had made this up; in his autobiography, Bosworth insisted he hadn't, and that the assembly line workers had done it as a method of fighting back against the impersonality of the system). After a while, his identity became twisted; it was hard for even Bosworth himself to know what was real and what wasn't.

"Somewhere in there, The Boz became this giant symbol for people and Brian became forgotten," he would say in his autobiography. The Boz, he said, "became the symbol of the anti-Christ, the symbol of everything that's wrong with 'damn kids' today."[4]

Everywhere he looked, The Boz claimed to see hypocrisy among his elders. In his autobiography, he detailed how his teammate Buster Rhymes fired warning shots from an Uzi out the window of his dorm after getting caught in the middle of a snowball fight; Switzer, he said, did little or nothing to punish him (Switzer later rebutted this story in his own book by claiming Rhymes was actually firing a pistol, not a submachine gun). The Boz had little regard for the rules and regulations of the NCAA, since he figured they and the school were benefiting from his image, including a poster of Bosworth that sold thousands of copies. He did not turn down money if it was offered to him; he once had a summer job that consisted of watching an oil rig go up and down for four hours. A friend in the district attorney's office fixed his parking tickets. He was railing against the establishment and using it at the same time, and in this way, the reporter who likened the dichotomy between John Shaffer and Brian Bosworth as Hardhat versus Hippie had, in fact, missed the point, for The Boz was anything but a hippie, and this was not the sixties. This was Reagan's America, and The Boz was an unrepentant capitalist, an opportunist seeking out stardom. He would later admit to joining forces with an agent named Gary Wichard a short time after the Orange Bowl, in order to craft his image. Here was the archetype for the modern age—all you had to do was turn on MTV to see it in action. Androgyny and satanic imagery and chains and big hair: The more it freaked out our elders, the more records it sold. It was anarchy, Republican-style.

A few months before the Orange Bowl, Dee Snider, the lead

---

4. Eventually, he would even distance himself from some of the claims made in his own book.

singer for a heavy-metal band called Twisted Sister, testified before Congress as to the contents of his song lyrics. It was a delicious and absurdist spectacle brought to you by the concerned mothers who formed the Parents Music Resource Center. Snider, dressed in denim and snakeskin boots and eye makeup, hair teased to the sky, pronounced himself a Christian, free of drugs and alcohol. Any implication that his music invoked images of sadomasochism and bondage, he said, simply meant that his accuser, Tipper Gore, had a dirty mind. The PMRC's lobbying efforts led to the placing of warning labels on albums with explicit lyrics. And yet the hearing succeeded in making Twisted Sister—and the heavy-metal genre—more popular than it had ever been.

So it went with Bosworth, who graduated into a polarizing brand of stardom in 1986. He would later admit to various sordid acts such as hiding in the closet to watch his teammates have sex with coeds, but insisted that he possessed a crude nobility beneath his threatening veneer. On drugs, for instance: He didn't do them. He claimed he'd had a meeting with some teammates in 1985 to convince them to stop freebasing cocaine on game days. Later, he made a big show about cold-cocking a persistent drug dealer he met at a club. His lunacy was always controlled, always at least a little bit calculated; empowered by the loose moral structure of his coach, he imported the iconography of hair metal to sports. He was all about imagery, about perpetuating a persona and lifestyle that was never entirely real, about enticing people to hate him for reasons they often couldn't articulate.

At least that was how it felt that evening against Penn State. Bosworth was everywhere that night, a crimson blur of fours dashing from one end of the field to the other. He finished with thirteen solo tackles, and he harassed the no-frills quarterback, John Shaffer, into a performance that was so ugly—ten-for-twenty-two, seventy-four yards, three interceptions—he gave way to his backup, Matt Knizner, late in the game. It all set up perfectly for Oklahoma: Miami, another burgeoning gang of malcontents, lost 35–7 to Tennessee in the Sugar Bowl, largely because they'd been partying all week long (in a newspaper diary, Miami's Jerome Brown wrote about his difficulty in determining which women at the New Orleans bars were transvestites). And so when Oklahoma tight end Keith Jackson outran a backup Penn State safety and caught a seventy-one-yard touchdown pass and danced into the end zone in the second quarter, The Boz scampered onto the field, helmet in hand, his mane glistening in the Miami night, and bear-hugged Jamelle Holieway. It seemed so over-the-top, so patently unnecessary, so pointedly disrespectful; the cameras caught it all. Oklahoma won, 25–10, and that night The Boz became something more than a football player: The Boz became a warning label.

III.

In Chicago, the Bears kept insisting that they were serious, that they were more than just an omnipresent media construction, that they actually planned on winning the Super Bowl and not just wailing about it in song. The time for "dancing and jiving" was over, Ditka said; the postseason had arrived, and there was a sense among them now that they *had* to win the Super Bowl, that anything less would be an embarrassment and a disappointment, that it would invalidate their whole ethos—not to mention the commercial viability of "The Super Bowl Shuffle," now playing in endless rotation on local radio. Even McMahon was subdued, at least for McMahon, at least for the moment—these would be the first playoff games of his career. Asked by a reporter if he would make a guarantee of a Super Bowl victory as his hero Joe Willie Namath had done long ago, he replied, "First we have to get there. If we get there, then yeah, I'll say we'll win it." Still, hubris was a key element of what had gotten them to 15–1 in the first place. In a peculiar way, the Bears had actually accomplished for their city what Reagan had accomplished politically: They brought hubris back, negating the decades-long failings of both their city and their sports teams. McMahon, the manifestation of that collective ego, was at his best when pissed off about something; now, wrote Don Pierson in the *Tribune,* because the quarterback had taken a month off in midseason to nurse his shoulder, he was angry that he hadn't found a reason to be angry for so long.

The Giants beat the 49ers in a first-round game, which meant a matchup loomed with Lawrence Taylor, New York's ferocious linebacker whose season had degenerated into an on-again, off-again binge of snorting and freebasing, and who was three months from vanishing into a rehab center for the first time. None of this was, at present, public knowledge, and yet the Bears seemed somehow determined to take advantage of Taylor's overzealousness (both emotionally and physically) and to bait him into distraction. Buddy Ryan had already "forgotten" Taylor's name when speaking of him as one of the league's most overrated players the season before, and now Otis Wilson stammered when discussing Taylor with reporters, saying, "Lawrence, Lawrence something . . . help me, I really can't think of his name."

And then they spent the evening running right at Taylor. They cut-blocked him, hitting him low on his body so as to slow him down and negate his strength. It was perfectly legal, but Taylor didn't much care for it. He swore and screamed. He called Bears fullback Matt Suhey a baby; even McMahon got under him once, and when wide receiver Dennis McKinnon knocked him head over heels late in the game, Taylor retaliated with a cheap shot. He jawed at Ditka and the Bears sideline; Parcells had to restrain him, and he left the game "kicking and screaming like a little kid," Pierson wrote. The Bears defense, mixing up its schemes, sacked the Giants quarterback, Phil Simms, six times, and Perry fell on top of the Giants' five-feet-seven running back Joe Morris, inducing a concussion and indefinite claustrophobia. New York's punter, Sean Landeta, somehow managed to whiff on a punt amid a swirling wind, and the Bears picked it up and scored the first of three touchdowns. They won 21–0, and McMahon threw two touchdown passes while taking the unusual step of wearing gloves to keep his hands warm.

"What kind of gloves were they?" a reporter asked.

"Black," McMahon said.

The NFC Championship game was next, against the team from Los Angeles; immediately, on the Monday after the win over the Giants, Buddy Ryan began complaining about the Rams' penchant for holding. It caught the Rams completely unaware, and it gave the Bears further cause to claim that the NFL held some kind of grudge against them, even as league officials acknowledged that the Bears were the best thing to have happened to the league in this decade, even as a clerk from the NFL's gift catalog admitted to the *Chicago Sun-Times* that more than half of the orders that had come in over the past few months were for Bears paraphernalia—they had become America's Team.

That same day, Ditka growled about uncalled late hits on McMahon, and then famously referred for the first time to his Bears as Grabowskis, as emissaries of the working class, and the Rams as the Smiths, as the fair-haired tools of the league establishment. Never mind that Fencik, the Bears' safety, had an MBA from Northwestern. Never mind that the Bears appealed just as much to the effete. The Chicago Symphony indulged in a version of "Bear Down, Chicago Bears," the team's fight song; amid the ostentatious wares at Neiman Marcus, one could purchase a seventeen-dollar submarine sandwich called "The Fridge"; and at an auction house on Ohio Street, the presentation of a football autographed by Ditka, accompanied by the playing of "The Super Bowl Shuffle," led to chaos, according to the *Tribune:* "Sophisticated, pearl-clad matrons went nuts; intense-looking gentlemen dropped their auction paddles to cheer and hoot."

But never mind objectivity and never mind perspective—this team was now shaping its own public legacy from day to day, in a town where the mayor had erected a giant television screen in Daley Plaza to play "The Super Bowl Shuffle" on a continuous loop. Over at the *Tribune*, Pierson and his colleagues never lacked for a story; Bears news bled over to every section of the paper. "Ryan and Ditka," Pierson later recalled, "were like matches to a fire." Ryan even bragged that his defense would make the league's best running back, Eric Dickerson, fumble three times. "I don't think we come in favor with some people," Ditka said of the team that had helped raise the NFL's prime-time ratings by 20 percent, that had sold one million copies of an utterly absurd rap record, that would wind up foisting approximately forty million dollars of team-related merchandise on fans who would also make the Rams-Bears NFC Championship the most-watched program in the history of Chicago.

And the NFL, recognizing the bonanza it had here, went right along. That week, just a few days after McMahon was featured in *People* magazine—"My offensive linemen spit on me," he told them. "I spit back"—the league gave McMahon another reason to get fired up: They came after him for his choice of apparel. True, he'd recently conducted an interview with a *Washington Post* reporter while wearing a fur-lined leather jacket, red tights, and wraparound sunglasses with polka-dot glass. But this was not the league's problem; the league's problem was with McMahon's headwear during the Giants game, a white Adidas headband that apparently violated standards because it was a blatant plug for a shoe company with which McMahon had an endorsement deal. He was fined five thousand dollars, and if the league's establishment hadn't seemed square enough before—if they hadn't seemed entirely out of tune to a generation of Americans who had grown accustomed to conspicuous capitalism on their television screens—well, they did now. Here was a self-professed heretic who now had an opportunity to use his newfound fame to rail against the establishment for suppressing his ability to make money: What could be more Ramboesque than this? McMahon played it to the hilt; he knew now that whatever he put on his head became a walking billboard. In the hours before game time, he acquired a felt-tip marker and carefully printed the name ROZELLE on a pair of white headbands, giving one to Payton and keeping one for himself. "That's publicity," he would say afterward. "That's football. That's politics, I mean."

("A great gag," Rozelle told the media.)

And this was football: The Bears smothered the Rams quarterback, Dieter Brock, and they forced Dickerson to fumble twice, one short of Ryan's brash forecast. McMahon audibled out of a draw and ran for a touchdown off a pass play in the first quarter, then threw a touchdown pass to Willie Gault. He called what he felt like and acted upon his instincts, and the only time he didn't, while sliding at the end of a run to preserve his body instead of crashing into a defender, he wound up getting hurt, a Ram helmet bruising his backside. "He was a crazy nut out there," Payton said. "He did everything but take his clothes off." In the fourth quarter, the snow began to fall, and the fans woofed and howled as linebacker Wilber Marshall returned a fumble for a touchdown. McMahon stuck out his tongue at the CBS cameras, and the Bears preserved a shutout: 24–0. On to New Orleans, to Super Bowl XX, where they were already ten-and-a-half-point favorites over New England, and where McMahon would further refine the art of outrageousness. Soon enough, he *would* take off his clothes.

IV.

It had been seventeen years since Joe Willie Namath's guarantee, since Rozelle announced that from then on, the annual AFL-NFL Championship game would be known as "the Super Bowl." With the thrust of Joe Willie's index finger skyward following the Jets' stunning victory over the Colts, the game had begun a journey into inordinate theatricality. In 1984, a small computer company named Apple had aired an advertisement during the Super Bowl, a dystopic vision based on George Orwell's *1984* that had changed the way we watched commercials; the cost to buy a thirty-second spot had soared to $550,000 in the two years since. A year earlier, President Reagan performed the coin toss via satellite from the White House. Increasingly, the game was becoming less about the game and more about the show surrounding the game; after Super Bowl XX, the league would ditch the dopey motivational troupe known as Up With People and start booking popular halftime acts like Michael Jackson.

And yet it still took a certain type of individual to seize the spotlight, to command the attention of an ever-expanding press corps. In the old days, Namath had accomplished it largely by exuding an unprecedented cool: He sat poolside and ogled girls and made a spur-of-the-moment proclamation at a dinner—"We're gonna *win the game.* I guarantee it"—that seemed positively tame but struck a societal chord amid the tumult of the era. Guaranteeing victory was not a novel concept—Muhammad Ali had already made a career of it— but "it was still jarring in the rigid ethical structure of team sports," author Michael MacCambridge wrote.

A decade later, self-promotion had become a more calculated enterprise. In 1979, at Super Bowl XIII in Miami, Thomas "Hollywood" Henderson purposefully made himself the story, stirring the drink by questioning the intelligence of the opposing team's quarterback, Terry Bradshaw, noting to the media that his intellect was such that he could not have spelled *cat* if you spotted him the *c* and the *a*. This was not a spontaneous assault. It was a premeditated attack from a linebacker whose team had won the Super Bowl the year before, from a man who was a natural-born wise guy, who also happened to be spiraling into a severe cocaine addiction.

Henderson wanted to be promoted (something he says the team's publicists declined to do), and he wanted to make money, to live a certain lifestyle; and if the Cowboys weren't going to do it for him, he would facilitate this by himself. He had heard a story from a Cowboys official that Bradshaw hadn't been smart enough to get in to LSU, and so he shaped his material to fit, formulating a one-liner that would invite the proper amount of attention. To his credit, it remains one of the all-time quips in Super Bowl history, as well as the tonal peak of the Hollywood persona he had bestowed upon himself and had been cultivating for several years. It was flippant and clever, laced with the sort of winking and ironic condescension that had carried from Ali's generation to his generation and on into the eighties.

The media flocked to Henderson all week long. He became both a pregame distraction and a multimedia superstar, referring to dentally challenged Steelers linebacker Jack Lambert as "Dracula," and leading one writer to call him the best thing that had happened to Super Bowl week since Namath. "It was the beginning of self-promotion," Henderson said. "Others had tried, but Hollywood Henderson was probably the guy in the NFL who did it. I knew, if you are the talk of the Super Bowl, which is the media mecca . . ."

Yet few people had taken advantage of the moment since Henderson. In general, Super Bowl week had become positively boring. Seven years later, into this holy land—into the city of New Orleans, where bars did not need to abide by such restrictive statutes as curfews—strode the apostate known as McMahon, merging Namath's attitude with Henderson's bluster and savvy with a postmodern sense of irony. Just a few days after the Bears beat the Rams, during the bye week before their departure for New Orleans, McMahon went on David Letterman's show, ground zero of the ironic hipster counterculture. He eased into a chair, wearing a sport jacket and jeans and sunglasses, handing out gifts and shouting out to his friends and exuding swagger. When Letterman pretended to bribe him to wear a *Late Night* headband on Super Bowl Sunday, McMahon pretended to accept the money. Who knows—maybe he *did* take it.

> LETTERMAN: Are you going to pay the five-thousand-dollar fine [to the NFL]?
> McMAHON: No. *(Applause)*

Soon after, McMahon signed with Warner Books to publish his autobiography for $250,000, the highest advance ever paid for a football player's life story; a *Rolling Stone* reporter would trail him during Super Bowl week for a cover story. Meanwhile, the Bears' superb defensive lineman, Richard Dent, was threatening not to play in the game because of a contract dispute. Scalpers were selling seventy-five-dollar tickets for a thousand or more. The Bears again fled their fan base, retreating downstate to the University of Illinois to work out in the school's new indoor practice bubble, shielded from fans and photographers, if only for a short time, getting serious for a few days before landing in the glittering distraction of New Orleans. Never before had a team been so hyped up before Super Bowl week even began.

Said Joe Willie Namath himself: "If Jim can go down there on Bourbon Street and be different, he really is something. Bourbon Street has seen just about every character there is except Jim McMahon."

V.

He did not wait long to get started. On Monday evening, January 20, the Bears arrived in New Orleans and held what was supposed to be an informal welcoming press conference in the ballroom of the Hilton. And here, immediately, McMahon began spouting off, dictating the narrative, establishing *himself* as the story. Perched on a platform, wearing (for once) a team-prescribed outfit of blue blazer and gray slacks, McMahon laid his sore buttock gingerly onto a chair and then fell into a rant about the illogical decision-making processes of the authority figures within his own organization. This latest flare-up had deeper roots: in the perceived stinginess of team officials McMahon had long considered to be his miserly adversaries, who had raised his salary to $500,000 a year but denied him the seven-figure contract granted to franchise quarterbacks like John Elway and Jim Kelly and Dan Marino; and in his natural stance against authority.

But the issue this time was not about money. The issue was much weirder than that, indicative of how skewed the spotlight on the Bears had become. This time the issue was with a Japanese man who spoke little English and whose last name McMahon did not even know. "Hiroshi-something," as McMahon referred to him, was actually Hiroshi Shiriashi, the trainer of the Japanese national team and an acupuncturist who had worked with Willie Gault (also a world-class sprinter) at a track meet in Tokyo, and had treated McMahon's sore rear end. (Gault, with his showbiz connections, had become the "fame broker of the Bears," according to acerbic *Tribune* columnist Bernie Lincicome.) On Monday afternoon, McCaskey refused to allow Shiriashi on the plane; the team's already put-upon public relations director, Ken Valdiserri, explained that McCaskey felt the Bears already *had* a trainer. And here, in front of a crowd of credentialed media that would swell to over two thousand by week's end (including twenty-seven reporters from the *Tribune* alone), McMahon fell into his default mode of defiance. "If it works, who cares if they approve or disapprove?" he said. "I don't really care if they approve or not. If it's going to help me play Sunday, I'm going to do it."

And then, after a few more questions, McMahon went off to tape a scene for a Bob Hope special. This is how the week began, and, lo, this is how it would unfold, in an orgy of controversy and confusion and excess piled upon excess.

By now, all McMahon had to do was speak of injustice, and thousands would flock to his defense. Why *shouldn't* he get what he wanted? Why *shouldn't* he get what he deserved? This *was* America, wasn't it? If the man requested needles be inserted into his posterior to help him feel better, then why shouldn't he be accommodated? On Tuesday, the Illinois State Acupuncture Association rallied to the cause, volunteering to pay to send Shiriashi to New Orleans, sparking a national debate about the effectiveness of Eastern philosophy, about a practice dogged by the notion that it was the medicinal equivalent of voodoo—the American Medical Association still considered acupuncture an experimental treatment.

But then, McMahon believed in experimentation. At Tuesday's media day, while he chewed gum and spat tobacco simultaneously, he denounced his newfound fame and denounced the media and denounced the very notion of work itself ("I don't want no job in no factory," he said when informed such a job would not burden him with such things as fame), and this continued cantankerousness only burnished his reputation. On the streets of New Orleans, a sketch of McMahon wearing the ROZELLE headband sold for a hundred dollars; a replica of the headband itself sold for anywhere from two dollars and fifty cents to five dollars. His agent, Steve Zucker, entertained offers from *Miami Vice* and MTV and from several movie producers who said his irreverence could make him a star, but McMahon wasn't interested. McMahon assured reporters that the Bears were not over-confident, that they had not been caught up in celebrity (even as The Fridge admitted, while trapped in a nearby scrum of several hundred reporters, that he might endorse a cat-food company, but had *definitively* turned down a part playing a bodyguard in a Cyndi Lauper film about professional wrestling). And then the quarterback kept on about the acupuncture, beating the drum, annoying the fogies in the press corps for whom this whole thing was never intended, for whom McMahon "served as a walking testimonial to the 'Me Generation.'"

Said McCaskey of Needlegate: "This is a noncontroversy controversy."

Said McMahon: "It *should* be a big story."

Facing a power struggle and a public-relations disaster, McCaskey had no choice but to relent. He joked that he would welcome Shiriashi to Florida with a brass band. On Wednesday morning, Shiriashi arrived at New Orleans International Airport, sans brass band, speaking through an interpreter.[5]

"I stick pins, we win," he said.

Off Hiroshi went to the Hilton, to the quarterback's room, where the subject yanked down his bikini tights and his purple underwear and took off his chintzy sweatshirt and tossed aside his baseball hat and his sunglasses. Then the subject lay down on the bed, head hanging over the edge so as to spit his tobacco into a paper cup, exposing the purplish flesh of his backside to the acupuncturist and to his roommate, lineman Kurt Becker (who was on injured reserve), and the coauthor of his upcoming autobiography, Bob Verdi of the *Tribune*. It was the first of several treatments over several days; it wasn't

---

5. Even amid the back-and-forth over Eastern medicine, there emerged a distinctly Western marketing angle in all of this, as well as an echo of the escalating hegemony of Nike, Inc. Shiriashi was, in fact, in Nike's employ, in its Japanese operations outfit, and the company issued a press release in which its director of corporate communications, tweaking Adidas, said, "McMahon may have put a company logo on his head, but Nike has left an imprint in a more important place."

always a pretty picture. "I felt sorry for the guy putting needles in his ass, because he was laying on his stomach blowing farts at him half the time," Becker said (*No like back window during treatment,* Hiroshi would reply). "I didn't even know where he *got* the guy."

That afternoon, McMahon showed up at a press conference wearing spandex tights, and at practice he wore a headband inscribed with the word ACUPUNCTURE; with a helicopter circling the field in search of fresh news, he once again delivered—he bent over, yanked down his pants, and "showed 'em where it hurt." Ditka, pulling a figure out of his own posterior, said McMahon's rear was "two hundred percent" better.

Front-page headline in the *Sun-Times* on Thursday: PUNCTURE PERFECT!

There was no official curfew, no bed check, no assistant planted in the lobby to note the exits and entrances of four dozen grown men. This team had thrived on the very Reaganesque notion of expansion of one's personal freedoms, and that mentality carried on into Super Bowl week. They would police themselves. Or maybe they wouldn't. The lure of Bourbon Street was powerful. McMahon, with the *Rolling Stone* reporter in tow, most likely felt a certain obligation to live up to his reputation, as well as a duty to take in the local culture, to expose himself (so to speak) to a town that had always been welcoming to bohemians. There was an element of exhibitionism about it that hadn't existed in Namath's day. On Monday night, McMahon hit the town hard, recording his part in the Bob Hope special, then posing for photos with Miss Hawaiian Tropic Oklahoma (who reportedly spent a good deal of time on his lap), and then he doubled back to Hope's hotel suite with one of his linemen, Jay Hilgenberg, sometime early the next morning to clean out what remained of the buffet. The next morning, he showed up late for a team meeting, and Ditka threatened to fine *Becker* a thousand dollars if he allowed his room-mate to get loose like that again. Briefly chastened, the roommates spent Tuesday night ordering room service and catching up on sleep.

"He's my friend, but I'm not his guardian," Becker would say in his own defense. "I'm not responsible for him."

They hit the town again on Wednesday. At Felix's Restaurant and Oyster Bar—where The Fridge had reportedly sucked down four dozen oysters and a vat of gumbo earlier in the week—a crowd gathered and began chanting, *"Rozelle! Rozelle!"* People passed along gifts, including headbands by the dozen, headbands made of blinking lights, headbands made of fur. At one point a strange man in a flowered shirt walked into the restaurant with a friend dressed in a bear suit. The man began speaking in gibberish and "Super Bowl Shuffle" verses and soon joined the group as sort of a de facto bodyguard, shooing away the photographers and autograph hounds. "Got to have violence," McMahon shouted. "Life is not complete without violence!"

On the way out, while being questioned by a *Washington Post* reporter as to the nature of his meal—oysters? catfish? boiled or fried?—McMahon urinated in a doorway on Chartres Street, then moved on to refill his bladder. And the next night, he and his posse did it again, eating at a steak house before retiring to Pat O'Brien's, where the men flocked to him and the women threw themselves at him, where McMahon himself acted as if he needed none of this while embracing all of it—the paradox of the punk superstar. "You've got to teach your body who's boss!" he shouted above the din of a piano player in an Adidas headband and an orange leisure suit playing a version of Thin Lizzy's "The Boys Are Back in Town." "If you're feeling down, go out and abuse it again. If you don't test your body, it will never learn how to respond."

And then McMahon and Jim Kelly, a star quarterback in the

USFL, retreated to Kelly's hotel room, where they hung out on the balcony and hurled fruit at the revelers on Bourbon Street. It was a moment of regression, to those days in San Jose when McMahon sat in the trees and threw prunes at the windshield of passing cars, to a simpler time when his insubordination did not inspire so many others.

On Thursday morning, the phone rang in the Hilton, in the makeshift Budweiser Suite, and McMahon rolled over on his purplish rear end and made the mistake of picking it up. "You rotten son of a bitch!" a woman said, and the quarterback, believing his memory intact, unable to pinpoint a precise reason for this particular insult at this particular moment, presumed it was the wrong number. But then it rang again.

"You fucking asshole!" said another stranger.

The quarterback, still groggy, hung up once more.

"Who the hell keeps calling?" Becker said.

"I don't know. Some pissed-off people."

Down to breakfast, where McMahon endured daggerlike stares, where his general manager, Jerry Vainisi, said, "Well, you've done it *now*, Jim. Did you say those things?"

"What things?" McMahon said.

Vainisi, huffing, dressed in rumpled clothes he'd pulled from his laundry bag in haste in order to get downstairs and get a read on the situation, walked away without saying anything else. In the buffet line, McMahon encountered Ditka. "Did you really say that?" Ditka asked.

"Look, Mike, I got woke up twice this morning. What the hell did I say?"

For once, it wasn't what McMahon had said. It was what he *hadn't* said. It was a complex telephone game of rumor and supposition brought to life, which had apparently begun when an anonymous person called the request line of New Orleans deejay Boomer Rollins. The caller said he'd heard McMahon had gone on a Chicago morning show hosted by anchor Les Grobstein, who was broadcasting from a local spaghetti restaurant. McMahon, the caller said, had called the women "sluts" and the men "idiots." Then Rollins got ten more calls, people saying the same thing, and then a television newsman named Buddy Diliberto called to prerecord a morning sports show on Rollins's station, WEZB, and said he would check it out. And without checking anything out, Diliberto went on the ten o'clock news and claimed it was true, that McMahon had said, "All the women in New Orleans are sluts and all the men are stupid." And he called for the women of New Orleans to show up outside the Hilton prepared to hurl rolls of toilet paper at McMahon. And the fundamental problem was that it all seemed quite plausible, given McMahon's behavior, given the swath he'd cut through this town over the past few nights. It was the kind of rumor that seemed just weird and specific and well sourced enough to actually *be* true, the kind of rumor that, in another era, might have been tamped down and gone unreported, but amid this orgiastic week, it became an accepted part of the narrative, if only because of Diliberto's lazy reporting.

The media had become a much larger echo chamber than Joe Willie Namath—who once called a few reporters poolside during Super Bowl week to dispute charges of a bar fight—ever had to deal with; in the years to come, it would only get more intense, but for the moment at least, public-relations people had only a vague idea about how to handle crises like these. It simply hadn't happened on this scale before, and flacks like Valdiserri were only just learning how to meld public relations and marketing, how to shape the message to positive effect. "I was twenty-six years old," Valdiserri said. "And it was just helter-skelter. Absolute helter-skelter."

And it could be argued that McMahon had brought this upon himself, given his loose behavior. "He did [say it]," claimed one of his teammates, Otis Wilson. "He just said it somewhere else." And it could be argued that perhaps this was the dark side of the bargain he'd made in order to build himself into a rebel superhero, in order to position himself in direct opposition to the media and the mainstream, in order to make the cover of *Rolling Stone:* People would inevitably seek to bring him down. Even so, it just enraged him to no end.

There were death threats and bomb threats, at least one of which was delivered in a Cajun accent: *Y'all bettuh git outta thayuh, 'cuz I'm gonna blow that place skah-hah.* Two dozen women really did show up to picket outside the Hilton, carrying rolls of toilet paper and signs reading, MCMAHON, PUT YOUR HEADBAND OVER YOUR MOUTH (though most of them appeared to be Patriots fans; at one point, they engaged in a heated conversation with an Adidas official who questioned if they had any proof of McMahon's transgression). And McMahon still had no real idea what had happened. When he did find out, when he heard that he'd supposedly been on Grobstein's show at six A.M. on Wednesday morning, his initial reaction was not to say anything about it at all, until Zucker, his agent, convinced him otherwise. So he went downstairs to a hotel ballroom, and he said this: "There's *no way* I'm going to *any* restaurant at six in the morning. And certainly not to talk to any goddamn reporter."

In truth, McMahon hadn't even appeared on Grobstein's show, and Grobstein, who worked for the Chicago station WLS, was suddenly surrounded by his colleagues asking for exclusive interviews regarding an interview that had never occurred. Diliberto would admit his mistake and accept a two-week suspension, but there was lingering discomfort, and it lasted the remainder of that week and beyond. McMahon wore a different number from his usual 9 during practice, so as to dodge any snipers who might be occupying the apartment buildings that lined the New Orleans practice complex; his roommate and his teammates avoided standing next to him. "It was fucking hell," McMahon said years later. "I can't even *remember* the game. I've seen Black Sunday and all those movies. If somebody wants to kill your ass, they're going to get a gun and do it."

He didn't understand it; he hadn't asked for this burden, to be tangled up in the complications of stardom. He hadn't asked for any of this bullshit; all of this bullshit had come to *him,* and he tried to take what he wanted and throw away the rest, but it didn't work that way anymore. It was all or nothing. "I can't go anywhere and not be bothered," he said soon after the Super Bowl. For a man who craved personal freedom and dreaded personal responsibility, fame was truly a bitch.

The game itself was exactly what they'd expected, what we all expected. The Bears fell behind by a field goal early on when Payton fumbled, and then they laid it down full throttle. In the team's final meeting before kickoff, before they fractured into a million pieces, before Buddy Ryan fled to become head coach of the Philadelphia Eagles, Ditka stood at the front of the room, wearing a headband and sunglasses. Then he mooned everyone, mocking the absurdity of the entire week, of the entire season, of the caricature even he had become.

The Bears led 23–3 at halftime. They talked in the locker room of scoring fifty points, of scoring a hundred points, of breaking every imaginable record; in the stands, large swaths of fans broke into verses of "The Super Bowl Shuffle" when it came up on the Superdome's video screens. With the Patriots defense shadowing Payton, McMahon thrived. Still wearing those black gloves—even though the game was indoors—McMahon ultimately took a charitable approach with the blank advertising slate of his headbands (*otherwise, they're going to crucify you,* his agent advised him). He promoted the Juvenile Diabetes Foundation and missing prisoners of war. He wore one that read PLUTO, the nickname for his college friend Dan Plater, whose brain tumor had ended his college career. He scored two touchdowns on short plunges, threw for 256 yards, and did not throw an interception before he was pulled from the game in the second half—not surprisingly, the media still chose to name someone else (Richard Dent) the most valuable player. The defense allowed New England *seven yards* rushing; the Patriots' starting quarterback, Tony Eason, went zero-for-eight.

And in the midst of all this, Ditka could not resist one last indulgence, one last outrageous flourish; in the fourth quarter, on a short-yardage play near the goal line, he inserted Perry into the lineup. For once, McMahon did not audible out of the play, handing off to The Fridge, who tumbled into the end zone, scoring the game's last touchdown, and depriving Payton, the veteran, the steadying presence in a clubhouse full of loons and savants, his only chance of scoring in a Super Bowl. Both McMahon and Ditka insist they didn't realize their mistake until later. Afterward, amid the requisite locker-room hysteria, Payton locked himself in a storage closet, alone. He did not speak much of it afterward; he did not speak much of it at all before his death from a liver disease in 1999. But it lingered, and it was a sign, perhaps, that this team had been so caught up in its image that it could not possibly sustain itself. All that resentment, between players and management, between players and players, between coaches and players, between coaches and coaches (both Ditka and Ryan were carried off the field, separately, after the victory)—it was as if a balloon had deflated. In the locker room, an argument broke out over the distribution of championship hats; some players suspected McCaskey had taken several boxes for himself.

Back at the hotel, the buffet for the victory party had been rav-

aged by the time Becker and McMahon arrived. A hotel official announced that the bar was closing in half an hour. So they took it
upstairs, calling room service, ordering cases of beer, arranging for a
chef to carve roast beef out in the hallway. They were among the
greatest teams in NFL history, and inarguably the most influential
collection of characters this decade; no one would ever re-create their
spontaneous bursts of egotism, no matter how they tried. Their narrative would be told and retold and embellished and adorned, so that
even children who had not yet been born would commit entire verses
of "The Super Bowl Shuffle" to memory. And yet this day, this game,
felt so empty, so anticlimactic—here they were, eating meat and
drinking beer in the hallway of a Hilton hotel. It was the journey that
mattered, and already they could sense that the journey was ending,
that they would never get back here again, that this was both the beginning of something and the end of something else.

They held a parade on Monday afternoon, on the frigid streets
of Chicago, while McMahon and Payton and seven other Bears broke
away and headed straight to Hawaii for the Pro Bowl, and a tipsy
Ditka went on the radio and told Chet Coppock the Patriots were
"loudmouths and cheap-shot artists." The parade was a raucous af-
fair, heavily liquored and celebrated from one end of Chicago to the
other, bottles of spirits tossed back and forth between players and
the crowd. The streets overflowed, forcing the freezing and the claus-
trophobic inside to watch from a big-screen television on the ninth
floor of Marshall Field's. Next (and final) stop: the White House, for
a celebration with the president, a ceremony that would be indefi-
nitely postponed once Tuesday morning dawned, once the hangover
settled in.

Again that day, people stood and gawked at the big screen in
Marshall Field's, this time at the images of a space shuttle carrying
seven astronauts—among them a New England schoolteacher named
Christa McAuliffe—launching into the sky above Cape Canaveral,

Florida, and then fracturing into pieces. The city froze; the nation froze. At a restaurant in downtown Chicago, a law-school student stared lockjawed at a television set and uttered a single baleful sentence.

"I thought the entire system was infallible," he said.

CHAPTER SIX

A Major Malfunction

At a news conference, Mr. Reagan . . . also blamed the January 28 loss of the Challenger *and the seven astronauts aboard on "a carelessness that grew out of success."*

—*The New York Times,* JUNE 12, 1986

I.

On the morning of January 28, 1986, President Reagan took a meeting with the Democratic House speaker, Tip O'Neill, during which he relied entirely upon partisan talking points gleaned from four-by-six cue cards prepared by his staff. It was a tactic that Reagan had used before, and even his Republican allies found it distasteful; this was Reagan at his worst, robotic and detached. He lamented the work ethic of "the fellow on welfare," telling O'Neill, "These people don't want to work." O'Neill and Reagan were generally civil, even friendly, but this time, the speaker came back at him hard, his patience worn thin. "I'm sick and tired of your attitude, Mr. President," he said. "I thought you would have grown in five years."

And then, a short time later, the day changed completely. On our television screens, an explosion: entrails of smoke and flame; a mosaic in the sky. On the ground, mass confusion: a shot of Christa McAuliffe's parents, their faces drawn and pallid, the *Challenger* coming apart before their very eyes with their child inside, intimate gro-tesqueries laid bare in real time. In our schools, we watched the whole sickening show (the explosion was caused, we would later find out, by a single faulty part known as an O-ring), and this became the first shared cultural tragedy of our generation, rendered sharply so by the rare presence of live television in our classrooms, and because one of our own—a schoolteacher—was on that flight. And immediately af-ter the explosion, the damndest thing: a disembodied voice from a NASA public affairs officer named Steve Nesbitt, droning on in the monotone of a filmstrip narrator, blindly calling out coordinates as if the shuttle were still in flight. While confused students in Christa McAuliffe's social studies classroom in Concord, New Hampshire, blew party horns, the voice uttered, several seconds later, the most chilling televised words since Walter Cronkite had delivered the news of a president's death twenty-three years earlier.

Flight controllers here looking very carefully at the situation.

Obviously a major malfunction.

The State of the Union Address scheduled for that night was post-poned. How could the president speak of budgets and policy at a mo-ment like this? Instead, he came on the air at five p.m. and gave one of the most empathetic speeches of his presidency:

And I want to say something to the schoolchildren of America who were watching the live coverage of the shut-tle's takeoff. I know it is hard to understand, but some-times painful things like this happen. It's all part of the process of exploration and discovery. It's all part of taking a chance and expanding man's horizons. The future doesn't belong to the fainthearted; it belongs to the brave. The *Challenger* crew was pulling us into the future, and we'll continue to follow them.

It was quintessential Reagan, professing optimism in the face of tragedy, and it foreshadowed what would soon become the most trying months of his presidency, a period that would call into question his promise that the era of self-doubt had subsided. This day, Tip O'Neill would later say, was Ronald Reagan at his best and Ronald Reagan at his worst, all in a matter of hours.

And for all the hyperbole that came to surround this televised funeral—for all the attempts to ascribe meaning to an essentially meaningless event—something about our view of the future, about the fundamental programming of our generation, really *did* seem different afterward. THE DAY GEN X GREW UP, one headline would describe it twenty years later, and in a way, it was true: What we had seen on television could not be taken back. If ever there were an antidote to the notion of American exceptionalism, here it was—the president himself would later blame NASA's failures on a sense of carelessness bred by success. We had taken a chance, and that chance had failed, and now we understood, if we hadn't before, that the entire system had never really been infallible.

II.

That night, undaunted by the sobriety of the moment, the fifty-four-year-old coach of a struggling college basketball team took the remarkable step of chasing one of his critics into the stands and confronting him. Aided by twenty-one points from its best player, Len Bias, Maryland had just broken a six-game losing streak, the longest of Charles "Lefty" Driesell's twenty-six-year career in Division I, against lowly Wake Forest. And when an unidentified fan shouted at

Driesell a garden-variety insult—*You're still in seventh place in the ACC!* was the precise taunt, according to Sally Jenkins of *The Washington Post*—the coach said, *Come down here and say that.* The fan said, *You come up here,* and Driesell obliged, leaping over a railing and standing chest-to-chest with the man. *Go on and push me,* Driesell then said, according to his own account. *And we'll get after it. You'll start it, and I'll finish it.*

For Driesell, life was an endless tussle with the myriad forces allied against him. He had once sold encyclopedias before beginning his college coaching career at tiny Davidson College in North Carolina, and he didn't deal well with rejection. He took over the job at Maryland in 1969, promising to turn a moribund basketball program that had won eight games in each of the previous two seasons into "the UCLA of the East." Ever since, he had been engaged in a struggle for respect, for recruits, for an edge, in the Atlantic Coast Conference where Dean Smith's dynastic University of North Carolina was the dominant force. And yet what Lefty had that Smith never did was an unmistakable flair. In the early years, he made a habit of throwing his sport jacket to the ground and stomping on it; when that got old, he left on the coat and just kept up with the stomping.

He was a manic presence, fiddling with the knot of his tie, hitching his trousers, waving and contorting and preening, wrote author C. Fraser Smith, like "the hybrid of a rooster and a clog dancer." He was a showman and a street fighter, and no one could question the physical courage of a man who had once received the NCAA's award of valor for rescuing ten people from a burning house. In 1970, he brought in a marquee recruiting class that included Tom McMillen—whom Driesell had stolen from North Carolina at the last minute with a carefully researched presentation to his family—and Len Elmore, two of the most talented (and most intelligent) teenage athletes in the nation. In the years since then, he had averaged more than twenty wins per season, and Cole Field House, the 14,500-seat on-campus gym that had generally drawn about 25 percent capacity for Maryland games before Lefty's arrival, was now sold out on a regular basis. He was "one of America's showman coaches, a group of manic professionals who borrowed more from Alice Cooper and John McEnroe than some idealized mentor," Fraser Smith wrote. "[He] operated constantly on the edge of public decorum and even, it seemed, of sanity."

Born in 1931, Driesell grew up in Norfolk, Virginia, and played basketball at Duke University in the early 1950s. He had a keen way of playing possum, coming off as a genial hayseed who despised intellectualism, who pronounced Maryland as *Merlin,* who had somehow charmed his way to a degree at Duke. He bragged that he never read much of anything, even as he often assailed reporters with early-morning phone calls questioning the veracity of their work (after a particularly harsh column, he challenged *The Washington Post*'s Ken Denlinger to a street fight). He couldn't even turn on a computer, but damn if he couldn't coach a basketball team—"Ah kin *coach,*" he'd say whenever challenged—and if that weren't the case anymore, he argued, then why had Maryland chosen to give him a ten-year contract extension in 1984? Out of the goodness of their hearts?

Fans, administrators, opposing coaches, reporters—Lefty fought them all, but most of all, his beef lately was with the system itself, presided over by the ruling forces of the National Collegiate Athletic Association, an organization whose bureaucracy and eggheaded hypocrisy stood in direct opposition to his folksy recruiting style. A few months earlier, Lefty had referred to the NCAA as a laughingstock, after hearing the organization had penalized nearby American University for violating rules against formal preseason practice. In Lefty's view, this was an example of the glaring hypocrisy of the NCAA, of its penchant for chasing after small problems while blatant lawlessness—the bestowing of cars and gifts on potential recruits—

ate away at it from the inside. "I've had (high school) coaches ask me for money" within the past six weeks, Lefty said.

The strain of what had become perhaps his most trying season seemed to have worn on Lefty's psyche; even the reporters could see it. After a loss to Virginia, he wondered if the pregame meal might have been to blame. His top recruiting target, a forward named J. R. Reid, would soon commit to North Carolina, despite Lefty's constant badgering, despite his insistence to Reid's father that J.R. could get all the playing time he wanted at Maryland. Lefty told Sally Jenkins that he had mellowed, but he changed plane reservations for Maryland's trip to Notre Dame ten different times, then chose to wear a sweater instead of a jacket, hoping it would bring him luck.

He still professed admiration for his players; he *loved* Leonard Bias, he would repeat time and again in the years to come, but he loved them all, in part because he'd worked so damned hard to get them to come to Maryland in the first place. *You're our number one recruit,* he'd written to Chris Washburn, who wound up at North Carolina State. Three months later, he wrote the same thing to Danny Manning, who committed to Kansas. He told Washburn that Maryland would win four national titles if he signed; he told Washburn and others that he'd signed Moses Malone, even though Malone had jumped straight to the NBA and never played a single game at Maryland. He did what he had to do to ingratiate himself. "Coach Driesell is like a brother," said one of his incoming recruits, Andre Reyes, who had signed the previous November after Driesell promised to make him an All-American by his junior season. Compared to Georgetown's John Thompson, who had built a successful program across town by stressing discipline and intimidation, "Coach Driesell is looser," Reyes said. "He jokes with you and he makes you feel comfortable. . . . [Coach Thompson] really stresses academics, which is good."

"I like talking to people," Driesell said as the '86 season wore on and questions arose as to whether the grind of coaching in this new age might be wearing him down. "It used to be that you could take a kid out to dinner and talk to him, talk to his family. As far as getting into a person's house and talking, I can out-recruit any of those other coaches."

But the modern age rewarded a different brand of audaciousness. In an attempt to keep up, Lefty had done what everyone else was doing: He had loosened his standards. He had recruited players with lower grades, with lower SAT scores; in 1977, four of his players were placed on academic probation. He questioned the utility of academic advisors for athletes, claiming that his assistant coaches could do the same job by rousing his players and making sure they were going to class. He cajoled administration officials to allow recruits into school even when their grades weren't up to Maryland's normal standards; his point guard, Keith Gatlin, had scored a 510 on the SAT, but Lefty pushed for an exception, and then, feeling brazen, he pushed for another exception in Terry Long, who had scored 640. The issues ran deeper than any single case study; at Georgetown, John Thompson continually questioned why athletes were being singled out amid the overarching failures of the educational system. What about the public-school children who were academically deficient and *couldn't* play basketball?

Lefty didn't concern himself with philosophy or public affairs. He knew what he knew, and he was convinced that the nabobs in charge didn't know anything about building relationships—about evaluating *character*—when compared to a man who had spent nearly three decades prowling strange living rooms, a man who slept in his car on recruiting trips and once allowed some kid's pet snake to crawl all over him in a quest to close a deal (it worked, by the way).

At times, Lefty appeared purposefully defiant, a rebel against the oncoming forces of political correctness. (One of his most ardent supporters was Robert Novak, the conservative newspaper columnist.) In 1983, a key player, Herman Veal, was suspended on charges of sexual assault before a key game against Virginia. Lefty, itching for conflict, insisted he wouldn't allow the suspension to stand. He called the victim, a twenty-one-year-old woman who said Veal had thrown her onto his bed and fondled her, and told her that her reputation would suffer if she went forward with her complaint. When the campus women's center came after him, Lefty came right back at them: "I'm the *men's center*," he said. "In my mind, Herman Veal's the victim."

Forced to apologize, "the role-model coach winked at his audience" during a press conference, Fraser Smith wrote. When his team arrived at practice that day, "they walked around laughing and slapping each other on the wrists—suggesting that the penalty was not a penalty, really, and exulting in yet another win for their coach." The woman was eventually forced to leave school, and life went on for Lefty, who won his first ACC tournament championship in 1984, signed that decade-long contract, and kept up the fight on all fronts. He appeared, to his more liberal critics, as demagogic and utterly out of touch. (Before the 1985–86 season, he circulated a memo that requested he be referred to as Charles G. Driesell, rather than Lefty, as if this might extend to him a certain gravitas; he had dropped the façade by February, after enduring much mockery.) At a coaching clinic in Rhode Island, he spoke of the good old days when players got into trouble for little things, like siphoning gas.

How, then, could a man whose impressions of youth culture seemed drawn from *American Graffiti* comprehend the pressures upon a contemporary star like Len Bias? How could he focus on anything but the all-consuming need to keep on winning? "Lefty didn't buy the drugs for Len Bias, and he didn't encourage him to take drugs," said Mark Hyman, a writer for *The Baltimore Sun*. "But the question is, was his style of discipline such that the kids thought it was OK to do this?"

All of it seemed pointed toward building victories. In suspending Bias and his teammates for violating curfew after the win over North Carolina State, Driesell claimed his main concern was that his team be ready to play Clemson in its next game. "You can't go out two nights before a game and stay out that late and be ready to play," he said.

"I understand Coach," said Bias in a *Washington Post* story published a few days later. "You get your points and your rebounds, and he's happy."

The question that haunted Lefty, the question that haunted the Maryland administration—the question that haunted virtually every major college athletic program in the nation—was this: What if changing your ways meant not winning anymore? Such a thought, at most schools, was unacceptable. The future did not belong to the fainthearted.

III.

While Lonise Bias continued to be haunted by nightmares and prophecies, another mother's premonition had already come to life: Four years earlier, Margie Hammock had dreamed of the hell her daughter would be put through by challenging the system; then she woke from a deep sleep and wrote out a detailed letter. *Let someone else do this,* Margie Hammock said, but her daughter in Georgia, Jan Kemp, had not listened, because Jan Kemp was already going through hell. On August 3, 1982, six months after having been demoted for reasons she deemed craven and perverse, she repeatedly stabbed herself in the chest with a butcher knife. On September 3, she overdosed on the antipsychotic drug Haldol; she lived. She was grim and miserable, twice hospitalized for depression, unable to cook a meal or read or write or even muster a smile. And then in 1983, after being dismissed from her job altogether, she filed suit in federal court against

her former employer, the University of Georgia, claiming her demo-
tion and firing had been entirely unjustified—claiming that they'd
had nothing to do with any supposed dereliction of hers and everything to do with feeding the machine of college athletics.

In January, opening arguments began in Jan Kemp's case against
a pair of administrators at the University of Georgia, alleging that
student athletes were being promoted out of remedial classes despite
poor grades, and if only for a moment, the lid was lifted: Here, in a
matter of a few weeks, was a treatise on the hypocrisy of amateurism,
and on the cost of victory in the 1980s, embodied in the plight of a
thirty-six-year-old English teacher.

In 1981, Kemp alleged, the university had chosen to allow nine
players to pass a remedial English course in which they had received
failing grades; this, in turn, kept them eligible and permitted them to
play in the Sugar Bowl. It was not the first strike against Georgia,
which was already on probation for rules violations, but this was the
apogee. A faculty member testified that athletes had been admitted to
school with grade-point averages of 1.88 and 1.96 (the NCAA minimum was 2.0); a study revealed that of the two hundred black athletes who had come to Georgia since the breaking of the color barrier
in 1969, only about thirty had graduated. In opening arguments, the
defense attorney for the university wondered whether educationally
deficient jocks weren't benefiting from college simply because they
could get jobs at the post office rather than work as garbagemen
when their careers ended. Georgia's football coach, Vince Dooley, admitted in testimony that he had taken chances on athletes simply because other schools were doing it as well. Students were promoted
out of the remedial programs despite GPAs as low as 0.29, and Kemp
testified that when she challenged this wisdom to her superiors, an
administrator named Leroy Ervin told her, "Who do you think you
are? Who do you think is more important at this university, you or a
very prominent basketball player?" After her firing, the university of-

fered readmission to a football player who had flunked out, on the condition that he write a letter condemning her teaching skills—a letter that accused Kemp of frequenting homosexual parties and of making lewd allusions during teaching sessions.

The majority of black athletes, Ervin (who was black) said in a secretly taped meeting with another instructor, were at Georgia "for their utility to the institution . . . to produce income. . . . They are being used as a kind of raw material in the production of some goods to be sold . . . and they get nothing in return. . . ."

There was nothing new to these sentiments; only the packaging had changed. The whole quaint notion of purity in collegiate athletics—and the slippery slope known as amateurism—had been rife with allegations of hypocrisy ever since 1852, when the Boston, Concord and Montreal Railroad funded a crew race between Harvard and Yale. In the 1890s, Michigan fielded a football team that included several players with no connection at all to the university; when universities took over the administration of college sports at around the same time, wrote Rick Telander in his 1989 screed *The Hundred Yard Lie,* "amateurism was just the lie that was needed. It was fine for the university to make money from sports, as long as the students didn't."

Now revenue had become the engine. All other purposes were secondary. The only way to defend the system was to affirm that pretty much everyone else was doing it too. Such was the capitalist instinct, and college sports were nothing if not a lucrative enterprise. No one but a Pollyanna could believe that the spirit of amateurism Ronald Reagan had romanticized as a youth—the wholesome schoolboy image of Frank Merriwell at Yale—was being utilized for anything other than to mask a financial purpose. CBS had paid more than thirty-two million dollars for the rights to televise the upcoming NCAA basketball tournament. Gross revenue for the tournament was forty million; each Final Four team made eight hundred thousand dollars in appearance fees. Total television rights fees for college sports: approximately a hundred million dollars per year. How could winning *not* matter if those numbers were the measure of success? In a perverse way, Vince Dooley was right, because it was not just Georgia, because there were dozens more programs like Georgia's that used the same policies—maybe fifty or sixty, according to the athletic director at Notre Dame (one of the few schools, like Penn State, that held themselves as self-righteous ascetics among the sinners).

Regard for the rule of law had been subsumed by the need to keep the revenue flowing; several coaches complained that they could not win without cheating, without enduring the inevitable meddling of their schools' prominent boosters. At Creighton, Willis Reed, who had guided the New York Knicks to a championship in a less complex era, resigned as basketball coach, citing those very reasons. And those who did cheat only gave way when they were cornered, when the local newspaper or the NCAA's undermanned enforcement arm managed to lift the veil. At North Carolina State, a star player, Chris Washburn, was suspended after stealing a stereo. At Memphis: potential ties between the basketball program and gamblers. At Kentucky: cash and gifts for basketball players. At Tennessee, quarterback Tony Robinson was arrested for drug trafficking. At Tulane, the basketball program was abolished following a point-shaving scandal. The NCAA had approximately ten investigators, led by director of enforcement Chuck Smrt, who acted almost entirely on tips and newspaper reports. The utopian ideal of a school "self-reporting" its own violations, as per the NCAA's code, was basically dead. And the stories the investigators heard were so unbelievably outrageous they seemed made up, even when they weren't—there was the one, Smrt recalls, about a booster and a coach who went to visit a prospect, and when a second coach showed up, they hid in the closet, and when the second coach began complaining about the first, the booster and the coach burst out of the closet and started throwing punches.

And then there was the proud tradition of the Southwest Conference, which had become a cracked fun-house mirror of good ole boys and high rollers, so corrupt that even the corruption itself had become a kind of sport. In the SWC, to *not* be on some sort of NCAA probation meant either you weren't buying the right recruits or you were from Rice. Seven of the nine members of the conference, all from schools located in Texas, got into some kind of trouble between 1985 and 1987. At Baylor, basketball coach Jim Haller resigned amid allegations that he gave a player money for car payments. At TCU, cash payments from boosters to football players. There were investigations at Texas, at Texas A & M, and at Texas Tech, but it was at Southern Methodist that things had gotten completely out of hand: sixty-one thousand dollars in payments to players between September 1985 and December 1986, and even a series of busts didn't curtail the pipeline. In 1985, after the NCAA put SMU on probation for the seventh time since 1958, Bill Clements, then the chairman of the school's board of governors (and later governor of Texas), approved of *continued* payments to players. "These wealthy businessmen–alumni compete with each other in recruiting these kids to their own schools, just like they compete in building the tallest bank building or cutting the sharpest cattle or oil deal," said one SMU official. "They just want to win, and if they can show somebody up by buying a kid a car, or slipping him a hundred bucks a week, they're going to do it."

At a special convention in June 1985, college presidents pledged to get more involved. Soon after, they approved Proposition 48, raising minimum academic standards. They approved drug testing, though only at championship events and bowl games. They approved the "death penalty," which would shut down for two years programs that engaged in repeated violations (in 1987, after Clements confessed, SMU's football program became the first victim). In Iowa, in an attempt to call attention to the issue, a state representative introduced a bill outlining procedures for paying athletes at Iowa's three state universities. There was talk of playing games only on weekends, talk of rescinding the 1972 ruling that permitted freshman athletes to be eligible to play right away. And at the University of Georgia, where Jan Kemp's trial had prompted the first campus protest of the decade on her behalf, a remarkable verdict: A jury awarded Kemp $2.5 million in damages, a massive and completely unexpected number, a decision that Maryland's athletic director, Dick Dull, said would force colleges to "reanalyze their own policies regarding the admission of athletes, some of whom may not have the credentials."

"The nerds were right all along—that we have been celebrating the wrong values," wrote Richard Cohen in *The Washington Post*. Our emphasis on an extemporaneous, carefree, and youthful lifestyle among schoolchildren, on the irreverence of athletes like Jim McMahon—"he drinks, he parties—and he hits his man the next morning"—had led us to this point, Cohen theorized; the problem was that we weren't working as hard as the Japanese, that we weren't as *serious* as they were. The answer was in a return to austerity in our schools.

Meanwhile, Len Bias, his star ascending, his college career drawing to a close, immersed himself in material thoughts: a new stereo, new suits, a leather jacket, and a hundred-and-fifty-dollar pair of shoes, marked down from four hundred by an admiring salesman. Where the money was coming from, no one seemed to know, though he would soon borrow fifteen thousand dollars on the strength of his impending professional contract. He pondered a lease on a sports car and he frequented a jewelry store in Silver Spring, where he bought a nameplate for his diamond ID bracelet and sized up a gold necklace. Cost: thirteen hundred dollars. He would soon put it on layaway.

IV.

And if any vestige of doubt remained as to his future, if anyone still pondered whether Leonard Bias was in fact the game-changing player the scouts had purported him to be, he put that to rest in six seconds in late February, in his second game back after his suspension. The whole night was his, really, and would turn out to be the zenith of his foreshortened career—"If Lenny Bias isn't the player of the world," Driesell said afterward, "I don't know who is"—and yet, in just those six seconds, in one extraordinary sequence, Bias illustrated how he could redefine the parameters of his position. His teammates and his coaches had both referred to him, in the past, as their "horse." This was why.

In those six seconds, with his team trailing by eight points at North Carolina and only three minutes left to play, Bias hit a twenty-foot jump shot from the wing, then galloped toward the baseline, stole the in-bounds pass, and, with a defender closing, dunked with his back to the basket before landing in a tangle of limbs on the floor. Maryland came charging back after that, and Bias scored thirty-five points from every possible angle, dunking over a pair of seven-footers, ball-faking, dribbling baseline, and drawing a foul, and then, moments later, delivering his "Basic Bias," as the *Post*'s Thomas Boswell called it, a "spraddle-legged, two-dribbles-and-good-bye corner jumper down the throat." He had entered the territory of legends and legends-in-the-making, of Bird and Erving and Magic and Jordan . . . and Carolina, which had never lost a game at its new arena, the Dean E. Smith Center—the DeanDome—could only exhale as Bias cut the lead to two, as the game went into overtime and he hit a twelve-foot jump hook while double-covered in the lane, as he leapt three feet into the air to block Kenny Smith's final attempt at giving Carolina the lead, as he bounded off the court following a 77–72 victory, shouting, "WHAT HAPPENED TO NORTH CAROLINA? WHO BEAT THE TAR HEELS?"

What happened? *He* had happened, and his victory propelled Maryland—which had once been 11–10, and 0–6 in the ACC—toward the postseason, and gave Lefty just his eighth win over Dean

Smith in seventeen years. In the ACC tournament, they beat North Carolina again, a cocksure Bias talking trash after his teammate blocked a shot and picking up a technical foul for starting an altercation with North Carolina's Brad Daugherty. And in Los Angeles, in the first round of the NCAA tournament, with the scouts now comparing Bias to Elgin Baylor, and an increasingly defiant Bias, tiring of the hype, stonewalling simple questions . . .

> Q: Your thoughts on being named ACC player of the year?
> A: No comment.

. . . the Terps defeated Pepperdine, 69–64. On the court, he talked constantly now, flirting with punishment. In the midst of a dispute between one of his teammates and a Pepperdine player, Bias pushed a hand into the Pepperdine player's face, prompting another technical foul, and a stomp and one-word scolding from Driesell: *"Leonard!"* All of it was attributed to Bias's competitiveness, to a style that had, ever since high school, been rooted in barely contained emotion. He was nothing like this off the court, his teammates insisted; he was laid-back Leonard, big man on campus, cool and calm and impeccably mannered. He came from a good family. He didn't even drink beer at parties.

Two days later, his career ended with a 70–64 loss to Nevada–Las Vegas. For a long time afterward, Bias sat in front of his locker, a towel draped over his head, his face in his hands, contemplating the end and contemplating his future. His disappointment was tempered by the fact, as his coach said, that he would soon "be a very rich young man."

In Dallas, at the Final Four, the future laid itself out in the form of an eighteen-year-old freshman, a six-feet-nine forward who played for

Louisville and whose nickname was Never Nervous. His coach, Denny Crum, was so apprehensive about corrupting Pervis Ellison's rhythm that he did not permit him to speak to the media, and sequestered him in the team hotel, no incoming phone calls allowed.

Ellison had been the catalyst for Louisville all season long, all tournament long, and he presided over the floor with a preternatural calm that prompted the nickname. He was a prototype, an example of how the next generation no longer seemed daunted by the transition from high school to college—and proof that youth no longer provided an excuse for losing. He scored twenty-five points and had eleven rebounds in a 72–69 win over Duke in the championship game, telling his teammates, "Just keep throwing it inside to me." He became the first freshman named Outstanding Player in the tournament since 1944, and in so doing, he seemed to quash any notion that a movement toward freshman ineligibility might somehow take hold.

The games were as pervasive as they had ever been, and the games, ever more visible, were a powerful distraction. At the same time Maryland was playing UNLV, Reagan spoke to the nation, appealing for funds to support the Nicaraguan Contras. The game had been shifted from CBS to ESPN, as the president held dominion over the networks; and yet at a Tampa bar filled with Reagan acolytes, no one seemed much interested in changing the channel. "I agree with Reagan's military policy," one said. "But why mess up a good game?"

CHAPTER SEVEN

Greed Is Healthy

The code of the Liar's Poker player was something like the code of the gunslinger. It required a trader to accept all challenges.

—MICHAEL LEWIS, *Liar's Poker*

I.

In February 1986, Bo Jackson shipped off to Buffalo to accept the fourteenth annual Dunlop Pro-Am Award as the amateur athlete of the year . . . and to face, once more, multiple permutations of The Question. Answering The Question had become second nature to Bo. It had defined him for so long now that hearing it, he told one reporter, was like shaving or getting dressed in the morning. He had learned to anticipate it before it was even asked, and he had learned how to answer it in a manner that was both truthful and completely open-ended. In Buffalo, he could see The Question rising from the mouths of several reporters, and he girded himself to respond accordingly:

Baseball or football, Bo?

And so he repeated the statements he had made previously, and he repeated them ad nauseam, for twenty minutes, as every nuance and angle of The Question came at him. He said that he would decide in June, after he had finished playing baseball at Auburn, after both the NFL draft and the Major League Baseball draft had taken place. He said that the answer to The Question wouldn't be determined merely by money, and that his indecision was sincere, and that he really *could* imagine playing baseball as much as he could imagine playing football. He said all of these things over and over again, and no one believed him.

He was not the first to face such a quandary, but he was certainly the most talented since Jim Thorpe at the beginning of the century, and the most intriguing—even more so than John Elway, who had gone to the NFL in 1983 to play quarterback rather than play for the Yankees. Bo repeated his talking points so often that his indecision became a national curiosity. The reporters remained incredulous, convinced that Bo was using baseball merely as a bargaining tool, that he would never actually deign to *play* baseball. He managed to be charming and aloof at the same time, and while his stutter had improved, he still struggled with certain letters, among them the letter *I*, which led Bo Jackson to refer to himself in the third person as "Bo Jackson," as if his body were taken over by some otherworldly force whenever he donned a uniform, as if he imagined himself capable of things that no other human being could even begin to fathom (as if he imagined himself as something larger than an individual, one baseball owner would later say).

He would play football, the writers presumed, because he was *better* at football, because he would be a number one pick in football, because he had made his name in football, because football would pay him more money. Why would the Heisman Trophy winner settle for less money to begin his career in the minor leagues? (This was the only hint Bo gave: He hated to ride buses, and minor-league life was something like one long bus tour of America, and that just made the writers feel even more like this indecision was all part of the game.) And while it was true that Bo wanted to get paid, it was also true that he did not have any grand vision for how to get there; either way, he honestly believed he would get rich, and he would be successful—so why shouldn't he choose whatever option gave him the most pleasure? And why, in a country where conspicuous consumption had become an enviable way of life, couldn't he eventually choose *both*?

The college baseball season began that same month, and amid all these distractions brought on by The Question, Bo took his spot in center field at Auburn. He played for Hal Baird, a former minor-league pitcher who had come to Auburn to coach in 1984; upon his arrival, Baird had been told by Pat Dye that he would have the privilege of coaching the world's greatest athlete.

Jackson had taken a year off from baseball in 1984 to run track, failing in his attempt to qualify for the Olympic trials. When he came back in 1985, Baird came to believe that what Dye had told him was undeniably and objectively true. Bo was a raw talent, and he swung and missed far too much (his freshman year, he had struck out twenty-one times in a row), and yet every day of practice, he seemed to get a little better; you could *see* him grow from Monday to Tuesday to Wednesday, from one at-bat to the next. Never had Baird seen a pair of eyes and a pair of hands and a pair of feet all work together in such harmony.

In a baseball uniform, Bo defied the geometry of the game in virtually every way imaginable. He could scurry from home plate to first base in a blur, and his time was faster than most of the veteran scouts had ever seen; he didn't even require a lead in order to steal a base. Against Tennessee, he hit a hard chop to the pitcher's mound, to a left-hander who made a 270-degree turn and threw hard to first base, which, somehow, Bo had already crossed. When he connected on a ball, the results were so colossal that he seemed to have simply outmuscled the angles of the park.

Against Mississippi State, a team with three future major-leaguers, Bo raced back to the warning track to catch a line drive, and when the man on second base tagged up and raced toward third, Bo did a pirouette and threw a ball on such a line that it "cut the base in half," according to Baird, and cut down the runner, and so confounded one scout that he tossed his clipboard into the air, resigned to the fact that for the first time in his three decades of chasing talent, the legend and the truth had merged into one synchronous form. *If that big donkey plays baseball,* said the scout, Kansas City's Dick Egan, *he'll be the first pick.*

Baird kept working with Bo on the fundamentals, always phrasing his tips as challenges in order to keep Bo engaged. When he tried to get him to plant his front foot earlier in his swing, he said, *I don't know if you can do it this way, Bo, it's pretty hard—Reggie Jackson did it this way, but only a few people can.* That would drive him, if only because Reggie was the closest thing Bo had to a hero in sports (though after encountering Reggie's colossal ego, he would change his mind). If the game wasn't close, if an at-bat or an inning didn't particularly matter, Bo could zone out, so the key was to keep him interested.

It wasn't easy. Bo had too many things on his mind already, and he struggled to maintain his batting average amid an existence now framed by The Question. On the road, he mostly stayed sequestered in his hotel room, and when he appeared in public, he was followed by a pack of fans and scouts and reporters and shadowy figures endeavoring to make deals on his behalf. He was hitting .246 with seven home runs in late March when he left Auburn for a brief diversion to Florida, to take a physical with the NFL's Tampa Bay Buccaneers, who were then charged with administering physicals to top prospects from a number of Southern schools in their region, and who, conveniently, also happened to hold the first pick in the upcoming NFL draft. It was not a secret that the Buccaneers coveted Jackson—because what team, in its right mind, would *not* covet someone who reportedly had run a 4.12 forty-yard dash at the NFL combine?—but it was also true that the owner of the Tampa Bay Buccaneers, Hugh Culverhouse, was not entirely in his right mind when it came to sharing his wealth with his players.

Culverhouse was a native of Bo's home state, a graduate of the University of Alabama, a Southern gentleman who had investigated organized-crime figures for the Kefauver Commission in the 1950s and was once a member of President Kennedy's tax advisory committee. He was, by all accounts, a brilliant investor and a generous philanthropist, except when it came to his football team; with the Bucs, he became miserly and unforgiving. In 1983, after Doug Williams quarterbacked the Bucs to the playoffs three times in four years, he asked for a six-hundred-thousand-dollar contract. Culverhouse refused to go higher than four hundred thousand, then tried to get Williams to go in on a real-estate deal with him in order to make up the difference. Williams, the first successful black quarterback in the NFL, was convinced that the slight was racial; he signed with a USFL team and later called Culverhouse "a perfect redneck asshole."[6]

Bo flew to Tampa on Culverhouse's private jet, after being assured by the Bucs that he was not violating any NCAA rules. He took his physical, stopped at a bakery to buy a loaf of Cuban bread, and flew back home. He had not yet hired an agent, but he was being counseled by a man he'd known from back in Bessemer; he used to mow the man's lawn when he was a teenager, and the man had given him gifts—a stereo, a pair of cowboy boots—and suggested to Bo that he should hire him as his agent. Bo was wary, but reticent to say no, and he agreed to take the man on as a "family advisor." And here, Bo would later say, he became aware of one of the complications of success in the modern age—the rise of street agents and other unregulated representatives in what was still, largely, a fledgling busi-

---

6. After his death, Culverhouse's wife, Joy, sued to gain control of her husband's estate, claiming he'd bilked her out of her share of the family fortune and that Culverhouse had cheated on her with several women, including the wife of television newsman David Brinkley. "I'd like to pull him out of the grave," she said, "and shoot him."

ness: "Young black guys are gullible to that type of thing because ninety-five percent of us grew up poor, with nothing," he said. "Somebody comes to you and says, 'Look, here's five hundred, here's a thousand dollars to hold you over for this month, and when you need more, just give me a call. And then when you get ready to turn pro, I'll give you the best deal.'"

This man, Bo later said, had been purporting himself to be Bo's agent (which would have been an NCAA violation in itself), and this man, Bo presumed, had made some sort of quid pro quo deal with Culverhouse. "I think what he did was Culverhouse said, 'Well, I'll give you this if you get him to come down, get him ineligible so that we'll know we have him,'" Bo later said. Whether this was a true story or a product of the inborn skepticism Bo inherited from his mother, his ride on Culverhouse's private plane *had* rendered him ineligible, according to the rules of the Southeast Conference. If a call had even been made to the SEC, somebody there had given out faulty information. He returned to Auburn to play his next baseball game, Baird asked him where he'd been, and Bo told him. Baird called Pat Dye, who was then the athletic director; they called the SEC office. Baird pulled Bo off the field and told him he was ineligible, and Bo walked behind the dugout and cried, both upset with himself and furious with those who had boxed him in.

The Buccaneers insisted they had no idea they'd done anything wrong, that they had made an innocent mistake. Publicly, they projected penitence and resignation. "Bo still has his baseball alternative," said the Bucs' general manager, Phil Krueger. "The scouts have seen enough of him."

This was the wrong answer . . . for Bo had been wronged, and when Bo was wronged, he did not forgive easily. First things first—he immediately fired the man who had become his advisor. He returned his gifts, and a few weeks later, when Bo went home to Bessemer and the man came to him, crying, Bo told him, *Get the fuck out of my house.* Years later, when he spoke about the man, he turned vicious and vindictive. He called him "the one person in the world I literally hate."

But he didn't trust Culverhouse anymore either. Because of the franchise's past, because of the Doug Williams fiasco and all the attendant rumors, because a team that had gone 10–38 the past three seasons with a patchwork offensive line did not bode well for his future, Jackson was already wary of the Bucs. And now he became convinced that he wouldn't play for them at any cost. "The culpability rested with Tampa," Baird said. "They made him mad, and they condescended to him, and that was the wrong way to deal with Bo Jackson."

He was a kid again, driven by his underlying anger at the world, and that anger would lead him to make a decision that would alter the legend, a decision that would open up a twofold path to stardom. "I refuse to be someone else's property," he said.

If it hadn't happened this way, if it hadn't been Tampa Bay with the first pick in the draft—if it hadn't been for the intransigence and condescension of Hugh Culverhouse—maybe Bo would have given in and gone the obvious route, and maybe he would have played professional football and never thought much about baseball. But now, faced with another crossroads in his existence, Bo Jackson once again took a flying leap across the chasm. To hell with convention. To hell with The Question and all the presumptions it engendered.

A few days later, he walked into Baird's office and took the first step toward beginning life as a professional superhero.

Coach, he said. *I really think I want to play baseball.*

II.

That winter had been an absolute hell for Michael Jordan. Stranded in a small apartment in Chicago, sidelined by injury for the first time in his career, Jordan asked permission from Bulls management to return to North Carolina, to a condominium he owned in Chapel Hill. He missed basketball, he confessed, like a man might miss a woman. He was headstrong and defiant, and he was convinced he would come back as soon as possible, and to hell with the conventional wisdom.

The bone he'd broken in his foot in that early-season game against Golden State proved especially tricky to heal, and the recovery was frustratingly slow, and all the momentum he'd built up seeped out; sales of the Air Jordan plummeted in his absence. The whole enterprise Nike had built around his game was put on hold, its future suffused with risk.

In February, Jordan could stand it no longer: He began surreptitiously testing it in pickup games, four times a week, with his friends and his ex-teammates. Like Bo Jackson, he had come to believe that he could figure these things out most effectively on his own; he did not trust his agent or his coach or the management of his team or even the *doctors* as much as he trusted his own instincts. When, during one of those pickup games, he took off from the free-throw line and dunked, he thought, *I'm ready.* And when his agent, David Falk, told him it wasn't worth the risk, when the doctors told him there was a 10 percent chance he could reinjure the foot if he came back *at all* this season, Jordan told them that he could take care of himself. Why was no one listening to *him*? He wore nonprescription glasses to a meeting with Bulls management, so as to appear serious; the owner of the Bulls, Jerry Reinsdorf, asked Jordan whether he would take a Tylenol if he knew the bottle was 10 percent cyanide. Jordan replied that he didn't have a headache. "What Michael is doing makes no sense," Reinsdorf said.

Jordan was activated on March 14, eighteen weeks after the injury was diagnosed. His minutes were limited to seven per half, then twelve per half after a probationary period. The Bulls had gone 3–0 with him, and were 21–43 without him, and were in contention for a playoff spot, though just barely. "While you can't question Jordan's desire to play," *Sports Illustrated* wrote, "you have to question his judgment."

Two weeks later, in New Jersey, he pleaded on the bench with his coach, Stan Albeck, for one extra minute of playing time; he had already scored twenty-two points in twenty-two minutes, but Albeck refused, and the Bulls lost. He scored twenty-three points in twenty-four minutes in a win over the Knicks at Madison Square Garden, and as Jordan became more comfortable, the Bulls kept winning—five of their last six, with Jordan averaging nearly thirty points per game—and slipped into the playoffs rather than the draft lottery (where one of the primary targets was a promising forward out of Maryland) . . . though Jordan suspected the Bulls management might have preferred the lottery, and he never quite trusted them again.

Instead, the Bulls would go up against the Celtics in the first round, who had by then formed a dynastic collective comprised of Larry Bird and Kevin McHale and Robert Parish and Dennis Johnson and Bill Walton and Danny Ainge, and had lost only one home game all season. The Celtics, and Bird most notably, epitomized old-school excellence: They played team basketball, unselfish and crisp, and Bird himself wore Converse shoes, a stolid and retro brand that had never quite caught on to the changes in the business (their market share had shrunk from 30 percent to 15 percent between 1974 and 1984). But then, Bird's entire persona somehow seemed shielded from the complications of the contemporary era; one night, perplexed by the activity at the team hotel, he asked a local sports columnist what was happening, and the columnist replied that Bruce Springsteen was in town that night.

Replied Bird: *Who's Bruce Springsteen?*

Bird's career had been (and always would be) defined by his lack of cultural awareness outside of basketball, and by his contrast with the Lakers' improvisational and ostentatious point guard, Magic Johnson: In a Converse commercial filmed that year, Magic glided into Bird's hometown of French Lick, Indiana, in a stretch limousine before stepping out to engage in a game one-on-one. But for one night at least, on April 20, 1986, Bird would be viewed through the prism of a new-age star/budding conglomerate who appeared to incorporate the most marketable elements of both men, who possessed both urban sheen and blue-collar grit . . . and who, given the odds of a relapse, given the admonishments of the adults who purported to manage his career, wasn't even supposed to be *playing* in this game.

That was the night Michael Jordan came of age, and that was the night we came to realize that the *possibilities* of Michael Jordan were more expansive than anything we had seen before. When he broke down Bird off the dribble on the Boston Garden's parquet floor, the executives at Nike let out a collective howl; suddenly, five million dollars over five years seemed a relative bargain. Later, they spliced the highlights into an internal corporate video—of Jordan spinning and driving and leaping and hanging in midair, of Jordan playing fifty-three minutes and making twenty-two shots and nineteen free throws and setting an NBA record by scoring sixty-three points in a playoff game. It didn't matter that the Bulls lost the game in double overtime; it didn't matter that they succumbed to the Celtics in three straight games to lose the series. Here, on our television screens, was the very epitome of the contemporary intersection of mythology and commerce. Here, preserved on videotape, was a highlight reel of Jordan schooling some of the best defenders in the history of the game, Jordan owning McHale and Walton and Dennis Johnson, Jordan going one-on-four and still scoring, Jordan making one of the best teams in NBA history often look grasping and helpless. And most notably, here was Jordan owning Larry Bird—"God disguised as Michael Jordan," Bird would say afterward—and in turn, here was Nike owning Converse. The games and the business of the games were now indistinguishable. And it was in large part because of this singular performance that Nike would one day, many years later, swallow up the entire Converse corporation.

III.

Nine days later, the number one choice in the National Football League draft sat on a dais in a New York hotel and addressed his inability to hit a curveball, speaking in the Jacksonian third person: *There's a lot of people out there who have criticized Bo, saying Bo can't hit the curveball.* He had become a master of dodging and darting and waltzing about The Question while its basic premise remained unanswered.

Options . . . those he had, now that he'd stood on a ballroom dais and posed for photographs with Pete Rozelle, now that he'd finally and officially become the Buccaneers' first pick. The draft proved a heady moment for the young man who had come of age in that three-room house in the backwoods of Alabama. He was the focus of everyone's attention in New York, the protagonist of an event that had blossomed from a glorified insurance seminar into a televised happening entirely because of ESPN. The network had begun carrying the draft in 1980, as an anchor for a station that was filling its hours with yachting and Australian Rules Football; this year's broadcast began at eight in the morning on a Tuesday, and Bo was the only player there in New York, at the league's epicenter. He had the cameras to himself. When his name was called, the five hundred fans crammed into the ballroom of the Marriott Marquis leapt up, chanting *BO! BO! BO! BO!* It was brief and it was anticlimactic, and nobody even bothered to hold up the orange Buccaneers jersey with Jackson's name on it.

The Birmingham Stallions had already selected Jackson in the first round of the USFL draft the week before, though the the league's future was cloudy due to a looming antitrust suit against the NFL. "I will not rule out anything," Bo said, but now that the Bucs seemed to intimate that they would find a way to sign him—now that Culverhouse had said he was prepared to make Jackson the highest-paid draft choice in NFL history—he seemed, from the outside, to be doing nothing more than posturing, stoking his value, massaging his ego. "Few persons in this room, with the possible exception of Jackson," wrote the *Chicago Tribune*'s Cooper Rollow, "were taking seriously the Auburn running back's statement that he plans to wait until after the June baseball draft to choose between the two sports."

Bo had secured new representation by then. Upon the suggestion of an Auburn alumnus, he chose the Birmingham law firm of Miller, Hamilton, Snider and Odom. It was an unusual decision, for neither Richard Woods nor Tommy Zieman, who would negotiate Jackson's contract, had represented an athlete before, and neither knew much of anything about the nuances of the business, or about the buzzwords of agenting: *skill guarantees* and *injury guarantees* and *annuities* and *signing bonuses.* None of this was yet common parlance, and Zieman enlisted the Washington, D.C., agency of Craighill, Fentress and Demoff—the group that represented Leonard Bias—to consult with them.

These men he had hired were lawyers, not agents, but what mattered to Bo was that he felt he could trust them, no matter their specialty. He took them to meet his mother, who fed them fried chicken and mashed potatoes, and the fact that they knew nothing of this world, that they were not among the legions of characters chasing his reflection, only made him trust these men more. And he was convinced by now that he *couldn't* trust Hugh Culverhouse. The weekend before the draft, Zieman flew to Tampa to meet for the first time with Culverhouse, who fancied himself a shrewd businessman, who

had made millions off investments, and who was determined to negotiate from a position of strength: He refused to do anything, he
said, until Bo gave up this ruse of playing baseball.

This was Culverhouse's mistake, and this was Zieman's boon—
his client's feelings of indecisiveness were authentic, and they also
facilitated a situation that gave him the most negotiating leverage.
For more than a month, the Buccaneers refused to do much of anything, and in that time Bo's mind continued to drift further toward
baseball. *To hell with this,* he thought, and with Baird's guidance and
Zieman's accompaniment, he began visiting baseball teams to convince them of his veracity. He went to Toronto and to California (and
here he came face-to-face with the straw who had once stirred the
drink, one Reginald Martinez Jackson, who told him that if all worked
out, Bo Jackson could someday become the next Reggie Jackson), but
his most intimate conversations came with Kansas City, the franchise
for whom Hal Baird had once been a farmhand, the franchise whose
scout, Ken Gonzalez, had been tracking Jackson since he hit puberty
and turned himself from a delinquent into an athlete. Zieman and
Jackson went to visit the team's general manager, John Schuerholz,
but even in the Royals clubhouse, they didn't take him seriously:
When Bo left the locker room, someone shouted, *See you in Tampa
Bay,* and Bo's anger and autonomy flared once more.

Whoever said that, Bo replied, *can go to hell.*

At Nike, Inc., Jordan's ascendance—his deification, as ordained by
the Reverend Larry Bird—had happened so fast that no one even understood what it meant. In January, morale at Nike was so low that
the founder of the company slagged on his own creation in a company newspaper: "The sad fact is that Nike's not a very good company," Phil Knight wrote, for he was a man who did not spare anyone's
feelings, even his own. "As befits a bad company, this newspaper, in

spite of a lot of very hard work by certain individuals, is not a very good newspaper."

But things *were* turning, even if Knight's dour outlook did not reflect it, even if the company's bottom line and market share had yet to turn around, even if they were still chasing after Reebok and the aerobic craze and anything else that might turn the bottom line around. Amid this internal strife, Nike had begun tapping back in to its creative roots, and they were on the verge of something unique: They were on the verge of becoming a *brand,* of discovering that the real work, as author Naomi Klein wrote, "lay not in manufacturing but in marketing." Air Jordan was a success, but they needed something more, and in the back rooms and laboratories of Portland, they'd come up with it: the Nike Air, a shoe known as a cross-trainer, a shoe that the average Joe (or Jane) could wear while running or doing aerobics or lifting weights or playing basketball.

In other words, it was a wholly modern shoe, in tune with the needs of omnivorous Americans: It was a shoe that allowed us to have it all. It was called Nike Air, and all it needed now was a face, a spokesman, someone to define it in the way Jordan had come to define his own brand. And at that moment, along came Vincent Edward Jackson.

And so with the professional baseball draft looming, with The Question nearing its inevitable resolution, Bo and his agents flew to Portland, to a house on Lake Oswego, where a woman named Karin Morlan lived. She was the head of Nike's "cleated promotions" (meaning football and baseball), and she had been courting Bo for months and pitching him to her bosses—to men like Rob Strasser and Peter Moore, the same ones who had engineered the rise of the Air Jordan shoe. Unlike Culverhouse, Morlan had studied her subject: They took Bo fly-fishing that day rather than spend money on an elaborate dinner. Then they pitched to him an entire line similar to what they'd once pitched to Jordan (though when asked how they'd made it work for Jordan, Moore shrugged and said, "I have no idea"). Morlan thought the shoe itself, a bulky contraption sealed with a strap (it was then called The Trainer), looked like a castoff from the production of *Ben-Hur.* Thought Zieman: *This shoe cannot possibly work.* In the presentation, presuming Bo would answer The Question by choosing football, they designed everything in Tampa Bay's colors, in that bile-like combination of orange and white, and Bo said nothing until the end, when he confessed to his animosity for Culverhouse and said playing for Culverhouse would make him feel like a "plantation stepchild."

There had been talk of a trade, of Tampa moving Bo to another team, perhaps even to the 49ers, to the team that Mike Ditka so resented because of its staggering genius of a coach, Bill Walsh (who had reportedly offered a package of players and draft picks to Culverhouse for the pick but was denied). And if that *had* happened—if, somehow, Culverhouse had let Bo off the hook—perhaps this would have become merely another deal for another football player (in a sport where endorsement contracts had never been as lucrative as their "noncleated" counterparts in basketball), albeit for a talent of rare pedigree. But it was all so uncertain, and while this gave the Nike people pause, they didn't want to miss the opportunity if Bo did get traded: Zieman asked for a hundred thousand dollars a year over three years, and this was *ten times more* than Nike had been willing to pay certain All-Pros and All-Stars in a baseball and football, and yet Morlan didn't balk at the price tag. They signed, and days later, it looked—as it once had with Jordan—like they'd made a terrible mistake, like they'd spent a fortune chasing ghosts. And it appeared that all of Phil Knight's worst fears about his own company were accurate. Not long after, when Knight found out who had pushed for the Bo Jackson deal, he called for Karin Morlan to be

Ronald Reagan spent four years at WHO Radio in Des Moines, immersed in the mythology of American sports. He would later call those years some of the most pleasant of his life.

Reagan poses with 1984 Olympic hero Mary Lou Retton. The '84 Olympics in Los Angeles, though marred by an Eastern Bloc boycott, became an opulent showcase of American triumphalism.

Bosworth (number 44) chases after Penn State's no-frills quarterback John Shaffer during the Orange Bowl. "I really trusted the authority of our coaches," Shaffer said.

Brian Bosworth, Oklahoma's flamboyant linebacker, poses with a teammate prior to the 1986 Orange Bowl. "I got so famous, so quick, I didn't know how to handle it," he would confess, many years later.

McMahon eludes the Giants' troubled and talented Lawrence Taylor during a playoff game. McMahon's fearlessness—both on and off the field—often led to trouble.

Quarterback Jim McMahon—defiant, supremely talented, and oft-injured— livens up Johnny Carson's show shortly after undergoing surgery on his shoulder.

Corbis Images

McMahon moons a helicopter, showing off his bruised backside during
Super Bowl week. The quarterback was the center of attention in New Orleans.

Len Bias soars over a pair of Duke defenders. By his senior season, Bias was widely regarded as the most exciting college basketball player in the country.

Mourners place flowers on the grave at Len Bias's funeral. His death would send shock waves throughout the country and greatly impact the trajectory of the nation's war on drugs

This poster of Bias was a common sight in Maryland dorm rooms. His death stunned the campus and affected a generation of American youth.

Bo Jackson cut a powerful figure in a football uniform and helped Auburn defeat hated rival Alabama for the first time since 1972.

Facing questions about his toughness, Bo ran for 142 yards against Alabama while nursing two broken ribs. A short time later, he won the 1985 Heisman Trophy.

In his brief time as a physical and commercial icon, Bo shattered bats over his knee, scaled outfield walls, leveled defensive backs, and defied conventional wisdom in two major American sports. "It's almost as if he choreographs his whole life," one of his friends would say.

In college, Bo ran a 6.18 in the sixty-yard dash and would later reportedly run a 4.175 in the forty-yard dash. "You think I can make any money in track?" he once asked his high school coach.

fired; he did not yet understand the psychology of the men who would become his two greatest creations. For just as Jordan had defied his doctors and his coaches and his team's owner in coming back for the end of the '86 season, thereby ascending to mythological status . . . so, too, did Bo Jackson envision a day when he could defy the proscriptions that had been set out before him, when he could answer The Question—*Baseball or football, Bo?*—simply by refusing to answer it at all.

The first press conference took place in Birmingham. It was Saturday morning, June 21, the day of the summer solstice, and when it was over, Bo Jackson flew straight to Kansas City to take batting practice with his new team. He had been offered four million dollars over five years by the Buccaneers; the Royals, who had drafted Jackson in the fourth round, with the 104th pick, offered him one million over three years. Soon after making his offer, Culverhouse told the media that if Jackson didn't accept the offer within the next week, he'd take it back and cut it in half, and Bo told his agents to tell Hugh Culverhouse, once and for all, to go fuck himself.

He proclaimed, once again, that he'd answered The Question on his own terms. He said that he wanted to avoid a catastrophic knee injury, that he wanted to have a long career, that he'd gone with his gut. "Was it for love?" led the Associated Press story. "Bo Jackson certainly didn't do it for money."

And in so doing, Bo had again achieved more than just internal happiness. He had set himself up as the kind of man who had bucked the cultural trend; in an era of spiritual materialism, he had not allowed money to cloud his judgment. In that way, he was a nostalgic cipher, a throwback to the romantic vision of Frank Merriwell at Yale. He was above it all; he really *was* like some kind of superhuman. "Let me state a fact," he said. *"Bo Jackson can play baseball."* (He'd been playing baseball since the age of ten, he later argued; wouldn't he have learned at some point if he *couldn't* play baseball?) And then: "I'm always going to do the opposite of what the public thinks. Just to make them sit up and swallow their Adam's apples."

He didn't tell anyone, but he hadn't given up on football. He wouldn't *allow* himself to give up on football, because this was the way Bo saw it—there were people who settled for whatever came their way, and then there was Bo Jackson. Years later, he spoke of it in terms of fishing: Some men are content to catch one small fish, but when Bo Jackson catches a small fish, he uses it as bait to catch something much larger.

That afternoon, he took batting practice in Kansas City. He had left his equipment on the private plane that had flown him from Birmingham to Kansas City, and so, using a bat borrowed from the Royals' Steve Balboni, he hit seven home runs, including one that landed at the base of the scoreboard, 450 feet from home plate. No one could remember ever seeing anything quite like it before.

IV.

This all happened a short time after a man named Ivan Boesky flew from New York to California via private jet to deliver the commencement address at the University of California's business school. Boesky, the son of Russian immigrants, worked on Wall Street; he was known as an *arbitrageur,* and he had made millions by placing brazen bets on corporate takeovers, sometimes in the very days before they occurred. Boesky showed up late that day, and in an interview with the local newspaper, he said that he "didn't give a damn" what the students wanted to hear. He spoke for a long time and said nothing of note, and then, in an instant, perhaps sensing he was losing his audience, Boesky said something remarkable and managed to capture the mood of Wall Street—and become a symbol of the dark consequences of the Zeitgeist—in a single flourish. "Greed is all right, by the way," he said. "I want you to know that. I think greed is healthy. You can be greedy and still feel good about yourself."

It would take time for Boesky's words to achieve resonance, for them to be adapted in a Hollywood film script and uttered by an actor who was playing a Boesky doppelgänger named Gordon Gekko, and whose character would come to represent the worst instincts of what author James B. Stewart called "the Greed Decade." It would take time for the excesses of Wall Street in the 1980s to lay themselves bare, but it was already coming, because six days before Boesky's speech, on May 12, a merger specialist at Drexel Burnham Lambert, Inc., Dennis B. Levine, was hauled in by federal officials on charges of insider trading. Levine lived in a co-op on Park Avenue, and frequented art galleries, and had already bought his father a new Jaguar and his wife a diamond necklace with his profits. And in order to save himself, he was willing to sing, to give up everything and everyone he knew, including Ivan Boesky. It was the beginning of the end of an ethic that had come to define a decade of American life; in November, Boesky would agree to pay a hundred-million-dollar penalty, and in December 1987, two months after the stock market crash, Boesky would be sentenced to three years in prison. "If ever there were people who believed themselves to be so rich and powerful as to be above the law, they were to be found in and around Wall Street in the mid-eighties," Stewart wrote, and in that moment, it felt as if the consequences were about to take hold.

Two Commonly Told Elements of the Len Bias Narrative That Are Almost Certainly False

1. LEN BIAS WAS EXPERIMENTING WITH COCAINE FOR THE FIRST TIME THAT NIGHT.

> *Origin:*
> Q: Could this have been his first encounter with cocaine?
> A: That is possible, yes.
> —*Maryland medical examiner John E. Smialek, news conference, June 24, 1986*

> *Contrary evidence:*
> A. Court testimony of Terry Long, who claimed "Len Bias introduced me to coke" and portrayed Bias as an experienced drug user. "One time he knocked on my door and he had a dollar bill and he said, 'Try this,'" Long told the court.
> B. "University of Maryland basketball star Len Bias apparently was not a stranger to the drug that took his life.

"State medical examiner Dr. John E. Smialek says detailed tests done on Bias's heart show the Terps' all-time scoring leader probably had used cocaine prior to his fatal dose on June 19.

"Smialek, who released the final autopsy report on Bias Thursday night, said tests on Bias's heart found microscopic damage to several muscle fibers, representing what usually is a cocaine-induced disease."—*Associated Press, July 5, 1986*

Why this matters:

Perhaps this doesn't matter at all.

"What can I do about what anybody says?" Lonise Bias told me. "The only thing I saw in 1986 was dirty laundry being put in a dead man's coffin who couldn't speak for himself. You don't know if there's another story that hasn't been told yet."

So perhaps this is one of those wishful notions—perpetuated by Len Bias's negative drug-test results (easily manipulated), and by the claims of friends and family, and by the medical examiner's initial opinion (later revised) that this might have, indeed, been Bias's first experience with cocaine—that benefits everyone and harms no one. Perhaps, in burnishing a legend, the claims of Driesell and Lonise Bias (who still believes her son had never tried cocaine before, and might, in fact, have tried it accidentally or even been poisoned) actually proved far more positive for society than the truth might have.

As evidence, I return to myself, at age thirteen, and all the other children of my generation, products of the skewed value system of the eighties, for whom the most potent advertisement for the Just Say No campaign might have been the notion that a single splotch of cocaine—and this is how I imagined it as a child, that Bias had simply touched several stray crystals of processed coca leaves to his nostrils and shortly thereafter departed this mortal coil—could kill us without prejudice. (Said one psychologist back in 1986: "The current generation of kids is shaped by incredible fear. . . . They are scared to death.") And there is no doubt that hundreds of thousands of Americans, upon experimenting with cocaine for the first time, thought immediately of Len Bias.

"All of us like to generalize our experience," says Eric Sterling, the congressional lawyer who has since become a vocal critic of the recidivistic churn of the American drug war. "But it's a big country, with a lot of different kids. I wouldn't say that it 'worked.'"

Still, I ask: Would Bias's story have achieved the same status as a cultural touchstone if we had known he—while probably not a habitual user—had dabbled in cocaine for months, or that his close friend was apparently dealing cocaine, or that the truth was far more nuanced than the mythology? Is there then something to be said, at least in this case, for a lie proving far more powerful than the truth?

2. LEN BIAS WAS USING CRACK COCAINE THAT NIGHT.

Origin:
"University of Maryland basketball star Len Bias died after smoking a pure form of cocaine free-base, the assistant state medical examiner who performed the autopsy on Bias has said. . . . 'Crack' is a relatively new and increasingly popular form of free-base cocaine extracted from the adulterated powder by using water, heat, and baking soda, drug experts say."—The Evening Sun, *Baltimore, July 9, 1986*

Contrary evidence:
A. Eyewitness accounts, court testimony from Long and Gregg.
B. "Smialek told reporters as he left the courthouse that it did not appear Bias freebased the cocaine found in his system. Earlier this month, Smialek's assistant, Dr.

Dennis Smyth, who performed the autopsy on Bias, said the redness in Bias's windpipe and a high concentration of cocaine in his blood indicated the athlete 'most likely' smoked cocaine rather than snorted it in powder form through his nose. 'We don't have any evidence to support that [freebasing] right now,' Smialek said."—*UPI, July 21, 1986*

Why this matters:

A. "In the month following Bias's death, the [television] networks aired seventy-four evening news segments about crack and cocaine, often erroneously interchanging the two substances and blithely asserting it was crack that killed Bias."— *From* Smoke and Mirrors, *by Dan Baum*

B. "Within a day of Bias's death, there was a previously scheduled planning meeting of presidential aides at the White House to discuss what issues President Reagan should focus on through the November Congressional elections. Drugs had not yet been officially linked to Bias's death, but one aide said he suspected that crack was involved."—The Washington Post, *September 14, 1986*

CHAPTER EIGHT

1103 Washington Hall

May you have champagne wishes and caviar dreams.

—Robin Leach

I.

And this was how the party ended:

At six-thirty-one in the morning, a man named Brian Tribble placed a phone call from a dormitory suite on a college campus to a 911 dispatcher whose Baltimorese hammered his consonants flat—and who, from his tone of voice, initially assumed this whole thing was a prank, a put-on by a bunch of rowdy university kids who had chosen to punctuate their festivities by abusing the goodwill of the people of Prince George's County. According to the notes of the technical services division of the Federal Bureau of Investigation, these sounds comprised the background noise of the call:

1. A male speaker saying "Washington Hall" near the beginning of the recording.
2. Moaning, heard throughout the recording.
3. Music, that may be from a radio or television.
4. At least two or three voices heard talking.

In the foreground, there was the voice of the caller, slurred and hesitant, repeating the victim's name over and over, as if willing this entire scene to go away. At that moment, we may presume, Brian Tribble was prodigiously high on cocaine and coming to realize that this was really happening to him: that his friend—and not just any friend but *Len Bias*—was seizing up on the floor in front of him.

> **OPERATOR:** P. G. County Emergency.
> **TRIBBLE:** Yes, I'd like to have an ambulance come, what, what room? What room?
> **BACKGROUND VOICE:** Washington Hall.
> **TRIBBLE:** What, eleven-oh-three Washington Hall. It's an emergency. It's Len Bias and he just went to Boston and he needs some assistance.
> **OPERATOR:** What are you talkin' about?
> **TRIBBLE:** Huh?
> **OPERATOR:** What are you talkin' about?
> **TRIBBLE:** I'm talkin' about, uh, someone needs, Len Bias needs help.
> **Operator:** Well, it doesn't matter what his name is, what's the problem?
> **TRIBBLE:** He's not breathing right.

On it went, for several more seconds, the operator clarifying the caller's name (*Operator:* Tribble?/*Tribble:* Yes, sir), and the caller's phone number (*Tribble:* I'm, I'm in Len Bias's room, I don't know the phone number there), and the caller's location (*Tribble:* It's, uh, I don't know, it's no address, it's just Washington Hall. Come up by Hun-Hungry Herman's and go straight up there and it's on the right side, so please come as soon as you can. It's no joke). And then one last plea—

TRIBBLE: This is Len Bias. You have to get him back to life. There's no way he can die. Seriously, sir. Please come quick.

A moment before this, Bias had sat up on a bed, bent over a mirror, and reminded his teammates that he was "a horse," that he could handle anything life threw at him, and then he'd snorted one last line of cocaine. A moment earlier, Bias was just another young man celebrating his future the way many young men have/will celebrate their futures: with music, with friends, with a party, with a mound of processed coca leaves piled onto a reflective surface. Then he got up to use the bathroom, and he stumbled, and he sat back down on the bed, and he began shaking, and he lapsed into a seizure. There were three other men in the room; together, they eased his body to the floor. One man, Terry Long, placed the handle of a pair of scissors in Bias's mouth to prevent him from biting his tongue; another, David Gregg, held Bias's legs. The third man, Brian Tribble, phoned his own mother, who told him to call 911. And through it all, Lonise Bias's eldest son lay on a cold hard floor, eyes at half-mast, a braided gold chain hanging about his neck.

But we are getting ahead of ourselves. First, we must come to understand how in the world Len Bias went to Boston in the first place. It is an improbable side trip that involves, among other things, a tricked-out lotto drawing and a cloud of stale cigar smoke. It begins in 1984, when the Boston Celtics traded journeyman guard Gerald Henderson to the Seattle Supersonics in exchange for Seattle's first-round pick two years on. And it continues into the following season, with the advent of a new system of order at the top of the NBA draft known as the Lottery.

The Lottery was invented to prevent bad franchises from tanking at the end of the season in order to win the top pick in the draft; it was an example of the NBA attempting to shield its product from corruption. That first year, in 1985, the Knicks won the Lottery and chose Patrick Ewing, and immediately allegations arose that the whole thing was rigged, that NBA commissioner David Stern had engineered Ewing's landing in New York in order to ensure the Knicks a healthy franchise in the foreseeable future. And then, on a Sunday in May 1986, it happened again: In the as-yet-unweighted drawing for the first eight picks—each team was represented by a single envelope with the team logo inside—the top two choices went to the Philadelphia 76ers (who had traded Joe "Jellybean" Bryant for the Clippers' first-round pick) and . . . the Celtics, whose team president, Red Auerbach, sat on a dais during the proceedings and nervously huffed cigar smoke about the room while Stern opened the envelopes, revealing the order of picks. "I think it's very fair," said Auerbach, who portrayed to the media a certain interest in Brad Daugherty, the seven-footer out of North Carolina, but could also not disguise his enthusiasm for only one player: Leonard Bias. Here was what Auerbach called a *ballplayer,* a prospect who had once coached at Auerbach's summer camp, a kid who could do it all . . . and he could fit seamlessly into the Celtics' system, into a rotation of All-Stars and Hall of Famers, and could spell Bird and McHale and keep their legs fresh as they grew older.

Even as the Celtics sliced through NBA playoffs that spring, even as they defeated the Houston Rockets in the finals, they could feel the advancement of time. Bird was only twenty-nine and had been named the NBA's Most Valuable Player for the third straight year, but all of that court time was beginning to take a toll on a man who had never been a natural like Bias, who had built his legend on labor as much as talent. "We're an old team," Bird said after the win over the Rockets, "and a little injury-prone."

In retrospect, certain events that spring, set against the emergence of an entirely new generation of heroes like Bias and Bo Jackson and Jim McMahon and Roger Clemens (the twenty-three-year-old Red Sox pitcher who had struck out twenty Seattle Mariners in May), took on an elegiac feel. Jack Nicklaus won the Masters at age forty-six; Bill Shoemaker won the Kentucky Derby at age fifty-four; and the Celtics won one last championship before the beginning of the end. Without Bias, Bird and McHale were forced to play more minutes, and injuries *did* take their toll, and an old team just got older and older, until they retired one by one and then faded from relevance. The repercussions of the modern age would eventually wither away a dynasty.

But first, before we take him to Boston, we must travel with Len Bias to New York. He went there with his father, James, and precisely forty-eight hours before his death, he woke with a start in a room at the Grand Hyatt, flustered by a nightmare: He was still at home in Maryland, and he had slept through the NBA draft, and he could not get to New York fast enough to be there when his name was called. He came to with a sense of relief—it was only six in the morning. The day was upon him, and his future had finally arrived. Now he could begin living the life he had imagined.

At the same time, in the same city, seventy blocks north of the Grand Hyatt, entire neighborhoods were gripped by a frenzied panic. A "new drug" had officially emerged, and reporters descended on the ghettoes to report on what had become the story of the summer. On the corner of 116th Street and Third Avenue, a *Guardian* reporter witnessed the frantic arm motions of a "young, bare-chested Hispanic man in leather pants" selling crack cocaine. The director of the 1-800-COCAINE hotline, Arnold Washton, told *Newsweek* that crack produced "almost instantaneous addiction," that it was a new and violent threat to America's inner cities. Freebasing cocaine had always been a dangerous pastime, but now that it had a new name and a simpler production process, now that it commanded the public's attention, crack became a monster, its effects exaggerated beyond the realm of possibility. It was dangerous and it was addictive, but there was a measure of hyperbole here. Crack was no more "instantaneously addictive" than any other drug had ever been, and the attendant violence had as much to do with the economics of this new market as it did with the potency of the drug itself. "The typical crack murder involved one crack dealer shooting another . . . and not, contrary to conventional wisdom, some bug-eyed crackhead shooting a shopkeeper over a few dollars," wrote authors Steven Levitt and Stephen Dubner, in analyzing the epidemic years later.

So, yes, it was bigger and faster and stronger and considerably cheaper, but it was *still* cocaine, the same drug that had been bouncing around downtown lofts and clubs for more than a decade, the same drug that had felled John Belushi, the same drug piled into a martini glass on the cover of *Time* magazine earlier in the decade, the same drug that author Jay McInerney had referred to as Bolivian Marching Powder in his 1984 yuppie gothic, *Bright Lights, Big City,* the same drug that one stockbroker said "made me feel like J. P. Morgan." Only now, it was new and improved and rebranded.

In the newspapers, the headlines had begun a daily portrayal of the bleakness of the situation uptown. From that week's *New York Times:* 3 SHOT, 2 FATALLY, IN BRONX VIOLENCE LINKED TO CRACK. Cocaine, the glamour drug of the early 1980s, was fast becoming a ghetto drug, confined to "base houses" in Harlem and the Bronx, passed on to the next generation by pregnant and hopelessly addicted mothers. Users were defined as inner-city-dwelling minorities; depictions of white cocaine users in the media dropped by two thirds, and depictions of black users rose by the same amount. A survey of voters in suburban Detroit found that many felt "not living with blacks is what makes a neighborhood a decent place to live." The Drug Enforcement Administration would soon issue a report stating that crack was virtually nonexistent outside the inner city, but the subtext—to suburban America, to those of us who grew up outside the urban bubble—had already fueled a panic: Were *we* next? That week's cover story in *Newsweek* was headlined AN INFERNO OF CRAVING, DEALING, AND DESPAIR. "It's everywhere," said a Florida law enforcement official, "and it crosses all racial, social, and economic boundaries."

Of course, all of this seemed a distant and unrelated concern that evening as Len Bias sauntered into Madison Square Garden looking sharp, sporting a gray striped suit and a skinny dark tie, as he took his place in the front row among several other talented young college basketball players who were on the verge of becoming millionaires. At that moment, it was not hard to wonder: What did sports have to do with *real life*?

And yet soon enough, this entire draft would become a cautionary tale. Of the first eighteen seniors picked, only seven had graduated from college; Bias, who had either failed or withdrawn from all of his courses that final semester, was not among them. More than half of the players picked in the first round would have their careers shortened by bad luck or bad decisions, by drugs or alcohol or injury or illness; among the top ten picks, Chris Washburn and William Bedford and Roy Tarpley all struggled with cocaine problems that ruined their careers. Norm Sonju, the general manager of the Dallas Mavericks, claimed to have compiled "six inches of paperwork" on Tarpley—including contacts with schools and churches—before choosing him. The men in charge had been misled, and they would never quite trust their sources again. After the Fiasco of '86, a number of NBA teams began hiring private investigators to back up their own information-gathering.

But on that night, none of these complications and connections had yet become apparent. On that night, there was only the image of a young man in a snazzy suit and a silk pocket square, rising from his seat, taking a green corduroy cap from the Celtics' equipment manager, and placing it askew atop his head. On that night, there was only a young man projecting happiness and relief. "I'm suspicious when Red Auerbach exposes himself to people," said John Thompson, the Georgetown coach who served as a commentator for the cable station TBS, which televised the draft. Thompson said this before the Celtics made their pick—he thought the Celtics might have thrown everyone off with their effusive praise of Bias, that they might choose William Bedford . . . and when Auerbach chose Bias anyway, Thompson expressed his disbelief once more: "I really thought Red was gonna trick everybody."

There were no tricks here. The Celtics desperately wanted Bias, and they got Bias; Auerbach would later admit he'd been scheming for three years to land this pick. And Bias wanted the Celtics (he had even made a hard pitch to the Celtics' GM, Jan Volk, a few months earlier), and he got them. It was, Bias said, "a dream within a dream." He was the best athlete in the draft, Auerbach said, and he seemingly had no major personal flaws; he was, after all, a born-again Christian. Driesell was telling anyone who would listen that his star player's only vice was ice cream. Larry Bird had already said he would show up at the team's rookie camp if the Celtics chose Bias. The rich got richer, and the commentators wanted to know from Auerbach how he would find playing time for another thoroughbred amid a stable of them. And for a moment, pondering the future, the old coach turned into a philosopher.

"Time goes," he said. "Time goes."

That night, Len Bias went to Boston on an airplane, accompanied by his father and his agent, Lee Fentress. It had been a long stretch since the season ended—he'd played in a series of barnstorming all-star games, and he'd negotiated with his agent and submitted to interviews and examinations from at least three NBA teams, who treated him like the commodity that he had become. They scrutinized *everything*. "Even your fingernails," Bias told his old rec league coach. It was the price of becoming a millionaire at the age of twenty-two, and hence the price of being able to engage in the conspicuous consumption Len Bias had dreamed of—to have your pick of Italian suits and stereos. (He told a reporter that he would now be able to afford a pair of Mercedes: one for himself and one for his mother.) It was not just about your game anymore; Michael Jordan had already changed the template. With a star like Bias, there were shoe contracts and endorsement deals to be cultivated and protected. It was unquestionably a business, and Bias was either self-aware or innocent enough to pass every drug test he ever took, and to emerge clean from all the predraft physicals. His advisors said they told him, in the days before the draft, that if he even happened to be in a car with someone smoking a joint, he should remove himself posthaste.

He took a week off at the end of May and spent it in Virginia Beach; when he returned, the phone rang constantly. He told a friend that he didn't trust women anymore because all they wanted was *money, money, money.* And yet he wanted money now too: One night he and Tribble took a job cleaning an office, and Bias made a hundred dollars—he was a guy, his friends understood, who was in constant search of a paycheck and a girl. He picked up women at the Chapter III nightclub, often in the company of Brian Tribble. Wednesday was Ladies' Night at Chapter III, and Thursday was Free Barbecue, and Saturdays and Sundays were Come As You Are nights and sometimes they stayed until closing, and Bias would sit up front, asking women for IDs and frequently leaving with a girl. None of it seemed especially harmful; most nights, Bias wouldn't even be seen drinking a beer at the club. Most people didn't suspect anything about it, except that Len Bias knew what was coming to him in the NBA and he acted like it.

In Boston, he conducted a press conference, then he went straight to the headquarters of Reebok and pressed more flesh and ate a hamburger and played video games and walked the halls in his Italian suit while his representatives negotiated a deal—and then, finally, it was time to go home. At eight-thirty that night, he and his father boarded a plane and flew back to D.C., and at ten-forty-five, Bias dropped his father off at their house and went straight to campus to celebrate. He did not see his mother, who was at a Bible study class; she used to kid him about his long legs, and when she came home, she joked that her long-legged rascal had run away from her again.

It was getting late, but after years of dreaming about it, of staring at the posters that hung on the walls of his dorm room, a young man who felt like he had waited his whole life had finally become a millionaire. The night was just beginning.

II.

There are things we know and things we do not know about the night Len Bias came home for good. We know that he called at least one of what appeared to be multiple girlfriends (an intern at a local television station), and we know that he called Brian Tribble, who had once played junior varsity basketball at Maryland before he hurt his knee when struck by a car while riding a motorcycle. (Tribble filed a personal-injury lawsuit against the driver who struck him, asking for a million dollars in lost income, the equivalent of what he might have earned during a career in professional basketball; a jury awarded him $10,000 in costs and damages.) We know that Tribble worked several jobs, and we know that he lived in a six-hundred-dollar-a-month apartment off campus and lifted weights and owned a silver Mercedes and three pit bulls named Assassin, Lady Devour, and Tan Man. We know that Tribble's father was a respected jazz drummer nicknamed TNT, and we know that Tribble was once voted most attractive in his class at McKinley Tech High School. His senior wish: *The ability to make it.* (According to a friend, Tribble was involved, at some level, in the distribution of controlled substances; Tribble declined, more than two decades later, to publicly discuss who provided the cocaine that evening. "Brian was a drug dealer back then," says that friend, Derrick Curry. "Still, I didn't have any idea about Lenny, not at all. There wasn't no drugs. Wasn't even no alcohol around. I'd never even seen Lenny *drink* before.")

We know that at approximately one A.M., Len Bias showed up at Town Hall Liquors on Route 1, still wearing his Italian suit and a diamond-encrusted gold bracelet and smelling rather nice, according to one of the young female clerks. We know that he bought two six-packs of Haffenreffer Private Stock malt liquor and then returned shortly afterward to buy an eighteen-dollar bottle of Hennessy and sign an autograph for the manager.

And here is where it gets confusing, as portions of the timeline of that night remain obscure and unsubstantiated. According to one account, Bias was allegedly pulled over for speeding on the Maryland campus as many as three times. Another woman said that Bias visited her at three A.M. and that she had loaned Bias several thousand dollars over the course of three years, though her testimony was later discounted. (Even in death, it seemed, everyone wanted a piece of him.) There was a report that he met another woman at a 7-Eleven and tried to invite her back to his dorm room. There was a report that he and Tribble may have visited a drug-infested section of the city known as Montana Terrace. What seems clear is that this night was all about escape—from his parents, from the friends who thought they knew him, from the reporters whose questions tried his patience, from the weeks of predraft workouts, from his role as a neighborhood hero, from the inherent responsibilities that would soon guide his adult existence, from the notion of authority itself.

At some point, perhaps around two-thirty, perhaps later, Len

Bias and Brian Tribble returned to 1103 Washington Hall. *WAKE THE FUCK UP*, Bias shouted, banging on the door of his teammate Terry Long. *WE'RE CELEBRATING.* Long woke up Gregg, and the four men sat in the suite and passed a mirror and snorted cocaine, using soda straws from McDonald's. They did this for several hours, breaking to hide the evidence from their roommate, Jeff Baxter, who had no idea what was going on, who went to bed sometime after three and woke up only when he heard the moaning in the next room.

One 911 call prompted a dozen more phone calls, the story quickly rippling outward. The paramedics arrived and transported Bias to Leland Memorial Hospital, as Tribble and two of Bias's Maryland teammates who had been partying with him began to clean up after themselves, emptying the leftover cocaine into a cookie bag, grinding what they'd spilled into the carpet using cleaning powder. Another teammate, Keith Gatlin, phoned Lonise Bias to tell her Len had had a seizure and was clinging to life; in their haste, she and her husband, James, rushed off to the wrong hospital. Before Bias even arrived at Leland, a source phoned television reporter Dave Statter, who did not cover sports but knew of Len Bias because everyone in D.C., and especially in Prince George's County, knew of Len Bias. Statter was a former firefighter, and he'd gotten a tip that morning that Bias was at the hospital, that he had somehow fallen into cardiac arrest. It seemed entirely absurd, but he called to confirm.

Statter phoned a woman at the dispatch center. She told him it was true and then hung up. He phoned his supervisors at Channel 9 in Washington. His supervisors phoned the station's sports anchor, James Brown, and Statter went live on the air as the first reporter at Leland Memorial Hospital. He knew Len Bias was in critical condition. He did not know why. At this point, only four people knew why, and one was dying and the other three were too freaked out to say anything, though the story has been revealed over the years in bits and pieces, through leaks and rumors and sworn testimony, most notably in a Prince George's County courtroom more than a year after Bias's death, when Brian Lee Tribble—either a scapegoat or a murderer, depending upon your point of view—went on trial, charged with providing the drugs that killed his friend.

At eight-fifty-one that morning, according to the autopsy report, Leonard Kevin Bias was pronounced dead. Larry Bird, reached by phone at his home in French Lick, Indiana, told a reporter that this was "one of the cruelest things I've ever heard." Bias's body was wheeled out of Leland Hospital, in front of TV cameramen and newspaper photographers who had been staked out for hours after chasing Statter to the hospital, in front of onlookers and teammates who had gathered near the entrance to the emergency room.

Meanwhile, Lonise Bias, who had arrived at the hospital a short time before and heard the doctors say they were doing all they could, felt the fulfillment of her prophecy was at hand. She listened, and she nodded, and then she told herself, "He's already gone."

III.

In the hours after Bias's death, there was nothing but shock on the airwaves. When the noon broadcast came on the air on Channel 9, an anchor bade her audience good afternoon and then said, "A local success story took a tragic turn this morning. . . ." And off they went, beginning an extended journey into one of the strangest and most sensational stories any of them had ever reported.

Cut to Statter, standing in front of Washington Hall, the details still emerging. "Doctors say he died of a heart attack . . . but at this point we don't know what caused that heart attack." Cut to a shot of the hospital and to a clip of the emergency room doctor who treated him and who was now surrounded by a battalion of television cameras. "All we know," Statter concluded, "is that Len Bias's heart stopped."

Over the years, of course, we have come to expect the worst from our public figures. But the television news was different back then, still in the middle stages of its transition from sobriety to sensationalism. (In 1986, let us remember, O. J. Simpson was still a football analyst.) The market was not yet saturated, the cable news channels were in their infancy, and the broadcasts themselves had not been subsumed by today's troika of scandal, cynicism, and splashy graphics. Despite the burgeoning presence of a twenty-four-hour all-sports cable network, an athlete's personal life was still sketchy territory, so no one really knew what to expect or even what questions to ask.

"I think today, it would be different," Statter said. "We've seen so many of these things happen to athletes, people expect it more now. We're so jaded now that if it's a real medical condition, we're almost surprised."

Over on Channel 4, the same thing was happening. "If you had to draw up a list of young people least likely to die of heart problems," began the reporter, Pat Collins, "Len Bias would be right up there on that list." And then: a shot of Bias's body being wheeled out on a stretcher and loaded into the coroner's van, an unmarked black Ford Econoline. For Statter, who had covered fires and murders and seen all manner of dead bodies, the sight of Bias underneath a sheet, his outline long and lithe, chilled him to the bone. At that moment, he realized just how bizarre and frightening this story had become.

The noon broadcast came and went, and already there were whispers of drug use, but it seemed no one wanted to believe them. They *knew* Len Bias, and the Len Bias they knew didn't take drugs; the Len Bias they knew was a Christian, and the Len Bias they knew acted as a role model in the community. Statter took another call from a source who told him cocaine had been found in Bias's system. The Eyewitness News team went to work: Statter, Brown, and their colleague Mike Buchanan confirmed it with two other sources, and then Statter went on the air with it, and the rumor spread throughout the day, and yet we all remained in willful denial.

Already that morning, Lefty Driesell had held a brief and tearful press conference. "Leonard would have wanted me to say something," he began, brushing a finger near his eye, and he ended with "I'll see you in heaven one day." At some point, he met with his players and they prayed together, and at this meeting, Lefty reportedly told them to be cautious with their public comments, and that would soon fan speculation about a cover-up, which only led to more confusion and sensationalism.

The news kept breaking all day long. Team coverage on the evening broadcasts, with reporters stationed at Washington Hall, and outside the Bias house in Landover, and at Cole Field House, where hundreds of Maryland students, upon hearing the news, gathered to cheer on a ghost. "Lenny elevated above mortal men," one of them told Tony Kornheiser, *Post* columnist. On Channel 4, sports anchor George Michael prepared to introduce a tribute package to Bias, broke down, and urged the camera to pan back to the anchor sitting next to him until he could gather himself. Another anchor, Channel 7's Frank Herzog, had taken his kids to see Bias speak at an event six weeks earlier; he imagined, like many others, that Bias must have had a congenital heart condition, something random and unpredictable. That was the dominant narrative throughout the afternoon and into the early evening; the cocaine story seemed such an outlier given Bias's public reputation, given his Christianity, given the testimonies of so many people who thought they knew him well. Why, George Michael asked, should any of us trust the unnamed sources spreading this rumor? Why should anyone believe such things about an athlete with a public reputation as honorable as that of Leonard Bias?

REPORTER (OUTSIDE WASHINGTON HALL): Any heavy
celebrating going on last night?
BIAS FRIEND: No. Not here.

In carefully crafted news reports on the medical aspect of heart con-
ditions, doctors testified as to the deadliness of a genetic disorder
called Marfan syndrome, which presented itself in long-limbed and
otherwise healthy people, and which had caused the sudden death of
Olympic volleyball player Flo Hyman in January. This, we presumed,
was the only explanation that made sense.

REPORTER: Some don't *want* to know if there's more to
this than a heart attack.

Outside the Bias house, Jay Bias, Len's younger brother, walked outside and made a brief statement to a television reporter, dedicating
the rest of his life to his brother. He was one day short of turning
sixteen, and that night, he left to go play in a summer league game,
citing his brother's instructions: "Whatever you do, don't leave the
court." He scored twenty, and his team won by nineteen, and he was
applauded for his courage.

By the time of the eleven o'clock news, the lead had changed completely. The next few days pressed forward with a new sense of urgency.
There was a chill on the airwaves, and we all began to feel as if we had
somehow been conned. Statter and his colleagues received death threats
for broadcasting what they had learned of the previous night, details
that suddenly seemed frighteningly intimate. All across the country, we
began to question everything we thought we'd understood about drugs
and athletes and our perceptions of celebrity. No one wanted to believe
it, but this was the new reality. There were no secrets anymore.

"Tonight," Pat Collins reported, "Prince George's County police
are suggesting it might *not* have been a heart attack."

"... and sources say police are looking for a man who goes by the name of *Tribble*."

The next day, a pair of reporters would walk out to the parking lot where Bias's leased Datsun 300ZX was still parked and they would spy white powder on the floor. The campus police impounded the car and found a baggie under the dashboard, filled with twelve grams of cocaine. Calls came in to the television stations, and a source with ties to the Maryland program spoke to Frank Herzog, and he said, *Listen, Len Bias wasn't just doing lines of cocaine. Len Bias and I did mounds of cocaine. Mounds.*

The new reality had become a litany of unanswerable questions: Who *was* Len Bias? What he had become? And equally confounding to Herzog, a question that seems incredibly innocent in retrospect, a reflection of the naïveté of the media when it came to cocaine: Where did a college athlete get the money for such extravagances? "It was awful," Herzog recalled. "But then, with everything after, you started to say, 'Yeah, what's your problem? What are you doing that we don't know about?'"

Eleven thousand people showed up the next night for a memorial service, held in the stale and sweltering air of Cole Field House. The Reverend Jesse Jackson presided, and called drugs a greater threat to the black community than the Ku Klux Klan, and then with a single hyperbolic flourish, he managed to elevate Len Bias to the realm of martyrdom. "God sometimes uses our best people to get our attention," he said. "God's only son, a good man, a young man, was crucified. Dr. Martin Luther King Jr., a good man, a young man, shot down in cold blood in the prime of his life. Mozart, Gandhi ... and others, young, gifted, strong, and militant, all taken in the prime of their lives to the drastic intervention of death.... God chose a rose ... a rose of our generation."

Outside Cole Field House, the whole case had busted wide open, and there were accusations of a cover-up, of Maryland athletes being involved in gambling rings. There were rumors that Bias had free-based, that PCP had somehow been involved; there were shots of cops crawling through the Dumpsters behind Washington Hall in search of evidence. We had to wait a week for the medical examiner, John Smialek, to issue his report, and he did it at a frenzied press conference five days after Bias's death. It was straight out of Holly-wood: Smialek sat at the front of the room, along with a member of the state's drug abuse administration, and the reporters shouted questions at him, demanding answers, demanding to understand, in plain English, what this all meant. The cocaine, Smialek said, reading from page eight of the autopsy report, had "interrupted the normal electrical control of his heartbeat, resulting in the sudden onset of seizures and cardiac arrest."

But how? Why? How much did he snort? ("I can't tell you how blood concentration would translate into blood concentration in an individual.") Was there any evidence of previous heart damage? (No.) So the cocaine killed him, period? (Yes.) Can you tell how he ingested it? ("It would be my opinion that it was snorted.") Can you tell whether he was a long-term user? ("There is no evidence of long-term use.") Could this have been his first encounter with cocaine? ("That is possible, yes.") Would you refer to it as an overdose? ("This particular concentration might not kill another individual.")

And finally: Is it as simple as here's this young guy, he signs, he goes out to celebrate, he has too much cocaine, and it *literally kills him*—it's just that simple?

Said the doctor: "That's exactly right. It's very simple."

It was a national story now, a medical story, a social story, a cultural clarion call. That evening, Peter Jennings interviewed the medical editor for *ABC News*, live on the air, and he asked what we were all thinking, about the story line that reinforced the new dominant narrative: "Do you mean to tell us that someone can die if they use it *just once?*"

Autopsy No. 86-999

Prince George's County

Leonard K. Bias

June 19, 1986

DIAGNOSIS:

1. Cocaine Intoxication

OPINION:

LEONARD K. BIAS, a 22-year-old Black male, died as a result of cocaine intoxication, which interrupted the normal electrical control of his heartbeat, resulting in the sudden onset of seizures and cardiac arrest. The blood cocaine level was 6.5 milligrams per liter. Toxicological studies for alcohol and other drugs were negative. Due to the ongoing investigation of the circumstances surrounding his death, the manner of the death is ruled UNDETERMINED at this time.

Of course, the doctor was speaking empirically and not emotionally. At some level, he could reinforce what we already knew: that the primary suspect in the death of Len Bias was now, and would always be, Len Bias himself. *It's very simple:* Len Bias caused his own demise. And yet the doctor was not equipped to comment on the system we had built around Leonard Bias, the system that had sheltered him and encouraged him and driven him to this point. He could not respond to philosophical questions. He could not speculate about anything beyond the presence of a specific drug in one man's bloodstream on the night in question. He could not discuss criminal investigations and societal implications or what all of this said about *us*. He could not address the mistakes of the institutions that had led such a man to his death (not to mention the distant possibility that Lonise Bias still clings to, that somehow Len Bias had ingested this cocaine by mistake). And so we asked ourselves: Was it somehow our fault? Were society's priorities so utterly skewed that we couldn't see the path down which we'd guided a star athlete?

What had we done?

"There was no *covering*," Lonise Bias said.

At the university, the scrutiny began immediately, and the scrutiny was relentless: Reporters from the *Post* and the *Sun* and the TV stations chased down leads daily for the next several months. A grand jury was called, and convened a few weeks later. A veteran Prince George's County prosecutor named Arthur A. "Bud" Marshall happened to be running for reelection (against a young black attorney named Alexander Williams), and what better opening was there than for Marshall to find the persons/places/things that had killed Leonard Bias, to ascertain the cause of what remained (officially, at least) UNDETERMINED? To Marshall, and to a certain segment of the public, suspects included not only Brian Tribble but the entire athletic culture at the University of Maryland. Marshall held a press conference on the day of Bias's funeral, stating that the university could not "handle its own affairs," and alleging that Driesell had sent one of his own assistant coaches to sanitize 1103 Washington Hall in the hours after Len Bias died.

And so the self-examination began: The university and its embattled chancellor, John Slaughter, reacted by launching several task forces to study the problems inherent within the system, to tamp down rumors that had now run wild, now that it seemed *everyone* was involved. *The Baltimore Sun* interviewed a track star who admitted to snorting cocaine, a football player who smoked marijuana, another football player confessing to steroid use, and a basketball player confessing to popping amphetamines after practice to keep from falling asleep while studying. It all fell under the same umbrella, since the war that had been called for by Jesse Jackson, one day after the medical examiner issued his report, was widespread and unrelenting and dated back to the presidency of Richard Nixon. "We must have a war on drugs," he said.

IV.

This is America, after all, and it does not take long for tragedy to be co-opted into a political stratagem. Still, it was a miracle of timing and geography: If it had happened elsewhere—in a lesser market, in another sport, with a lesser NBA team involved, outside of the East Coast circuit—*none* of this self-examination might have occurred. But it did . . . and it just so happened that the Speaker of the House of Representatives at the time was a Democrat named Thomas Phillip "Tip" O'Neill Jr., and Tip was an old-school Boston politico, and you can imagine how a politician with ties to both D.C. and Boston, two cities devastated by the Bias tragedy, would react the morning after such an event.

On June 20, a young lawyer for the House Judiciary Committee came in to work and could hardly believe the response. Maybe it was because of O'Neill's ties to Boston, and maybe it was because Len Bias had played his college basketball approximately ten miles from the Capitol Building, and maybe it was because the House gym had a basketball court, and maybe it was because the news reports and the medical examiners' reports could not combat the misconceptions that permitted the melding of the two major news stories of that summer: the death of Len Bias and the rise of crack cocaine. The lawyer, Eric Sterling, had heard of Len Bias and had read in the newspaper about his death, but he didn't think much more of it until he arrived at work that day and realized the entire landscape of Congress had changed over the death of a basketball player.

Overnight, America's "vulnerability" to drugs had become the seminal issue in Washington. O'Neill was thinking about the mid-term elections in November 1986; he was thinking about regaining political momentum from a popular second-term president. He was thinking about out-cowboying Reagan himself, for once. And it didn't matter that Len Bias, as far as we know, had had little or nothing to do with crack—because that summer, Len Bias was the story, and crack was the story, and to conflate them would simply be good politics, both for Reagan and for his adversaries. O'Neill thought the Democrats should take the lead on getting tough on drugs, and that meant stricter sentences for drug offenders, and it meant both Democrats and Republicans were immediately swept up in hyperbole and emotional appeals, in trying to out-tough each other, in a debate swept clean of nuance. If you proposed a bill stating drug dealers should be drawn and quartered, one congressman said, you might have a chance of getting it passed that summer. Crack had altered the media's image of a typical cocaine user from white to black, from rich to poor; in 1986, for the first time, more blacks were imprisoned than whites. Now, here was the perfect call to action, a young man of modest means on the verge of becoming rich, an athlete who had instilled pride in white and black communities, suddenly gone . . . and for no good reason.

"People were generally fat and happy," said one California congressman, asked about the mood in his district. "The one issue they talked about with emotion was drugs."

There was no time to waste: *Write me some goddamn legislation,* said O'Neill. *The Republicans beat us to it in 1984. I don't want that to happen again.*

It had officially become a nationwide scare, on par with HIV and global thermonuclear war. If it could happen to Len Bias, we began to think, maybe all the Reagan-era propaganda had been true. Maybe this really *could* happen to any of us. Calls to cocaine hotlines, especially from young users, jumped precipitously. For a moment, it seemed that perhaps one event might actually change the attitudes of an entire society. And then, just nine days after the death of Len Bias, the damndest thing happened: At ten in the morning, at a home in Sacramento, California, a scream could be heard—a scream so loud that an old man who lived next door later said it was "the kind of sound you never forget." Two houses away, a woman presumed an animal was being tortured; she scrambled to lock her doors, knocked over a table, ducked under a windowsill, and phoned the police.

Inside the house, a young football player named Don Rogers, a defensive back for the Cleveland Browns, had collapsed to the floor for no apparent reason, twenty-four hours before his wedding day. This was on Friday. Like Bias, Don Rogers was the oldest son in his family. Like Bias, Don Rogers had no known history of drug abuse. Like Bias, Don Rogers was loved, even worshipped, in his own community.

The next day, at a press conference held at almost the precise moment Don Rogers was supposed to have gotten married, the coroner's report revealed that yet another athlete had died of a heart stoppage due to a cocaine overdose. Suddenly, the death of Len Bias meant nothing (at least in terms of its effectiveness as a deterrent), and yet at the same time it meant twice as much as it had before (there were now *two* needless deaths to point to). And at the same house whence the scream had originated a day earlier, Don Rogers's own mother collapsed into the arms of her younger son, the victim of a heart attack that nearly killed her as well.

CHAPTER NINE

What a Performance!

*Bigness apparently wasn't going to be a problem in the new
era of unbridled capitalism.*

—JAMES B. STEWART, *Den of Thieves*

I.

Now, *here* was a modern-day spectacle.

In late June, at a minor-league ballpark in Memphis, an alphabet
soup of cameras (ABC, CBS, NBC, ESPN, CNN) lined up to capture
footage of the man who had made a most curious decision about his
immediate future. He swerved into the players' parking lot in his new
black Alfa Romeo (for he was *still* a millionaire, if only just barely)
and stepped into a tent that had been set up to accommodate the
crush of reporters. He apologized for being late, claiming he had lost
his hotel room key for the second time that day, and it was in moments like these—when that inherent psychic neurosis played against
his tremendous physical confidence—that Bo Jackson set himself
apart from any athlete who had come before. When he stepped up
for batting practice that day, wearing jersey No. 28, a reporter asked,
"Where's his blue ox?" And Bo obliged, playing Paul Bunyan, using
his ax to drive four balls that were "last observed approaching the
suburbs of Nashville," according to one report.

To see him in a place like this, to see "the best pure athlete in America" (according to Royals scout Ken Gonzales) confined to the purgatory of Double-A, playing the outfield for a team known as the Memphis Chicks, swatting at bugs with his glove while standing in front of an auto-parts advertisement . . . it was mercurial, it was fascinating, it was surreal. It defied logic. (And it transcended sports: Even *People* magazine sent along a reporter.) But then, Bo had always defied logic—the scouting report issued by the Royals likened him to Mickey Mantle and Roberto Clemente, and the manager of the Memphis ball club, Tommy Jones, had to scan the report several times to be sure he was reading it correctly.

Everyone wanted to read something into Bo's decision to play baseball instead of football. The psychology was captivating and didn't fit in with our presumptions about 1980s athletes: How could anyone pass up *all that money*? There was still an underlying feeling, at least among reporters, that this was some kind of stunt—that eventually, Bo would return to football, that his impatience would get the best of him, that he just wasn't meant to be here, that even the best pure athlete in America could not learn to hit a curveball on a whim. Perhaps, thought *Sports Illustrated*'s Douglas Looney, Bo merely wanted to prove he could do something beyond the thing that he was most known for, in the same way Joe Namath had once imagined himself an actor.

But at least for the moment, Bo would give away nothing about returning to football. He ducked all questions about it (a few months down the road, when the speculation heightened, Bo taped a sign over his locker: DON'T BE STUPID. NO FOOTBALL QUESTIONS PLEASE). He insisted that the focus remain on baseball. He said publicly that he wished to be treated like any other minor-leaguer on any other team, and on that first night, in front of three hundred reporters and seven thousand fans (twice the normal attendance) chanting, *Bo! Bo! Bo!*, he singled to center field in his first at-bat. He didn't bother to ask for the ball, he said, because "my trophy case is already full."

Of course, he *wasn't* like every other minor-leaguer. He was, in fact, unlike any other minor-leaguer who ever lived ("I can't come up with anybody," said the president of the National Association of Professional Leagues), and nobody wanted to mess with him, for fear of screwing up the finished product. Even the Royals minor-league hitting instructor joked that if he tinkered too much with Bo's swing, he'd be tossed in the river.

In another time, perhaps Bo could have hidden away in a place like this, could have developed his tools in relative peace, but this was the eighties, and there were cameras in every city, and there were wire services transmitting Bo's nightly statistics to every newspaper in America. And it did not start well: He had two hits in his first thirty-one at-bats and four in his first forty-two, with twenty-one strikeouts and two errors in center field. He was raw; he was still learning, struggling to hit any pitch that actually *moved* on its way to home plate, and the directive from Kansas City was simply to let him find himself, without any intrusions. For George Lapides, the general manager of the Memphis Chicks, his own interpretation of the directive was simple: *Treat him like everyone else, but also give him whatever he wants.* He put up Bo's mother in the best hotel in town, on the team's dime. And on the night of Bo's first road trip of the season, six hours by bus from Memphis to Chattanooga on the heels of a night game *(Welcome to the minor leagues, kid!),* Lapides took a midnight phone call from a stuttering superstar. And Bo, fighting terribly to finish his words, said, *I—I could not get on the bus.*

It took a moment for Lapides to process what Bo was saying. And then Bo said, *I—I'm going to have to fly to Chattanooga.* Lapides covered for him. He told the media Bo had stayed behind to shoot television commercials for the team, and Bo drove his Alfa Romeo to

Lapides's house and stored it in his garage until the road trip was over. So much, the GM thought, for a lack of special treatment.

Still, even Lapides, whose relationship with Bo quickly soured, admitted that most of his star player's transgressions were minor, in large part because Bo was incredibly cautious about his public persona—tied, as it was, to his financial future as a pitchman for Nike, Inc. Bo claimed to have lost his patience with Lapides only when the GM asked him for one too many signatures, and then asked him to submit to an interview with a high-school-aged friend of his son (Lapides says he doesn't know what set Bo off about him). In fact, Bo asked two of his minor-league teammates to be in his wedding (though Lapides said one of those two men told him that Bo was "damn near insufferable"). But both the GM and the superstar, amid all their little clashes, knew the truth: Bo never really fit in Memphis as a Chick. He was just too *big* for the place. This town already had its Elvis; they didn't need another.

Later that summer, Bo started hitting, just when everyone began wondering if he ever would. His batting average steadily rose, up toward .300, and he continued to defy logic and common sense: In a game against Greenville, Bo hit the longest home run Lapides had ever seen—over the lightbulb second from the left on the standard above the left-field fence. Lapides swears one of his maintenance people measured it, and it soared approximately *645 feet* from home plate, then rolled fifty more before coming to a stop against a wire fence.

In September, Bo was promoted to the major leagues, to the big club in Kansas City. He left Memphis without saying good-bye, without even telling his manager; he stopped on the way to visit with his wife and his newborn son. The Royals were then the defending World Champions, and Bo settled right in to a clubhouse of All-Stars: George Brett, Mark Gubicza, Bret Saberhagen. In his first major-league at-bat against Steve Carlton, a lock for the Hall of Fame, Bo sat on a hanging curveball and drove it into the left-field stands: It was, just barely, a foul ball. So Bo, who had already rounded second, came back to home plate and hit a chopper between first and second base, and beat it out for a base hit. A few days later, he went four-for-five with four infield hits, and a few days after that, he hit his first home run—it carried 475 feet to left-center field, one of the longest in the history of Royals Stadium. He was a leadoff hitter and a cleanup hitter and a cultural phenomenon, and yet he was still learning: During that month in the majors, he hit .207.

At Nike, Inc., amid the currents of fear about the company's future, amid Phil Knight's fury over the fact that they were paying a hundred thousand dollars that summer to a Memphis *Chick* . . . one of the men who had chased after Bo on the company's behalf, Bill Frishette, saw something happening. This investment, he wrote in an internal memo after visiting Bo during his months in Memphis, would pay off eventually. Frishette understood: Bo would adapt physically (because he always did). His headstrong self-interest—and his stubborn refusal to compromise, to give in to public expectations—fit the ethos of a new generation. Bo *knew* what he was doing, even then. "His talent combined with his decision to walk away from a sure million," Frishette wrote, "will make the 'Bo Jackson Story' a sports legend of the eighties."

II.

Of course, none of this would have happened were it not for the convergence of a filmmaker and an adman. The adman was a sly little fellow who had taken seven years to graduate from the University of Washington (earning three separate degrees in philosophy, history, and communications), who had grown up on *Mad* magazine and *Monty Python* and had fallen into the ad business for lack of a better idea. The filmmaker was named Spike Lee, and he will come into the picture momentarily. But first, the adman: In 1984, Jim Riswold left his hometown of Seattle and moved to Portland to take a job at a small agency called Wieden and Kennedy, and not long after Riswold arrived, Wieden and Kennedy got the contract from another local business, Nike, Inc., to promote their young basketball star, Michael Jordan.

Up to then, the Jordan commercials (crafted by a New York agency, Chiat/Day) had focused exclusively on Jordan's basketball skills, on his physical beauty. Such was the nature of the business when it came to athletes and commercials, but Riswold wanted to get beyond that, to get at the Jordan persona, to somehow render this mythological figure as a human being.

"I mean, ESPN was doing half the selling job for you," Riswold said. "Why repeat what you could see on ESPN? Before this, that's what Nike ads were—they were highlight films. But these things with Michael, and later Bo, made Nike a part of the popular culture."

That summer, while shooting a commercial in Los Angeles, Riswold and his executive producer went to see a thoroughly forgettable Rob Lowe–Demi Moore vehicle called *About Last Night,* but it was the trailer for *another* movie that caught his eye: *She's Gotta Have It,* by Spike Lee. The movie, shot for $175,000, came out in August, and one of its main characters was Mars Blackmon, a bike messenger so obsessed with his Air Jordan shoes that he refused to take them off even when he made love. So Jim Riswold called Spike Lee and enlisted his help in humanizing Michael Jordan. It took eighteen months after the release of the movie for the vision to come together, but the connections made that summer would set the tone for everything that came after: There was Spike dressed as Mars in those thick black glasses and that ridiculously huge gold MARS chain, hanging on the rim, standing on Michael Jordan's shoulders, rhapsodizing: *Do you know who the best player in the game is? Me, Mars Blackmon. And I'm way above the rim, demonstrating some serious hang time. . . . Do you*

know how I get up for my game? Doyouknowdoyouknowdoyouknow?
That's right. Air Jordan, Air Jordan, Air Jordan.

And Jordan does not even have to say anything. He leaves Mars
hanging on the rim, he dunks, he grins, and we cut to the Air Jordan
logo.

And a campaign was born: *Money, it's gotta be the shoes!*

But something else was also birthed with that ad, not to mention
the dozens that came after, flooding the airwaves in the latter half of
the 1980s, supplementing our nightly dose of *SportsCenter,* accomplishing the nifty trick of cutting these men down to our size while
simultaneously building them up (and cutting race out of the equa-
tion almost entirely)—hence, selling product. "In the modern entertainment culture, in a society obsessed with celebrity, deeds performed
on celluloid often seemed to become substitutes for reality," David
Halberstam wrote. "The commercials were brief, but there were so
many of them and they were done with such talent and charm that
they formed an ongoing story. . . . So it was that an American icon
was born."

The ads were irreverent, and they were steeped in irony, and Riswold believes they were the kind of spots Nike could *never* get away
with now that they are a conglomerate. But back then, this company
was searching for anything that would work, for anything that would
connect to this new generation, to those of us who had been raised
on television and all the mythos that surrounded it. That Jordan
could back up this narrative on the court—that he could pour in
sixty-three points in a single afternoon against one of the best teams
in basketball history—only made his commercial self seem that much
more authentic. He made the impossible seem possible, and if he
could do that merely by playing one sport, it was not hard, a short
time later, for the adman to imagine what Bo Jackson could do by
mastering two of them.

III.

It is difficult to pinpoint exactly when Bo's mind officially turned back to football. Perhaps in October, when the weather turned, when the baseball season ended, when the leaves changed color, when his instincts kicked in and told him he *should* be donning pads. More likely, despite his public pronouncements that he was entirely focused on baseball, he had never turned away from football at all. His rights still belonged to Tampa Bay, and so he could not act on it yet, but that feeling . . . that he should be at football practice right now, as much as he despised it . . . was inescapable. "That's what I'd done all my life," he said years later. "I did it in elementary school, I did it in junior high, I did it in high school, I did it in college. I know—the things I'm good at, I'm *good at*."

That summer, the National Football League seemed weakened and uncertain of its future; the Bears and their antics and their attendant publicity had provided a needed boost, but a lengthy story in the August edition of *Fortune* (IT'S 4TH & 10—THE NFL NEEDS THE LONG BOMB) detailed the league's problem with an impending television contract, with "monster salary demands," with the drug issues that had continued on into '86, including the post–Super Bowl claim by Patriots management that several of the same players who had been carved up by the Bears in New Orleans were dealing with substance abuse problems. And then there were the proceedings taking place in Room 318 of the federal courthouse in Manhattan, with six jurors—five women, one man—prepared to determine the future of the game itself.

This was the long-awaited antitrust case of the United States Football League against the National Football League, in which the USFL accused the NFL of conspiring to keep their league off television and generally encouraging its failure in order to preserve their monopoly. It was a case of millionaires suing millionaires; there was no little guy. The underlying issues were complex, but the hyperbole was plentiful: The attorney for the USFL, Harvey Myerson, wore tailored suits with silk handkerchiefs and repeatedly evoked Franz Kafka in his opening arguments to the jury. For eleven weeks, Myerson pranced about the courtroom, sparring with witnesses, speaking in his own flamboyant lexicon, portraying the NFL as a corporate behemoth and the USFL as the David to the NFL's Goliath. He presented evidence of a "smoking gun," a seminar held in February 1984, at which a Harvard Business School professor named Michael Porter declared that the NFL was in the midst of guerilla warfare with the USFL and proposed strategies for vanquishing the enemy. This, according to Myerson, was evidence of a grand conspiracy, and he even elicited testimony from one of the NFL's own: Al Davis, owner of the Raiders, and a perpetual malcontent, who complained that league officials had conspired to destroy the USFL's Oakland franchise. At one point, called to testify for the USFL, Howard Cosell delivered a rambling and bombastic four-hour testimony that alluded to the Iranian Hostage Crisis, Michael Jackson's Victory Tour, the Reagan administration, two of his own books, Coca-Cola's recent attempt to acquire Dr Pepper, and an honor he'd been given by the National Order of the Leather Helmet. ("What a performance!" Cosell exclaimed to a reporter as he exited the courtroom.)

And then there was Donald Trump.

Trump . . . the most skilled self-promoter and publicity seeker of the era, a man who courted enemies and the attendant press these feuds brought to him, a man who had built his empire with money acquired from his father, a man whose portfolio of garish properties—a Fifth Avenue condominium with pink marble walls, a casino, a twenty-nine-million-dollar yacht with gold-plated bathroom fixtures—exemplified eighties immoderation. In 1983, Trump bought in to the USFL, purchasing a struggling franchise known as the New Jersey Generals, and immediately, he began thinking ahead, to the day when the USFL could move its schedule from the spring to the fall, to the day when it could go head-to-head with the NFL and its considerable television revenue. It was, he later said, a "long shot, a lark that I could afford to take." This, to Trump, was the Art of the Deal (later the title of his first book, which became a best seller "partly because of Trump's own purchases" of it, according to *Time*); at his first owners' meeting, a month after he purchased the Generals, he laid out his strategy and urged his fellow owners to fight to sign as many as top players as they could. Trump inherited a star running back in Herschel Walker, the oversized and yet ultimately unfulfilling legend out of Georgia, and he would steal away Doug Flutie, the 1984 Heisman Trophy winner out of Boston College, a diminutive and charismatic quarterback whose height (he was five feet nine) seemed to inhibit his potential. "Doug Flutie," Trump said, "had the potential to be the USFL's Joe Namath," and when Flutie played well, Trump wrote a letter to the USFL's commissioner, declaring that because of Flutie's promotional value to the league, the cost of his contract should be shared league-wide. The idea was shot down, but what did it hurt to ask? This was the Art of the Deal.

There were so many showmen present that the courtroom could barely contain them all. Rozelle was not immune to hyperbole either; he testified that he had fallen physically ill—as in, *sick to his stomach*—when he'd gotten word about Porter's presentation to the NFL owners. Trump claimed that Rozelle had told him he'd have an opportunity to own an NFL franchise in New York if the USFL kept playing in the spring rather than the fall, and if they promised not to bring a lawsuit. Rozelle claimed that Trump had asked him for ownership of an NFL expansion franchise in New York, and that if he got one, he would sell the Generals to "some stiff." The NFL's attorney, Frank Rothman, remained a voice of calm and assurance—even as Cosell, once Rothman's client, questioned his intelligence on the stand—and he argued that Porter's combative recommendations to the owners had never been actually implemented, and that the USFL was moving its schedule to the fall only in order to force a settlement. In the end, even Trump admitted that Myerson's histrionics—*"Nail 'em!"* he shouted during closing arguments. *"That's what this country is looking for you to do!"*—may have overwhelmed the jury. How could any organization that had *Donald Trump* on its side possibly be considered an underdog?

In late July, on the day the jury reached a verdict, Pete Rozelle ate lunch at a Chinese restaurant, then climbed into the back of his car with the NFL's vice president of programming, Val Pinchbeck. On the radio, they heard the headline:

The United States Football League won its court case against the NFL. Details to come. . . .

Whatever damages the USFL was awarded would be tripled, according to antitrust law. They braced for the worst. For a moment, Pinchbeck thought Rozelle might have a heart attack. And then the news came back on, and Rozelle ordered his driver to bring him down to the courthouse, to stand outside the room where, just a few hours earlier, the forewoman of the jury had stood and announced the damages the NFL would be forced to pay out. . . .

"One dollar," she said, and with that, the game that had ruled as the American pastime since the days of Namath was *back,* and despite an ugly strike the next year, it would soon be more popular than ever. The same league that had lost the last four Heisman Trophy winners—either to the USFL or, in Bo Jackson's case, to a rival sport—had found stability in that courtroom. Within months, the USFL would go under, submarined by a yearning for the next big deal, by its payout of larger and larger salaries . . . and the NFL would sign its first-ever television deal with a cable network, ESPN. Working together, they would both become unimaginably huge.

Meanwhile, the same rogue owner who had testified against his colleagues in court would soon take yet another outrageous chance,

drafting the best pure athlete in America despite all the pronouncements that he was concentrating solely on baseball. Al Davis gambled,
which made sense, because only someone as autonomous as Al Davis
could understand someone like Bo Jackson, whose entire rationale
for playing football was that he didn't want to "cheat myself out of
some fun," who didn't want to regret in twenty years that he'd for-
gone a once-in-a-lifetime opportunity to set himself apart from anyone who had come before him. He would risk his longevity, and he
would inevitably shorten his career and risk his chances at greatness
in either sport—but Bo didn't care about such things. Bo wanted
what he wanted, and Bo just wanted to have fun.

The Raiders chose Bo in the seventh round, with the 183rd pick
of the 1987 NFL draft, throwing the bones on the notion that a young
man with his gifts, in this day and age, could accomplish everything
at once.

CHAPTER TEN

Money Days

You don't understand. The wife expects a new Jaguar every
year, and the three houses aren't paid for yet.

— ANONYMOUS MERRILL LYNCH EMPLOYEE,
AS QUOTED BY *Newsweek,* OCTOBER 1987

I.

In August, the traveling circus known as the Chicago Bears shoved
off to London for an exhibition game against the Dallas Cowboys.
Billed as "American Bowl '86," this was a newfangled invention, an
opportunity for the NFL to carry its post-USFL mojo over to a country that had become tangled up in the soap opera of American football. In fact, England had become fascinated largely because of the
two men Rick Telander referred to, in *Sports Illustrated,* as our nation's "weirdest sports duet."

The Fridge, having already appeared in a commercial for a British supermarket, was the hottest U.S. import since the Big Mac. And
the other half of this dynamic duo showed up at the airport in a cam-
ouflage suit, dressed to play his part in an intercontinental burlesque
show. Here was the Punky QB, swaggering through the halls of
O'Hare, carrying a plastic cup of beer and gnawing on a massive cigar, and what could be more representative of the American attitude

in the summer of '86 than this, a cinematic snapshot worthy of a Stallone film?

That day marked the end of a tumultuous off-season for Jim Mc-Mahon . . . months spent diddling around in celebrity golf tournaments and filming commercials and making token public appearances for amounts of cash so absurd that he began to regard it all as Monopoly money. The man and his look had become the representation of an ideal. Outrageous individualism was the hot new thing: *Everyone* was doing it. At the University of Georgia, members of the baseball team began celebrating home runs by butting heads. "Jim McMahon must've inspired us," one of them said.

In the gossip pages, Liz Smith reported that McMahon had dinner at Calvin Klein's apartment in Manhattan. Sunglasses and headbands—peddled by entities as diverse as the Chicago White Sox and the Jane Austen Society—became the must-have accessories of the summer; even Ditka wore a headband when he threw out the first pitch at the White Sox opener in April. McMahon posed for *Town & Country* in a Calvin Klein tuxedo. He posed (clothed, sans sunglasses) for *Playboy.* He headlined the Nabisco Dinah Shore Pro-Am, ahead of a former president (Gerald Ford), a recording legend (Perry Como), and several dozen Hall of Famers (including Joe DiMaggio). He filmed an ad for Taco Bell (he skipped out of a team meeting to shoot it, and met with Bruce Willis to pick up acting tips), and he did another for Honda scooters, part of a rogue campaign featuring well-known iconoclasts—Lou Reed, Sandra Bernhard—that was the brainchild of the same Portland adman, Jim Riswold at Wieden and Kennedy, who would soon connect with Spike Lee and Michael Jordan and Bo Jackson. Five secretaries offered McMahon fifteen thousand dollars just to have lunch with them. He signed five thousand photographs at a shopping mall in Kokomo, Indiana. He hosted the opening of a Hard Rock Cafe in Chicago, mingling with Robert Palmer and Oprah. He attended a roast in his honor at Caesars Palace. He posed for a promotional poster (*Mad Mac: Grid Warrior*) dressed in black leather and accompanied by a live bear.

He sure as hell wasn't in Utah anymore.

One lazy afternoon in March, McMahon took a call from his agent, Steve Zucker—The Fridge had canceled his appearance at a company cocktail party, and they needed a last-minute replacement. They were offering ten thousand dollars for an hour's work standing around, telling stories. McMahon said he wasn't interested; he was going to dinner with his wife. A couple of minutes later, Zucker called back: They were up to fifteen. McMahon told his agent to tell them to stick it.

And then Zucker called again. They were offering twenty. They had also offered to send a limo to pick him up and to drop him off at the restaurant, where he would be able to meet his wife in time for their eight o'clock reservation. So it went, McMahon twenty grand richer merely for being himself in a nation all too eager to spend the money it had accumulated in this gilded age. In those first few months after the Super Bowl, he took in almost a million dollars and still said no to dozens of other opportunities, including a *Miami Vice* appearance (because they wouldn't take his linemen, Becker and Van Horne, to appear with him) and a four-hundred-thousand-dollar movie deal (because it would suck up five weeks of golf in the off-season). *Advertising Age* had written, in the days after the Super Bowl, that McMahon's "shades-and-swagger act did him more harm than good with corporate America," but *Ad Age* (which later named The Fridge its Star Presenter of the Year, the first athlete to take the honor since O. J. Simpson) did not see the outline of the future—the notion that, in the modern age, controversy and salesmanship were not mutually exclusive concepts.

"I made more in endorsements than I did in football," McMahon said. "That kept me afloat. But it was a pain in the ass. How does it take you nine damn hours to do a thirty-second commercial?"

Still, as much as McMahon complained about the actual labor, he needed to maintain his cultural relevance long enough to stick to his plan of never having to work a real job for the remainder of his life. He had made it there before the '86 season even began—in June, he told one reporter he'd never have to work another day if he didn't feel like it, that he'd probably sit around and watch *M*A*S*H* all day long, if he could get away with it.

He blamed the media for fanning his image, for turning him into a caricature, and yet he could not help himself. In London, he showed up at a trendy West End club wearing a black leather jacket and sunglasses, his hair profusely gelled and spiked; in an attempt to humor the photographers following him, he hoisted a pair of women onto his shoulders. The only thing that kept him from the front page of every tabloid in the UK was the presence of The Fridge, whose girth was a source of endless fascination among the Brits. In England, soccer's popularity had been derailed by waves of hooliganism, and "American football" had emerged, if only for the moment, as a viable alternative, largely because of the Bears and their antics. Twelve million Britons stayed up until the middle of the night to watch the Super Bowl; ratings for a Sunday-night NFL highlight show on the BBC's Channel 4 had steadily ascended, mostly due to the presence of this enormous kitchen appliance and his rebel sidekick. It was like the importation of a bad network TV show.

The Fridge's appeal was simple: He was a walking giant, a physical curiosity, and for the tabloids, he was that globular manifestation of American excess. A story circulated that The Fridge practiced by running into (and through) walls. Because of his size, because he endorsed British chocolate bars and cereal packets—spots that soccer players could no longer get, due to the sullied reputation of their sport—The Fridge was easily the most recognizable football player in England (decades later, that is still the case). He was dragged along reluctantly into the material world by his own wife: While in London,

Sherry Perry posed sprawled on a bed for a British tabloid (FRIDGE IS RED HOT IN BED, SAYS WIFE!); later, she reportedly bought a pair of matching Mercedes with engraved door handles. It seemed that The Fridge was simply being swept along in this wave, that he was an innocent here, a genial fat man with a gap-toothed smile who had little idea what he'd become.

McMahon's overseas appeal was more complex. After a week of performance art at the Super Bowl, he truly had become the representative of the American id, the Ambassador of Arrogance. *Your Outrageousness,* Walter Payton dubbed him, upon their excursion to London. Even kids in England had taken to wearing headbands. When McMahon stepped off that plane at Heathrow, still dressed in his camos, chomping on his cigar, yearning for a beer to soothe his jet lag and allow him to forget how far from home he was—it was only then, wrote the *Washington Post,* "that the fans knew the real Americans had arrived."

The game was secondary to the presentation and to the trappings of celebrity—Phil Collins showed up at practice, and several players attended a party hosted by the Bee Gees—but the game was sold out nonetheless, and eighty thousand largely confused fans stood in a steady downpour and took in a sport they did not quite understand, if only because the men playing it seemed to represent something about America itself. They yelped at the Dallas Cowboy cheerleaders, screamed at The Fridge as he plowed one yard into the end zone for yet another touchdown, howled at a streaker who zipped across the Wembley turf in the fourth quarter, and cheered for McMahon, who had co-opted the British punk aesthetic in a distinctly American fashion.

The Bears won, 17–6. McMahon, belly weighed down from an off-season spent curling twelve-ounce Mooseheads, played two series. On the second one, he tweaked his hip flexor. The only thing he did more effectively than pissing people off was finding a way to hurt himself in the process.

II.

But then, it was only a matter of time before the sideshow unraveled. The petty jealousies that had emerged in the locker room after the Super Bowl—in that postgame tussle over championship hats—had carried over into the off-season. It was every man for himself, and on a team that felt perpetually underpaid and disrespected by its own management, there was reason to grasp for whatever they could get. McMahon led the charge; by saying what no one else could get away with saying, he made it acceptable. Around the locker room, Mondays and Tuesdays became known as "money days," littered with opportunities for Rotary Club speeches and in-store autograph sessions. Dan Hampton and Steve McMichael, two defensive stars, feuded over an appearance in a tire ad starring The Fridge. "Our cause," said Kurt Becker, McMahon's roommate, "got kind of convoluted."

Never, for any team, in any sport, had there been a moment quite like this one. It was fraught with commercial potential, and not just for McMahon and The Fridge: A backup tight end was making fifteen hundred dollars an appearance on the banquet circuit, and by July, he'd had twenty-five engagements. On an off-season Caribbean cruise, Shaun Gayle, a defensive back, and Emery Moorehead, a tight end, only had to walk on deck to draw a swarm of fans. They had become something more than a football team; they were now folded into the popular culture. In April, The Fridge and offensive lineman Jimbo Covert appeared at Wrestlemania II, contributing to yet another rebirth in the cyclical life of professional wrestling. In San Diego, an indoor soccer team recorded a knockoff of "The Super Bowl Shuffle," with a number of equally mindless rip-offs soon to follow.

It was all so much, and it spilled over into the unlikeliest of places: At baby showers for team members' wives, a two-hundred-dollar stroller was no longer an untoward gift. Everyone began competing, in terms of conspicuous consumption. "It was like *Wheel of Fortune*," said Cathy Butler, wife of the kicker Kevin Butler. "'Big money, big money.' There was such materialistic competition. . . . Guys were getting dealer cars. . . . Who has the bigger house? Who's got the newer Mercedes? It was like a monster."

There was no one to control it, because even Ditka had gotten tangled up in the material opportunities of the moment. He was a celebrity, too, marketing his derangement and forming his own cult of personality and writing his autobiography (with the aid of the *Tribune*'s Don Pierson); he had lent his name to a popular restaurant and had commercials running on multiple channels within the confines of metro Chicago. In Platteville, the Bears convened for training camp, fully conscious of the fact that they were still the most talented team in football, that they could only derail themselves, and that they were on the verge of doing quite a job of it.

Ditka had given them golf shirts during minicamp in the spring, embroidered with a motto: ARE YOU SATISFIED? The answer, for the most part, seemed to be in the affirmative. The Bears—or at least some of them—spent training camp in Platteville dodging the crowds and frequenting the local taverns, coupling with groupies atop pool tables, receiving oral sex in the parking lot, and sliding oiled-up women down the lanes of a local bowling alley in a team-bonding exercise. McMahon, who immediately chopped the sleeves off his ARE YOU SATISFIED? shirt, cut a roly-poly figure of 212 pounds by the time training camp arrived (he had taken to wearing pants with elastic waistbands on the golf course). Most nights, he led the charge to the bars. Ditka had called him in and asked him to become more of a leader. McMahon didn't know what the hell *that* was supposed to mean. He considered beer to be a key component of his existence, and he figured he had weeks to prepare himself for the regular season. He would run his way back into shape soon enough. Except his body was not so forgiving, and McMahon's hip soon became a serious problem, and this only set off Ditka further.

So began the recycling of past grievances, the coach griping about his fat quarterback and the quarterback insisting he didn't have any reason to even *speak* to his coach anymore, and maybe he wouldn't speak to the media, either, if they kept buying in to Ditka's company line. McMahon was convinced that his being out of shape had nothing to do with his inherent fragility.

> DITKA: He's full of it.
> McMAHON: He says a lot of things nobody cares about.
> DITKA: If the whole thing is to pout anytime you disagree with somebody, forget it.
> McMAHON: He knows I'm hurt. I'm a little bit overweight. More weight is more padding, right?

But there was something stale about the feud this time around. Ditka versus McMahon was no longer fresh, no longer curious: Both sides were negligent, McMahon for being McMahon, and Ditka for being tone-deaf in terms of handling the ego of the contemporary quarterback. In this new age, the cycle spun faster, and it worked against a team like the Bears, a team that had risen so fast and had become so pervasive and had so fully embraced its self-image. The difficulty in forming a dynasty was now confounded by marketing and popular culture. "The inability of teams to get the same incentive every year" made it nearly impossible to win anything more than once, said the Cowboys' Tom Landry, Ditka's old-school mentor. "It was interesting to me to read about The Refrigerator . . . [and how McMahon] is set for life. You want to repeat, but you don't want to pay the price to do it."

The new season began, and McMahon published his autobiography, written with the *Tribune*'s Bob Verdi. It spent twenty-one weeks on the best-seller list and cataloged a litany of complaints against Bears management, and against the team's president, Michael Mc-

Caskey. "Can you imagine a bunch of players sitting around the night they win the Super Bowl and talking about how much they'd like to be traded?" McMahon wrote.

They opened the regular season against the Cleveland Browns, and they won 41–31, but in the midst of an on-field assault, McMahon landed awkwardly on his right shoulder, his throwing shoulder. He could feel something popping in and out all day long, and he re-aggravated it while trying to prevent one of his children from falling down the stairs later that evening. He sat out one game, and then another, and then he took a shot of painkillers and played in three straight blowout wins, the defense carrying them on sheer momentum, Ditka and McMahon going back and forth to try to assuage the tension. And even as they continued to win, even as they went 6–0 for the second consecutive season, you could feel the moment slipping away. "I think," one player said, "we're getting a little oversaturated by hearing about ourselves."

McMahon couldn't figure out what was going on with his shoulder—it hurt, and then it didn't hurt, and the doctors told him the joint he'd messed up initially was healed, but something wasn't right. It still clicked when he moved it, and the clicking brought on pain. And on top of that, he bruised his kidney and once again found himself urinating blood. The status quo was increasingly unsustainable. The rebel quarterback was coming apart at the seams.

III.

And yet it was clear that the Bears had already put their stamp on the cultural landscape: In April, on the second day of the baseball season, the New York Mets recorded a rap record called "Get Metsmerized." It was virtually unlistenable, not to mention an utter commercial failure, perhaps the worst incarnation to date of the regrettable genre "The Super Bowl Shuffle" had inspired, but nevertheless the point had been made: The Mets embraced the self-aggrandizing ethic of Ivan Boesky and Wall Street as well as the ethic of McMahon—they were, according to pitcher Bob Ojeda, "a bunch of vile fuckers." As could be expected of a team that had recorded a song celebrating its own success one game into the season, they were also unapologetic; they won their division by twenty-one and a half games, and all season long, they partied on charter planes and in nightclubs and popped amphetamines in the clubhouse. Their two best young players, Daryl Strawberry and Dwight Gooden, would soon succumb to cocaine addiction, and their first baseman, Keith Hernandez, was still recovering from his own long dalliance with cocaine, revealed during the Pittsburgh drug trials the previous fall. Borne entirely upon a wave of arrogance, the Mets won the National League pennant in a tense six-game series against the Houston Astros, then, aided by perhaps the most horrible and ego-crushing mistake in modern history—a ball trickling through the legs of the Red Sox's aging first baseman, Bill Buckner—the Mets went on to win the World Series in seven games.

Looking back, it is not hard see that baseball would never be quite the same afterward, that one of the greatest postseasons of all time would be remembered as much for the characters it eventually destroyed as for the myths it created. It was not just Buckner; it was Gooden and Strawberry, who never did live up to their potential, their careers marred by cocaine; it was Donnie Moore, the California Angels pitcher who gave up a game-winning home run in the American League Championship Series and eventually committed suicide; and it was Roger Clemens, the intense Red Sox rookie who had struck out twenty batters in a game earlier that season, whose career would bridge decades of scandal and heartbreak and greed and steroid use in a sport whose commissioner had stated, after the revelations in that Pittsburgh courthouse, that baseball's drug problems were a thing of the past.

Two decades later, as baseball blundered through another series of drug-related scandals (this time, steroids), the judge who had presided in Pittsburgh, Gustave Diamond, marveled at the naïveté he had seen displayed in his courtroom, and at the propensity for men to continually give in to their worst instincts—at their ability to sabotage the bodies he referred to as "God-given machines."

And life goes on, he said.

And those Mets, those impeccably gifted and swaggering Mets, never won another World Series.

IV.

In a way, the height of the McMahon craze ended where it began: On October 19, the Bears went to play at Minnesota, just as they'd done a year earlier. They were undefeated, and McMahon, with the bad shoulder, was declining to practice but still intimating that he could play. And Ditka was refusing to play McMahon if he did not see himself fit enough to practice. Everything had changed, and yet nothing had changed. It was a rerun, the same argument that had triggered this cultural extravaganza a year ago in the week before the exact same game, except this time two things were different: Ditka was ever more determined to get his way, and McMahon was genuinely injured.

Ditka had started McMahon at the last minute the week before, and the quarterback had struggled through an ugly victory over Houston, and Ditka insisted this time that he wouldn't do it again. He was the coach, and he had to draw the line somewhere. And so, against the advice of many in the Bears hierarchy, he began angling to sign another quarterback in addition to the three the Bears already had (McMahon, Fuller, and Mike Tomczak). As was Ditka's tendency, he had become fixated on one quarterback in particular—a five-feet-nine signal-caller, a refugee from the USFL who had the potential to work miracles and the potential to flop. Ditka wanted Doug Flutie.

Flutie was an innocent in this psychodrama, used by the coach as his next project now that The Fridge had graduated into the cultural elite, and used by McMahon as a foil. Flutie was trapped in the midst of the most famous squabble in Chicago since Al Capone versus Bugs Moran. "He never had a chance," Don Pierson said.

What, McMahon wondered, did they need with this Oompa Loompa when they already *had* three quarterbacks? Why did Ditka feel the need to screw with the chemistry of an undefeated team? Why not sign another wide receiver? Three days before the Minnesota game, the Bears made it official—Flutie was one of them now. McMahon showed up at practice wearing a red jersey with the number Flutie had worn at Boston College, 22. Ditka ignored him, just as he had ignored several members of the Bears front office in insisting upon signing Flutie in the first place. This was *his* team, and this was *his* call.

Flutie carried a reputation as a clutch player from his days at Boston College—like McMahon, he had become famous for throwing a Hail Mary, this one a last-second bomb that defeated the University of Miami—and yet he was also the All-American boy, handsome and genial and Catholic, with big brown eyes and an inherent respect for the establishment. Ditka, reluctant to berate his newest acquisition, took to calling him Bambi and invited him to Thanksgiving dinner at his home.

Bambi? Thanksgiving dinner?

In that way, Flutie came to represent everything McMahon was not. "I admire him for standing up and saying what he feels," Flutie had told *Ad Age* in February, asked about the McMahon phenomenon. "This is something I would like to do every now and then, but I guess I'm a little afraid of the ramifications. In Jim's case, I don't think he cares."

And it was true: Unlike Flutie, McMahon didn't bother with such outmoded concepts as tact and deference. If Ditka was going to screw with him like this, he was going to screw with Ditka right back. He went straight to the media, questioning Ditka's loyalty and questioning the effect Flutie's presence would have on the locker room. But it was hard to know what was real and what wasn't anymore. Were the insecurities of McMahon's youth, and the patterns of his on-again, off-again relationship with his father, resurfacing in his relationship with Ditka? Was this a predictable reaction from someone who had grown accustomed to being the center of attention in this town? Or was McMahon voicing legitimate concerns for a team that had become used to taking its cues from him?

"What we are seeing here," wrote the *Tribune*'s Bernie Lincicome of McMahon, "is outright, naked envy."

Either way, many of his teammates remained on his side. *What's this fucking Flutie shit?* one of McMahon's linemen, Keith Van Horne, asked Ditka upon learning of the signing.

That Sunday at the Metrodome, the Vikings gave away headbands to their fans; their cheerleaders wore headbands and sunglasses, "courtesy of Jim McMahon enterprises." And the CEO of this cult of personality sat on his helmet on the sideline, as far removed from Ditka as he could possibly be, and watched in silence as his team lost, 23–7. In the same building where he'd worked miracles, he could do nothing but pout and wonder what had happened to the empire he believed was rightfully his.

And then it got worse, so that even as the Bears continued to win, you could feel their spirit draining away. They had become emotionally dependent upon McMahon, and that in itself was an unsustainable situation, for McMahon's strength as a leader (not to mention as a commercial pitchman) was the fact that he didn't embody the traditional characteristics of a leader, that he was self-interested and driven by spontaneity and conflict. Every hero since Achilles has been flawed, and what made McMahon unique, Rick Telander noted, was that his flaw was also his strength: He was uncontrollable.

The Bears finished the regular season as the unhappiest 14–2 team in NFL history, and McMahon's absence had everything to do with it. After the Minnesota loss, Ditka called a team meeting, and Hampton went after McMahon, questioning the nature of his shoulder injury, questioning whether he was even hurt at all. Ditka had the same thoughts. It was a legitimate complaint, as no one seemed to know how hurt McMahon was, including McMahon himself. Still, given his behavior, he had set himself up for this. All he could do was keep on insisting that he really *was* hurt; he now says that the team's trainers were telling members of the defense that he wasn't hurt at all, which led to charges that he was faking the whole thing, that he had stopped caring, that he'd rather be playing golf and guffawing in a lounge chair at the antics of Hawkeye Pierce. "I shouldn't have played after the first game," he said. "But I tried to play for ten more weeks, and I played six games, and we won all six."

So he kept going, raging all the way until the end. He didn't want to cede his role to anyone . . . let alone Doug Flutie, Ditka's newest pet. Because McMahon didn't welcome Flutie to Chicago, no one in the Bears locker room welcomed Flutie, who was continually mocked for his size; one day, when the team ordered pizza for lunch, they ordered a personal pan pizza especially for Flutie. McMahon brought him a bag of miniature footballs during practice, and then found further reason to rage at the whole situation when the Bears released wide receiver Ken Margerum, one of his closest friends (a happening McMahon found too suspicious to be coincidence).

It was not unprecedented for a team with inherent psychological issues to work through them by winning yet another championship. "Remember the Oakland A's in the seventies?" McMahon said at one point. "They argued and kicked and screamed all the way to three World Series titles in a row." But this was a different time, a different age—the distractions were bigger now and would continue to grow and mutate, as per Tom Landry's maxim. And maybe McMahon could have held all of this together by wire and string and by force of personality, as he'd done the year before, if only his body had held together, if only the repercussions of his own hubris had not come crashing down on him in one vicious and borderline-criminal act.

The attacker was a Green Bay Packers defensive lineman, a troubled soul laboring for a once proud franchise, who had been accused of indecently grabbing a woman in a bar the month before (he later apologized, and no charges were filed) and who would, soon after, check himself in to an alcohol rehab program. His name was Charles Martin, his nickname was "Too Mean," and his moment of infamy came on a Sunday in late November, after McMahon threw an interception. Martin came upon the quarterback in a vulnerable position: walking away from the action, toward the sideline. It was all premeditated. Martin had scrawled the numbers of several Bears players, McMahon foremost among them, on a towel he wore in his waistband—he had crafted a hit list. Several seconds passed, perhaps twenty in all, and then Martin approached from behind, picked up McMahon, and dropped him on his head, reaggravating McMahon's injured throwing shoulder once more. The referee, Jerry Markbreit, had never seen anything like it; for a moment, he couldn't quite believe what he'd just witnessed.

In that moment, Charles Martin, suspended for two games by commissioner Pete Rozelle, became a stand-in for many concerns, including what was perceived as a spiraling cycle of violence in football and in America: In *The New York Times,* columnist Dave Anderson wondered whether drugs could have been a factor, and suggested that any player who engages in an unnecessary act of violence should immediately be tested for drugs. There were threats of lawsuits and calls for criminal prosecution. In the ensuing years, Martin would come to terms with the outrageousness of what he'd done, and he would apologize for it, would express his regret. And yet, by resorting to guerrilla tactics, Martin had accomplished something that had once seemed impossible: He had succeeded in getting Jim McMahon to shut his damn mouth.

Two days later, McMahon flew to Los Angeles to meet up with a renowned orthopedic surgeon, Dr. Frank Jobe. "As soon as Frank opened up my arm, he went, 'Holy shit,'" McMahon said. "There was nothing left in there. I was lucky to ever play again."

He needed surgery. His season was over. Without McMahon, the Bears thought, at least their season would not be couched in uncertainty; but without McMahon, they also had no spirit to unify them or to energize them. The conflict that had driven them was gone. Flutie started the Bears' opening playoff game against Washington, and he was confused and overmatched; he began calling out formations from Boston College and from the New Jersey Generals playbook. The Bears lost, 27–13, and a strange sense of relief swept over them: This wild laboratory experiment into the extremes of human behavior had come to an end.

V.

That span of twelve months, the rise and fall of Chicago's team, became the signature moment of McMahon's career. The unraveling was gradual but unmistakable: The Fridge's ballooning weight, McMahon's continual state of disrepair (mental and physical), Payton's impending retirement, Ditka's egotism (the restaurant that bore his name had become a multimillion-dollar operation)—all of it contributed. There was no way to recapture what once had been. "It was new, and it came together once, and it was gone," Telander said.

But the ideas behind it had already helped to craft a new reality. You could see it happening in New York, first with the Mets and later with the Giants. In January 1987, as Lawrence Taylor temporarily clung to sobriety, New York won the Super Bowl, and they developed a unique signature along the way: After victories, players hoisted a bucket of Gatorade and splashed it onto their coach, Bill Parcells. It was, said Ken Valdiserri, the Bears' PR man, yet another example of the newfound pervasiveness of product placement in sports, something the Bears had wrought, both wittingly and unwittingly. Much later, they would take credit for this as well: The Bears' Dan Hampton insisted he had dumped a bucket of Gatorade on a teammate as early as 1984.

"What happened during that time in Chicago was nothing you could prepare for, nothing you could read about in a blue book and learn how to handle," Valdiserri said. "But it changed the face of marketing in sports."

McMahon would spend two more seasons in Chicago and play a total of sixteen games, including seven in the strike-shortened 1987 campaign; for the remainder of his career, he would never play more than twelve games in one season. It was the quarterback who had started this revolution, but now the quarterback already had everything he wanted. He was set for life. He wasn't much into long-term legacies, anyway. He lived in the moment, the way *he* wanted, and if people couldn't understand where he was coming from—if they couldn't see the truths he saw—that was their own damn problem.

CHAPTER ELEVEN

A Casual Defiance

*It wasn't a sustaining issue. It was the epitome of the fad is-
sue, a classic really. It came and went in three weeks, max.*

—LEE ATWATER, REPUBLICAN CONSULTANT,
ON THE REAGAN ANTIDRUG CAMPAIGN

I.

On the morning of June 19, 1986, Derrick Curry's mother shook
him awake and delivered the news that would alter the course of his
life. Curry sat straight up in bed, fell into a daze, and shared in the
universal sentiment of the moment: *There is no way this can possibly
be happening,* he thought. He was sixteen years old, a basketball player
at Len Bias's alma mater, Northwestern High, who was spending his
summer as a volunteer counselor at an elementary-school camp. He
was a teammate and friend of Bias's younger brother, Jay, and he was
a friend of Brian Lee Tribble, the voice on that heartbreaking 911 call;
he'd made a cameo appearance at Washington Hall the evening before, sitting vigil for Len's return from Boston with Jay Bias and David Gregg and some of Len's other Maryland teammates. He and Jay
had gone home before the party began. They were asleep by the time
it ended. What happened in between, he simply could not imagine.
The Len Bias he knew—the Len Bias most everyone knew—did not

do drugs, no matter what his friends—no matter what Brian Tribble—might be rumored to be into.

But time goes, and as it did, Curry would come to bear witness to the moral complexity of this saga, to the ongoing fallout of June 19. He would mourn the death of at least one friend and the incarceration of many others, and he would eventually become swept up in the considerable vortex generated by this night . . . in repercussions that rippled outward from Prince George's County to the University of Maryland to the District of Columbia to the White House and beyond.

"So many different turns of events came about over Len's death," Curry said. "It's sad and ridiculous. And I found myself in the middle of this whole crazy thing."

II.

"Like everyone else, I, too, felt the loss of Len Bias," wrote Nancy Reagan in a *Washington Post* op-ed, shortly after the events of June 19 set off a nationwide panic. She went on to discuss a disquieting conversation she'd had with a reporter who had been present at a cocaine party and done nothing to stop it—"She should have gotten up from the table, told people what she thought, and left"—and the damning influence of television and movies, and the impact of drugs on a generation of schoolchildren. It was July, and Bias was dead, and Don Rogers was dead, and the first lady had been laboring for years to reach this moment, however unfortunate the impetus. Just Say No's full-on mainstream moment had arrived: Fifteen million viewers tuned in to a CBS program, hosted by Dan Rather, called *48 Hours on Crack Street*, during which New York senator Alfonse D'Amato and Rudolph Giuliani, then a U.S. attorney, purchased crack in the Washington Heights section of Manhattan. *Newsweek* wrote that crack was the biggest story since Vietnam and Watergate; *Time* called it "the issue of the year."

In fact, the problem remained largely isolated to urban neighborhoods, and in fact, cocaine use among high school seniors would decrease 37 percent between 1985 and 1988, but this was a nationwide crusade now, and we had been conditioned by the images in our newspapers and on our television sets. The shock of this situation—of a healthy young man dying while drugs infiltrated our cities, while suburbanites feared for their own communities—led the media to begin taking its cues from law enforcement officials and politicians . . . and the politicians, for one, were facing a crucial midterm election in the summer of '86, and cocaine/crack and its attendant panic was one issue without an obvious downside. The White House pollsters reported back that drugs had become a growing concern among the general populace. A national antidrug campaign was proposed, and exacerbated by the righteous anger O'Neill encountered when he returned to his hometown of Boston shortly after the death of Len Bias, both Democrats and Republicans were willing to move fast, in what Eric Sterling, the lawyer for the House Judiciary Subcommittee, deemed a "legislative frenzy." They evoked the Bias name early and often. They did not bother with procedural hurdles such as public hearings. "The chemistry to create an issue was all there, and Bias lit it," said one member of Congress.

A congressman from California proposed that any merchant who took money from a drug dealer should have their business seized, and called for the criminalization of any drug "which has a stimulant, depressant, or hallucinogenic effect on the central nervous system," seemingly unaware of the fact that this would include coffee and alcohol. A congressman from Florida called drugs "the biggest threat we have ever had to our national security." A congressman from South Carolina called them "a threat worse than any nuclear warfare or chemical warfare waged on any battlefield." (He sponsored a measure requiring the president to halt all drug smuggling within forty-five days, which was, according to one of his colleagues, the equivalent of asking Reagan to cure the common cold by Thanksgiving. Still, the measure passed.) The House majority leader, Jim Wright, a Democrat, said they were "slowly rotting away the fabric of our society and seducing and killing our young." Congress demanded revocation of probation for drug addicts, the death penalty for dealers, an end to suspended sentences, and a billion dollars to build new prisons. They asked for everything they could possibly get, because what sold in the heartland better than law and order? A representative from Oklahoma admitted the situation was "out of control," but added, "of course I'm for it."

"In death," wrote author Dan Baum, Len Bias "would become the Archduke Ferdinand of the Total War on Drugs."

In August, William Rehnquist, the president's nominee for chief justice of the Supreme Court, admitted to a nine-year addiction to sleeping pills; a thirteen-year-old girl in California turned a trash bag filled with her parents' marijuana and cocaine over to police after listening to an antidrug lecture at her church; and the president submitted to a voluntary drug test. In September, the president and his wife went live on the air during prime time from the private quarters of the White House, shaping the drug war as a moral imperative, as antithetical to the American experience, as the great and unifying cause of our time.

> RON: America has accomplished so much in these last few
> years, whether it's been rebuilding our economy or
> serving the cause of freedom in the world. What we've
> been able to achieve has been done with your help—
> with us working together as a nation united. Now, we
> need your support again. Drugs are menacing our soci-
> ety. They're threatening our values and undercutting
> our institutions. They're killing our children.
>
> NANCY: Our job is never easy because drug criminals are

ingenious. They work every day to plot a new and better way to steal our children's lives, just as they've done by developing this new drug, crack. For every door that we close, they open a new door to death.

RON: My generation will remember how America swung into action when we were attacked in World War II. . . . Well, now we're in another war for our freedom, and it's time for all of us to pull together again. . . . As we mobilize for this national crusade, I'm mindful that drugs are a constant temptation for millions. Please remember this when your courage is tested: You are Americans. You're the product of the freest society mankind has ever known. No one, ever, has the right to destroy your dreams and shatter your life.

It sounded *great:* like FDR on poverty, or Kennedy on the space program, or LBJ on civil rights. The reactions were universally favorable, for this was what the country wanted to hear in the wake of an athlete dying young, as they lamented a problem that felt much larger and more threatening to middle-class America than it actually was. And this was one of the last great edicts the president would issue while at the height of his powers, before a burgeoning scandal swept away his aura.

In October, a $1.7 billion bill, the Anti-Drug Abuse Act of 1986, rambled through the House and the Senate; most notably, it added twenty-nine mandatory minimum sentences for drug offenders and decreed that possession or sale of one one-hundredth of an amount of crack cocaine as compared to powder cocaine (five grams versus five hundred grams) would trigger those mandatory minimums. That number was based entirely on fears of this new drug. What it had to do with Len Bias, who had overdosed on powder cocaine, no one seemed to know. But it was all part of the same narrative now.

The president signed the bill into law on October 27, two weeks before the midterm elections.

III.

Meanwhile, back on campus, the Lefthander kept on sparring.

On the same day the Maryland medical examiner issued his findings regarding the death of Len Bias, an academic counselor named Wendy Whittemore resigned from the university, citing concerns that education was not Lefty Driesell's top priority, and revealing that five of his twelve players had flunked out of school the previous semester. She stated that the players had seemed frustrated as they left for the West Coast in March for the NCAA tournament; she said that Bias was sometimes upset when the coaches steered him toward recreation courses, and that he had chosen to major in general studies rather than art or interior design simply because it fit his time constraints. Driesell snarled that he had no idea what this woman was talking about ("What the crap?" he asked the *Post*—as if he didn't have enough to deal with). Another academic counselor did not seem surprised by Driesell's reaction. He claimed that Lefty *asked* the right questions, but there was a larger, overarching question "of articulated values and actual practices."

"M-o-n-e-y," James Bias would lament in the weeks afterward, his tone growing increasingly bitter even as his wife refused to engage in recrimination. "That's what it's all about. It's all about making money for the university. It's not about athletes. It's not about athletes and how you feel about them."

Driesell would deny all of this. He would deny virtually everything and would keep at it for decades. He would vehemently deny that, amid the panic and confusion of June 19, he had attempted to obscure any truths about Bias's death. (He would eventually testify in court—he told the press that, despite having been told of the cocaine in the immediate aftermath of Bias's death, he couldn't be sure that drugs had killed Bias, and "I wasn't going to say that unless I was positive.") He would deny that Len Bias had flunked out at Maryland because of what Lonise Bias had called a *lack of covering*. He would deny that his standards might have eroded over seventeen years of coaching, and he would not comment about a report that he often insisted on flying to road games early and arriving home late, thereby forcing his players to miss additional classes. He would refer to Whittemore as someone who was "trying to save her butt" and would describe John Slaughter, the university president, as a "jerk."

He was a brawler, and he would fight like hell until the end. Backed into a corner, Lefty clung to the notion that personal responsibility outweighed the value of institutional oversight. He also had leverage, in the form of a ten-year contract he'd signed in 1984, and a high-powered lawyer, Edward Bennett Williams, serving as his representative. Ultimately, Lefty and his attorney argued, the decision that killed this man had had nothing to do with him. He'd *loved* Leonard Bias, and the Leonard Bias he'd known was a born-again Christian, but the meaning of this incident, to him, was simply that life is random and unpredictable. The meaning was this: "Some guy was doing cocaine, and he died."

He had his defenders: One newspaper columnist viewed the characterizations of Lefty as "a caricature complete with horns sticking out of his head . . . [he was] a sitting target for a bloodthirsty mob." The coach was, wrote his conservative ally, Robert Novak, "the scapegoat. . . . The wonder is that Len Bias was so close to graduation after four years of big-time basketball, when students carrying no such burden quietly drop out."

On the final day of September, Driesell held a press conference at which he defended his academic record, utilizing charts and graphs that backed up his case. He spoke for an hour and a half. A lot of people, he said, think that "Lefty is some sort of animal out of the sky." His players, he contended, had a graduation rate of 81 percent. The university's figures put it at 56 percent. (The discrepancy came about because Driesell declined to include players who had transferred, or died, or joined a professional team before reaching their senior year.) He outlined nine "suggestions to aid academic performance of athletes," including the notion that they should no longer play games from Monday through Thursday, that they should play no more than twenty-five games per season, that freshmen should be ineligible to play varsity. This was his retort to his critics: See, the coach *did* care.

An academic task force, commissioned by the university, would soon offer similar ideas: *We recommend that coaches and other team officials charged with the coordination of competition schedules endeavor to minimize the number of classes missed. . . . We believe that postseason games, tournaments, and all-star games should be restricted to occur over semester or holiday breaks or after the end of an academic year. . . . The Task Force recommends . . . an end to freshman eligibility in men's and women's basketball and in football.*

The task force was chaired by J. Robert Dorfman, then the chair of the College of Computer, Mathematical and Physical Sciences, who was not a basketball fan. Dorfman had published papers on "Time Correlation Functions and Transport Coefficients in a Dilute Superfluid" and "Kinetic Theory of the Drag Force on Objects in Rarefied Gas Flows"; now he found himself facing down a basketball coach and engaging in a semantic discussion about the meaning of statistics. Dorfman's view had always been that the university, as its mission, should focus strictly on education; what he encountered while chairing the task force made him realize that there were others whose thinking was entirely antithetical to his own. "It's a little hard for me to describe how he viewed things," Dorfman said of Lefty.

This was one of the conclusions of the report: *For some coaches, there is an implicit set of priorities: athletic performance first, academic performance second, and the personal development of students last, mostly as it has an impact on playing.*

The task force did succeed in implementing small changes—for instance, in tighter regulation of the athletic department in relation to academics—but many of their sweeping recommendations were never implemented. It was too late to pull that far back. The Frank Merriwell of Ronald Reagan's childhood, the amateur athlete engaged in sports as an innocent pursuit, had died long before Len Bias. The games had become too important, too lucrative, to be neutered in such a way; how could freshmen be deemed ineligible when a freshman had just won Louisville a national championship in basketball? How could games be relegated to weekends when more games were being televised than ever before, when more games were needed in order to feed the beast of cable television? We suffered through a moment of reexamination, and then the moment passed.

Still, at Maryland, the status quo would not stand. This was a fight Lefty could not win; he had pushed too far, and angered too many people, and overstepped his authority. "There was nothing I did wrong—what did I do wrong?" he said. "Leonard Bias was a great kid. I loved him. But he was not under my jurisdiction in any shape or form. It wasn't anything I had something to do with. He made a bad decision to try cocaine for the first time."

On October 29, four weeks after his studious but unconvincing presentation on academics, Charles Grice Driesell entered Cole Field House, bent his considerable frame over a bank of microphones, cracked a joke about the size of the crowd ("Maybe we should have charged admission"), and then admitted defeat. He announced his resignation from coaching (the school's athletic director had already left, and Slaughter, the president, would leave soon as well). Then he turned away from the crowd and toward the door, arm in arm with his wife and two daughters. It made for a sad postcard on the front pages of the papers, a poignant farewell image of a coach who had unwittingly—and perhaps unfairly—become an emblem of the era's indulgences, and who remained pathologically convinced of his rectitude.

"Leonard Bias didn't change a thing," he would say, still brawling over twenty years later. "You're bringing up all this crap that happened, but there's nothing to it."

In the end, there was no reason to turn back. Eighteen months later, the coach, courted by James Madison University in Virginia, accepted a new job.

One week after the resignation of Lefty Driesell, the Republicans lost control of the Senate, despite Reagan's fervent campaigning on their behalf, despite his pleas to "win one for the Gipper." He had abruptly shed his reputation as a political magician, wrote his biographer Lou Cannon, but this was not the worst of it. The worst had taken place the day before, with the publication of an article in a Lebanese magazine that detailed the administration's covert attempts to barter arms for hostages in Iran without the knowledge of Congress (efforts that would later be linked to the administration's under-the-table funding of the Nicaraguan Contra rebels, long a pet cause of the president). By the end of the week, the American media had picked up on it, and the story burst into scandal. Reagan gave a prime-time speech that proved unconvincing to the public. A week later, he held a contentious news conference.

It was a complex story, fraught with equivocations and denials, and what was most disturbing was that the president seemed as confused by it as we all were. For the first time, he appeared to have lost his way. Asked ABC's Sam Donaldson: "Sir, if I may, the polls show that a lot of American people just simply don't believe you. But the one thing that you've had going for you, more than anything else in your presidency, your credibility, has been severely damaged. Can you repair it? What does it mean for the rest of your presidency?"

"Well," Reagan responded, "I imagine I'm the only one around who wants to repair it, and I didn't have anything to do with damaging it."

In December, his approval rating dropped from 67 percent to 46 percent, the sharpest single-month tumble since polling began in 1936. There was talk of impeachment, and this bothered him; here was a man, his wife said, who had never had his integrity questioned. Here, also, was a man who was stubborn and prideful and reluctant to admit his mistakes. History, and his own attempts at damage control—his pleas of ignorance, his undeniable charm and good-heartedness—would eventually restore his reputation, but this moment marked the decline of the singular ideal that had guided his presidency. "He was no longer the magical sun king," Cannon wrote, "no longer the Prospero of American memories who towered above ordinary politicians and could expect always to be believed."

To Reagan's opponents, and even to some of his allies, the Iran-Contra scandal became a symbol of the president's lack of regard for the very system of government he presided over, an exemplar of a revolution in national values that encouraged greed and self-interest above all else. *Don't worry about laws,* said one Republican senator, grasping to explain the metaphor of the moment. *Just get the job done.*

IV.

It took nearly a year for Brian Lee Tribble to go to trial in Prince George's County, charged with supplying the drugs that killed Leonard Bias. Terry Long testified for two and a half hours; David Gregg claimed Tribble had said he'd gotten the cocaine "from the bottom of the stash." But Long also said Bias had introduced him to cocaine, and he claimed that he and Tribble and Bias and David Gregg had snorted cocaine for hours while at Tribble's apartment, after a home game against North Carolina State in January. Terrence Moore, a seventeen-year-old with an extensive criminal record, said he had sold cocaine on Tribble's behalf, and the prosecution attempted to portray Tribble as a dealer and Bias as a "courtesy middleman." The case was inherently weak—the overzealous state's attorney who had originally brought it, Arthur Marshall, had lost his reelection bid the previous fall after a messy grand-jury proceeding—and the evidence was circumstantial. Mostly, the trial succeeded in raising further questions about Bias himself, about his associations, about his predilections, about his own level of innocence or guilt. "I have no doubt that Brian loved Lenny," Curry said. "People still don't realize how much it ate him up. To this day, it still haunts Brian. But I think if Brian was a real friend—and I know personally that he loved Lenny, and I have seen Brian break down from talking about what happened to Lenny—he shouldn't have put him in that situation."

On June 3, 1986, after deliberating for six hours, a jury acquitted Tribble on all charges. The defendant wept and nearly collapsed in his chair; outside the courthouse, he told reporters, "I loved Lenny Bias. I always have and I always will."

The whole saga had already dragged on far too long, but it wouldn't end there. It couldn't end there, because now the Bias name carried a strange cachet, an aura of myth that suffused and obscured any objective truth.

For Jay Bias, who had played in a basketball game one night after his brother's death, the legacy of Len Bias ate at his own sense of identity, at his own passion for basketball. He sought solace on the court, but what he carried, both within himself and through the projection of others, was an unfulfillable set of expectations, as if Jay should continue what his brother could not. On the court, he resembled Lenny, and he was endowed with undeniable talent: In their junior year, Curry and Jay Bias led Northwestern High to the state championship. Jay scored twenty-eight points in the finals, which were played at Cole Field House, the gym where his brother had made his name.

Jay Bias averaged twenty-five points and twelve rebounds his senior season, and was generally regarded among the top recruits in the nation. But something wasn't right; Derrick Curry could see it. Jay clashed with his coaches, and he got into fights, and he fell into inexplicable tantrums. His grades and his test scores were subpar, and he chose to enroll at a nearby community college. After a year and more problems, he quit school and took a job, hoping, at some point, to enroll at American University. "After Lenny died, it took away his love for the game of basketball," Curry said. "Part of him wanted to play and be the second Lenny, but the pressure people kept putting on him took its toll. Finally Jay said, 'Man, I'm just tired.' He used to keep so much stuff inside."

Meanwhile, swept up in the perverse and counterintuitive logic of contemporary celebrity, Brian Lee Tribble was seen as a rising star. He considered writing a book; he hosted parties at a club called East Side, where the taped telephone message said, *Every Tuesday, you're invited to a dance party with Brian Tribble.* He was besieged at his ten-year high school reunion by classmates who wanted to take a picture with him. He had accomplished his senior wish: He now had *the ability to make it.* At some point, according to prosecutors, he went to Miami and made connections with high-level drug dealers. They trusted him; he was *Brian Tribble,* and he had beaten the rap. But because he had beaten the rap, the FBI kept tabs on him.

Eventually, guilt led Brian Tribble back to Jay Bias. "Brian used to look out for me and Jay, particularly after Lenny died," Curry said. He gave them money to take their girls to the movies. He gave them money to go shopping, and he asked for nothing illegal in return.

Everybody knew what he was into, but as long as he didn't involve *them*, what did it matter? In a way, given the economic realities of the moment, it was hard to blame him. "I think what happened with Brian," Curry said, "is that Brian is a very likable person, and Brian knew a lot of people, and they said, 'Do you want to make some easy money?' And Brian probably figured, 'Well, doggone, this is easy.' I can say that from his family's standpoint, he wasn't living in the ghetto. His family wasn't doing bad. Brian is, and was, a very intelligent person.

"But sometimes people get into it so much that they can't get out of it."

In August 1990, Brian Tribble met a connection at a parking lot in New Carrollton, prepared to purchase 8.8 pounds of cocaine for the price of a hundred thousand dollars. When federal agents moved in, Tribble fled by car and then on foot. He turned himself in a short time later, pleading guilty, acknowledging that he and his associates had sold over 110 pounds of cocaine in an eighteen-month period.

Three months later, on December 4, Jay Bias, then twenty years old, went to a shopping mall. He told Derrick Curry he planned to buy an engagement ring for his girlfriend, and Curry was going to go with him but chose instead to get a haircut from a friend. Midway through his haircut, Curry saw a television news report about a shooting at the mall; when he heard the victim was Len Bias's younger brother, he leapt out of his chair and raced to the mall, and then he found himself at Leland Memorial Hospital, in the same emergency room where Jay's brother had been taken four years earlier. According to reports, the shooter had accused Jay of flirting with his wife, a salesclerk at Kay Jewelers, and Jay left and got into his car, and the suspect drove up behind him and shot him in the back. Curry later heard that Jay Bias and the man who murdered him had gone together in a limo to their prom. At the hospital, Eric Bias, the last living male progeny of Lonise and James Bias, kept repeating these words: *My brother's not dead.*

It made no sense, but what *did* make sense anymore? What logic could anyone extract from this without clinging to the notion of divine inevitability, to the theories of predestination and martyrdom favored by Lonise Bias?

Derrick Curry was twenty years old then, the son of a high school principal with a Ph.D., but he was given to sucking his thumb during moments of extreme stress. He was timid, a slow learner. He had enrolled at Prince George's Community College, but he still harbored aspirations for a Division I basketball career at Georgetown; he was a playground virtuoso, his vertical leap supposedly measured at forty-three inches. He did not take drugs, and he insists he never profited from drugs, but his friends—well, they were his *friends,* and what they did, he figured, was their own business. He knew the D.C. drug kingpin Rayful Edmond, and Edmond would hang around and play ball with stars like Alonzo Mourning of Georgetown, but Rayful would never jeopardize Mourning's basketball career (Mourning testified in 1989 that he'd never seen drugs at Edmond's home). "He had ballplayers around him strictly for playing basketball," Curry said. "He wasn't subjecting them to any illegal activity."

He presumed, if it came down to it, that his friends would do the same for him.

In fact, his friends had formed a drug ring known as the Woodridge Group. In order to further their business, they had traded crack for cellular phones, and those cellular phones had been supplied by undercover federal agents. And in October, a little over a month before Jay Bias was shot outside a shopping mall, Derrick Curry went to run an errand for his friend, a man named Norman Brown. Curry looked up to Brown for reasons he couldn't quite explain, for reasons that may have had to do with the defiance of his father and his establishment, for reasons that may have had to do, the

Washington Post's Richard Leiby later noted, with Brown's "casual acceptance of crime and danger; a casual defiance of the American power structure." (And it is not difficult to wonder whether the relationship between Brian Lee Tribble and Len Bias was guided by those same elements.)

Something about this didn't feel right. Curry saw suspicious cars in his rearview mirror, blocky sedans of the sort that only the feds drove. He pulled his station wagon into a parking lot and bolted. He beeped Norman, and Norman called him right back, and Curry muttered something unintelligible.

"I can't hear you," Norman said. "Take your hand out of your mouth."

Then Norman asked: "Where the shit at?"

"In the car," Curry said. "I parked it at the rec center."

This was all caught on tape. And one day after the death of Jay Bias—in part, Curry says, because the feds feared the Woodridge Group would retaliate for his murder—federal agents broke up the entire ring, arresting twenty-eight people. Inside the station wagon, agents found Derrick Curry's college textbook on criminal justice, a spiral notebook bearing his name, and a one-pound rock of spongy and poorly cooked crack cocaine, the size of a Nerf football and the consistency of a brownie. When they raided the house where he was staying, at four-thirty in the morning, they asked Curry, "Who are you?" Then, Curry says, they asked him what he knew, and he told them he knew nothing.

This wasn't entirely true: He knew his friends were dealing drugs. And he understood, upon being apprehended, that he would have to pay a price for his compliance. His father had warned him—his father had asked him, upon hearing of his friendship with Brian Tribble: "Isn't that the guy who killed Len Bias?" Curry didn't understand the connection, didn't realize that his casual association with these people could somehow impact his own life. There was a sense, among those friends, that they could get away with this; what most puzzled the feds about the Woodridge Group was that none of them were poor. None of them needed to sell crack in order to support their family. But they had come of age at a time of 50 percent unemployment among young blacks. Even if you made it through college, said Shambra Mitchell, a good friend of Curry's, "you might end up working at Popeye's." And so you took what you could get. You did what you had to do.

Don't worry about laws. Just get the job done.

Curry imagined he would serve a short jail sentence and then be given a chance to atone for the sins of his gullibility. He had no criminal record. He had $150 in his savings account; he drove his mom's 1981 Chevy Citation. He was Norman's errand boy. One FBI agent called him "a flunky."

But there were federal laws, hurriedly passed in the months after Len Bias had himself defied the law and the American power structure. And these laws decreed that drug offenders were subject to mandatory minimum sentences, and those who trafficked in crack rather than powder cocaine were especially susceptible, even as we began to question whether one was really a hundred times worse than the other. Despite sympathy from a judge who could do nothing to help him, Derrick Curry was sentenced to nineteen years and seven months in prison for his role in a drug conspiracy, a sentence three times that served by most murderers in America. This punishment was made mandatory by laws passed in the summer of 1986, in the midst of what the president had deemed a national crusade. By the time Curry had his sentence commuted in 2001 by President Clinton, thousands of low-level drug offenders had been imprisoned in an attempt to redeem the sins of June 19, 1986. Curry was thirty-one, and any real hope that he might resume his basketball career had long since passed; he went through a tryout with the Knicks, blew out his knee, and it was over.

He had time to think in prison, and he had time to talk, and he had time to forgive. He saw his old friends. For a while, he shared a prison cell with Brian Tribble, whose sentence for conspiracy to distribute cocaine was only half as long as his own, and they would talk about what had happened, and they would talk about what might have happened if that night had never happened at all.

CHAPTER TWELVE

The Old College Try

Miami Vice typically focused on conventional two-sided tensions between good and evil and how Crockett and Tubbs negotiated the space in between. . . . Good-versus-evil plot lines usually masked the ways in which institutions like the police force were connected to larger social and economic tensions.

—JIMMIE L. REEVES AND RICHARD CAMPBELL, *Cracked Coverage*

I.

All through the month of December, scandal and its attendant commotion kicked off the evening news. The president was reeling: According to a *Newsweek* poll, only 10 percent of Americans now believed that he'd been entirely ignorant of the Iran-Contra arms-for-hostages deal; according to a *Los Angeles Times* poll, 78 percent perceived a White House cover-up. A defiant Reagan blamed his troubles on "great irresponsibility on the part of the press." Wrote the *Economist* magazine: "The image of Mr. Reagan as a decent, honest and aboveboard statesman has, in many minds, been superseded by that of a run-of-the-mill, arrogant and evasive politician." When asked by reporters if he was tuning in to the hearings of the House Foreign Affairs Committee and its broadening exploration of Iran-

Contra, Reagan joked, "Oh, now and then when I can't find a ball game."

Such was the real-world backdrop for one more ball game, the culmination of the college football season, yet another youthful collision between social order and chaos, between statesmanship and arrogance. This year, it was Penn State versus the University of Miami, the new and improved progenitors of bad behavior, a band of extremists who had knocked Oklahoma from the pedestal with a 28–16 victory in September. Miami, whose starting tight end had been arrested and charged with possession of cocaine and a handgun; Miami, where one linebacker had become entangled with a sports agent and another linebacker had been charged with possession of steroids, battery of a police officer, disorderly intoxication, and fleeing a police officer; Miami, where a wide receiver named Michael Irvin had driven over the feet of a pair of university law students and where a defensive lineman named Jerome Brown had misplaced a handgun in a shopping cart on campus and where at least three dozen players charged more than eight thousand dollars in phone calls to an MCI phone-card number that was posted on the wall of a dorm room.

At Miami, they had come to believe that style and substance could coexist, if not always in perfect harmony with the legal system (though the school's athletic director dismissed these transgressions as "minor incidents"). Their coach, a shrewd and immaculately coiffured taskmaster named Jimmy Johnson, had recruited some of his best players from impoverished neighborhoods, and used his background in psychology to manipulate them into working harder than they ever imagined they could. In turn, he also permitted them to act out. He viewed their boisterousness as a coping mechanism for adjusting to a college atmosphere that felt unfamiliar and unwelcoming to minorities: "to mask nervousness, anxiety, and insecurity, some of our players behaved quite the opposite on the football field: cool, supremely confident, joyful. They exulted in their success, and they were demonstrative about it."

They adopted their collective persona from a pastiche of cultural influences: from the imagery of MTV, from the swaggering Bears, not to mention from the pastel noir of the most-watched television program of the moment, *Miami Vice*. They cut their jerseys short to reveal their midsections; at the beginning of the fourth quarter, they held up and waved four fingers in the air. When they played Oklahoma, they refused to shake hands with their opponent before the coin toss. They placed obscene prank phone calls to Brian Bosworth and Jamelle Holieway the morning before the game, an idea that Johnson rather enjoyed when told of it. All around them, they saw college football programs that seemed soft and bland and emotionally suppressed and trapped, by their elders, in the mores of the past—"If you asked the majority of college players, they *wished* their coaches would let them play like us," said Miami's Alonzo Highsmith—and nowhere more so than at Penn State, where everything seemed tinged in sepia, where the coach resembled a history professor and the quarterback, John Shaffer, back for his senior season, only vaguely resembled an *actual* quarterback. (This, too, was an exaggeration: "They made us out to be bunch of choirboys, but that wasn't the case," said a Penn State linebacker named Trey Bauer, who had a penchant for running his mouth, often to Paterno's chagrin. "It wasn't like we were locked in the library twenty-four/seven.")

Miami had lost a New Year's Day bowl game—and with it, a chance at a national championship—the year before, falling 35–7 to Tennessee in the Sugar Bowl. And the Hurricanes decided that, this time around, they would be required to make a forceful statement, something that would establish their seriousness and yet also affirm their status as rogue visionaries. They believed that they could win games before they even took the field, by sheer force of intimidation. And no one can remember who among them came up with the idea, but in late December, when they stepped off a plane and into the Arizona desert, arriving for what would soon become the most bloated and self-important college football game in history, the Hurricanes were wearing the same outfit in which John Rambo had accomplished his defiant cinematic reboot of history.

For Miami, the combat fatigues they wore that week were a statement of purpose, a reaffirmation that the old rules did not apply to them: This time, they were going to *win* the war.

II.

Such hyperbole had been an essential element of Don Meyers's vision: He had the audacity to imagine a college football game as an event as big as the Super Bowl, grandiose and bold and capitalistic, and he was unwilling to compromise on the scope of it. He exploited every angle. He stroked every ego. He played the parties off against each other. The whole system of college bowl games, a twisted landscape of backroom negotiations and handshake deals made by men in cacophonous sport jackets, had reached a financial fault line, and Meyers saw a way to work this to his favor. In the modern age, Meyers understood, you did what you had to do. *Just get the job done.*

Once Miami beat Oklahoma in September, the two best teams in the country were independents, with no ties to any conferences, meaning no affiliations with any specific bowls. The Fiesta Bowl, for which Meyers served as chairman of the selection committee, had always been second-tier, unable to stand up to the cabal of Rose, Cotton, Sugar, and Orange, but here was a quirk in the system, an opportunity for the Fiesta to elevate itself and, in so doing, to poke a thumb in the eye of the bowl system and its antiquated sense of propriety, and to make everyone involved a hell of a lot of money in the process. A true number one versus a true number two, both undefeated, playing on a neutral field: In college football, this almost *never* happened.

And so Meyers went after Penn State, and he went after Miami. He didn't imagine he'd have much trouble with the Nittany Lions; all they wanted was another opportunity to win a national championship after they'd been overwhelmed by Oklahoma the year before. *If we have to play in a parking lot,* Paterno told Meyers, *we'll do it.* But Penn State was never the number one team that season, and in the end, the decision would not be Penn State's.

There was never a question that Jimmy Johnson possessed the best team in the nation that year; the only question, in fact, was whether this might be the most talented team in the *history* of college football. Their quarterback, Vinny Testaverde, would win the Heisman Trophy; they had a top-flight backfield anchored by Highsmith, an unbearably cocky wide receiver named Michael Irvin, and a defense rife with size and speed and bubbling over with attitude. This was a new breed of college football team, an NFL developmental squad disguised as amateurs. They had outscored their opponents by more than a three-to-one margin. Whoever they played, wherever they played, it would be a formality, the culmination of a season guided by destiny.

Meyers began traveling to Florida to speak to Miami's athletic director, Sam Jankovich, and Jankovich assured him there was no way his team would leave Miami when they could play in the Orange Bowl, which would essentially be a home game. But Meyers did not give up; he did not believe in impossibilities where financial rewards were involved. He worked his way up the ladder at NBC, and he eventually twisted enough arms in the entertainment division that he convinced them to move the game from January 1 to January 2, if he could secure the matchup, thereby permanently altering the notion that college football's national championship be decided on New Year's Day, while also persuading network executives to preempt the most popular show on the network: *Miami Vice.* Meanwhile, his colleague Bruce Skinner, the Fiesta Bowl's executive director, had scored a coup of his own: The game itself would henceforth be known as the *Sunkist* Fiesta Bowl. Skinner had generated the notion of a title sponsorship in the wake of the 1984 Olympics, upon realizing that corporations were in search of sporting events to throw their collective weight behind. In short order, title sponsorship of college bowl games would become commonplace, a chintzy display of the corporatization of sports. But for the moment, it fit; and it secured a hefty portion of the money needed to generate the spectacle that Don Meyers had envisioned.

Still, Jimmy Johnson saw no real reason for his team to leave Florida to play its bowl game. What was the point of hauling across the country to play a team that might have been undefeated, yes, but had nearly lost to Cincinnati and barely beaten Maryland? So even after Meyers had secured more money from his sponsors, even after he'd coaxed more money out of NBC, even after he'd set up a fundraising banquet with Bob Hope, even after he'd delivered black satin sweatsuits to the entire Miami team, even after he'd arranged for the wives of the Miami coaches to get free treatments at a highbrow desert spa—even after he'd raised the payout for each team to nearly $2.4 million dollars—he *still* needed one more flourish, one last appeal to the considerable self-regard of a coach whose adamantine hairstyle had already achieved mythological significance.

Meyers began calling reporters.

Jimmy Johnson doesn't want to play Joe Paterno on a neutral field, he told them.

Jimmy's afraid.

When anyone at Miami asked him if he might be the anonymous source responsible for such statements, he denied it. But he understood the fundamental motivator behind Miami's rise from a nondescript program to the number one team in the nation; he understood the importance of ego. And immediately after Miami's final victory of the season, over East Carolina, Jimmy Johnson confirmed that his team would play in the Fiesta Bowl, in prime time, on January 2, 1987, against Penn State, in what was already being billed as the twentieth century's umpteenth *Game of the Century,* more as an attempt to gin up the circumstances than because of the competitive nature of the matchup. ("The Game That Modesty Forgot," a writer for the Penn State student newspaper would later call it.)

Johnson wasn't concerned. His team feared nothing except itself.

III.

In December, a seventeen-year-old student at South Plantation High School confessed to a *Miami Herald* reporter that he'd been injecting himself on a weekly basis with one hundred milligrams of Equipose, a steroid used to build muscles in show horses. The story ran on the front page, a lengthy and disturbing exposé about the newest threat to the Just Say No generation, quoting concerned experts and young boys whose primary neuroses revolved around their physical appearance on the beach. At South Plantation, steroids had become an accepted part of the culture: Sixty-five percent of the students surveyed by the school newspaper said they knew someone who was doing them. One senior whose bedroom had become the epicenter for injections had taken to calling it "the Doctor's Room"; another senior confessed that the drugs made him feel like "punching his grandmother."

Days later, Brian Bosworth and his Oklahoma teammates arrived in Miami to play in the Orange Bowl, against the University of Arkansas. The Boz insisted that he did not take steroids, that his teammates may have regarded them like baby aspirin but he saw no purpose in abusing his body: He believed bulking up would only slow him down.[7] And yet a moment had arrived, early in 1986, when

---

7. His coach, Barry Switzer, would later say: "Anybody could tell The Boz had used steroids at some time or other just by looking at him."

Bosworth felt he had no choice; after the win over Penn State, his shoulder was *killing* him. It had gotten so bad he couldn't comb his own hair, and on top of that, he had a deep thigh bruise, and he wasn't certain he could make it back for spring practice. So he found a doctor who promised a quick cure-all: a course of a steroid known as Deca-Durabolin.

Bosworth did not inform the team's doctors. He said that the physician who prescribed the drug carefully monitored his liver and kidney functions to assure he would not suffer any complications. The problem was that Deca-Durabolin stayed in one's system for an extremely long time; the problem was also that in January, the NCAA had decreed that it would begin testing for anabolic steroids, as well as everything else on a fifty-nine-page list of prohibited substances. On December 10, while he was laid up in the school's infirmary with a stomach infection, the NCAA arrived to administer a drug test, and Bosworth, dehydrated and barely able to muster enough urine to satisfy the requirements, tested positive. He was suspended for the Orange Bowl, and hence one of the first high-profile steroid controversies of the age was born, for The Boz did not suffer indignity quietly. He immediately went on the offensive.

Steroids were *legal,* he said during a contentious thirty-five-minute press conference at a Miami hotel (and he was technically correct: they were not deemed illegal under the Controlled Substances Act until 1990, in the wake of Ben Johnson's steroid-tainted victory in the hundred-meter dash at the 1988 Seoul Olympics). Steroids had been a tacit element of sports culture for thirty years, Bosworth said, and unlike cocaine, steroids "aren't destroying society." Mostly, he decried the hypocrisy of the NCAA, for its ignorance and shortsightedness. He bemoaned the fact that they'd penalized him for something that he'd taken months earlier, when the drug testing rule had yet to be put in effect. It wasn't like he'd been smoking or snorting: Even Nancy Reagan hadn't put much thought into Deca-

Durabolin. "I'd certainly rather it be steroids than cocaine or marijuana," said Barry Switzer, and The Boz, being who he was, continued
to hammer at this perceived moral relativism. He refused to leave it
alone. He refused to let the moment wither away.

Never mind that he had surreptitiously taken steroids despite
the warnings from his own coach, and after the NCAA announced
its ban: He saw this whole episode as but the latest in a series of efforts by an overzealous governing body to curtail his liberties. Earlier in the year, the NCAA had prohibited him from writing on his
shoes, in the same way the NFL had launched a crusade against Mc-
Mahon and his headbands. Well, *screw that*, Bosworth thought:
This was America, not Russia, and The Boz remained, beneath the
Mohawk and the earring, a hard-line capitalist in a Corvette. After
he'd been forced to paint his sneakers black to cover up messages
he'd written before a game against Colorado earlier that season,
Switzer told him the NCAA were "a bunch of goddamn Communists," and The Boz had filed that line away. Now, he thought, it
might make for a good T-shirt, so he and his roommate cruised the
streets of Miami Beach, driving an official Orange Bowl vehicle, in
search of a silkscreen shop. The finished product read NCAA: NA-
TIONAL COMMUNISTS AGAINST ATHLETES. And across the bottom:
WELCOME TO RUSSIA.

Bosworth later claimed that Switzer hid the T-shirt when he
found it in the locker room, and this was what convinced him to wear
it. He was permitted to stand on the sidelines with his team, and in
the third quarter, with Oklahoma winning 28–0, he slipped off his
jersey to reveal the shirt. As was typical for The Boz, the cameras
found him immediately, and then he made things worse; of his drug
test, he told a sideline reporter that it appeared as if the NCAA, acting
indiscriminately in enforcing their new rules, "took a shotgun into a
dark room and started blowing people away."

For Switzer, a coach whose permissiveness was considerable, a coach who abided headbands, bandanas, Afros, earrings, gold teeth, and silver shoes, this T-shirt was the final straw. The Boz's lucrative act—this zany and uninhibited role he now owned, a role would envelop him to the point that it subsumed his actual identity, until it became, in his own words, "a monster"—had come to outweigh his value to his football team. He had caused such an outrage that he would not return for his senior season. He would never play another game at the University of Oklahoma. But he didn't have to; the monster had already slouched from its cage.

IV.

At a news conference during which he referred to Paterno (anointed that week as *Sports Illustrated*'s Sportsman of the Year) by the pejorative "St. Joe," Jimmy Johnson affirmed that he didn't care much about how his players dressed or how they went about motivating themselves. He told the assembled horde—and in the end, about fifteen hundred media members flocked to Phoenix to cover a game that was beginning to feel like a Super Bowl—that he couldn't wait to see what they came up with next.

Johnson had other things on his mind. In fact, Meyers had never seen a coach so terminally *uptight,* so preoccupied with gamesmanship and psychodrama. Johnson complained about the carpeting in the locker room, so at the last minute Meyers had carpenters flown in from Los Angeles to replace it with something that matched the shade of green in Miami's school colors. And on the day before the game, each team was scheduled to do a walk-through on the field at Sun Devil Stadium. Meyers called Paterno and asked him what time he wanted. "Four o'clock," Paterno told him.

He called Johnson. "What time does Joe want to go?" Johnson asked. Meyers told him four o'clock. "Then we want to go at four," Johnson said.

Meyers called Paterno back. "We're going out at four," Paterno said.

Jankovich, Miami's athletic director, called Meyers around midnight. He was upset, citing favoritism toward Penn State, and according to Meyers, Jankovich might even have cried, though Jankovich said he couldn't recall. All he knows is that the Hurricanes had been promised certain things. They wanted the bigger locker room; they got the smaller one. They wanted to be the home team, but Penn State wore its home blue jerseys.

When four P.M. came, Miami showed up for the walk-through. Penn State never did.

By then, the Hurricanes were primed to implode in an orchestrated display of rebelliousness that took place on the final weekend of 1986, at a steak fry with a country-western theme, a historically innocuous occasion that suddenly became a stage for social protest. At the steak fry, both teams were supposed to deliver a brief (and ideally, playful) skit. Penn State's players wore suits and ties. Miami's players wore their black sweatsuits, only because, Highsmith insists, the Fiesta Bowl officials had told them to. The Penn State punter, John Bruno, fell into a monologue, dragging out a garbage can labeled with masking tape as JIMMY JOHNSON'S HAIR SPRAY, and making a crack about the racial harmony at Penn State: "We're one big family," he said. "We even let the black guys eat with us at the training table once a week."

So now it was Miami's turn. They bristled at the racial implications of Bruno's joke—they were already uneasy just being in Arizona, a state where public officials remained openly contemptuous of the celebration of the first Martin Luther King Jr. Day in January 1986—and they would not stand for their coach being reduced to a punch line. They were not here to eat rib eyes and make small talk; when a mariachi band boarded their bus upon their arrival and handed out oranges, they shooed the band off with extreme prejudice. And so at the steak fry, defensive lineman Jerome Brown, the ringleader of the tormentors, stood up and unzipped his sweatsuit to reveal his fatigues. "Did the Japanese sit down and eat with Pearl Harbor before they bombed them?" he said. "No. *We're outta here.*"

Out toward their buses went the men in the fatigues, adhering to a plan they had apparently formulated before the event had even begun—a walkout on the old ways, a thumb in the eye of their staid and predictable foe—and thereby cementing the reputation of a football program whose players would believe they had come to embody the legitimate savagery of the era. ("They were a bunch of young guys who weren't very smart," said Penn State's Trey Bauer. "No way that shit would have happened at Penn State.") But not before Bruno stood up, made a joke about Miami having to leave so the players could begin filming *Rambo III,* and then delivered the last, best punch line of the evening.

"Excuse me," he said. "But didn't the Japanese lose the war?"

V.

A year and a day removed from the first and only loss of his entire football career, a year and a day removed from the moment when he had insisted on accepting the blame for his team's 25–10 loss to Oklahoma in the Orange Bowl, John Shaffer stepped onto a football field in Tempe, Arizona, and tried not to think of anything except the first play of the game. It was going to be a pass. They were going to *throw* on first down, to try to catch Miami sleeping, to liven things up, and then Shaffer found himself distracted by the presence on the sideline of David Hartman, one of the anchors of *Good Morning America.* And he saw all these famous faces—alumni, celebrities, hangers-on— and the whole thing began to sink in: This was bigger than any college football game he had played. This was bigger than any college football game *anyone* had ever played; it had become such a spectacle that the president, in search of a way to speak to the American people without saying much of anything at all, had agreed to a five-minute halftime "chat" with NBC's Bob Costas.

And for just a moment, in the midst of this chaos, Shaffer thought: *What am I doing here?*

Meyers had fulfilled his vision: The Fiesta Bowl lived up to its hype as the Game of the Century in one crucial way—the ratings were enormous, larger than even the network could have expected: 25.1 percent of households with televisions (more than seventy million viewers) were tuned to NBC that night. Cable television would soon fracture audience shares, as would the waxing shadow of ESPN, and no college football game has matched that rating, before or since. With its sheer audacity, with its clash of personalities (both real and exaggerated), with its bright colors and expensive graphics, this game validated the notion that televised sports were fully grown; it wasn't just the Super Bowl or the Olympics that could pull in corporate interests and a mass audience. "When you look at it," said Skinner, the Fiesta Bowl director, "that game pretty much captured America."

In the din before kickoff, Michael Irvin, the Miami wide receiver, approached a Penn State defensive back named Ray Isom. "*You're Isom?*" he said. And then he laughed. All week, Miami had been ridiculing Penn State's defensive backs, likening them to Smurfs; they'd spent the remainder of the days following the steak fry engaged in rhetorical brawls with Penn State's entire way of being. They refused to sign autographs for children at Fiesta Bowl functions; they declined to shake hands with Penn State's captains before kickoff. It was, wrote *The Dallas Morning News,* the most blatant confrontation between the righteous and the evil since Reagan had bombed Gadhafi in Libya. "I think they're nothing," Jerome Brown had told a press conference. "Shaffer thought he had a bad bowl game last year. That was nothing. After this game, he'll wish he'd graduated. The dude's about to star in a nightmare."

Penn State got the ball first. Shaffer called that pass play. He looked into the eyes of his offensive linemen, and they were glassy and unfocused. *They're not here yet,* he thought, and he wasn't sure if *he* was either. He took the snap, faked a handoff, and dropped back four steps, five steps, and one Miami lineman came charging in from the outside, unblocked, and Shaffer ducked away, but here came two more, charging straight into him. The quarterback wound up twisted in the grass, fourteen yards behind the line of scrimmage. He never had a chance. It would go like this all night for Penn State's offense; Shaffer finished the game five-for-sixteen for 53 yards, and Penn State finished the night with 162 yards of total offense, and Miami finished with 445.

"To this day," said Highsmith, the Miami running back, "I have no idea what happened."

Somehow, Penn State kept it close. The game settled into a rhythm: Penn State stalls on offense, Bruno punts the ball deep into Miami territory, and Miami turns the ball over. Miami went up 10–7 on a field goal with 11:49 remaining, but Testaverde threw a pass into the arms of Penn State's Shane Conlan, who returned it to the Miami five-yard line. Penn State's tailback, D. J. Dozier, scored a touchdown soon after, then dropped to a knee and said a prayer. Penn State 14, Miami 10.

In the end, on a fourth down at the Penn State thirteen-yard line with eighteen seconds remaining, Testaverde dropped back to pass and threw his fifth interception of the night; all evening, Miami's receivers had been knocked silly by Penn State's defensive backs, and Testaverde, confounded by Penn State's rotating coverages, could never find a rhythm. A linebacker named Pete Giftopoulos cradled the ball in his arms, and then, unsure what to do, scrambled aimlessly, like a foal lost in the woods, before dropping to the ground. On came John Shaffer, who clutched tightly to the final snap and took a knee.

And for the first and only time in his college career, the quarterback who had always trusted in authority rode off the field on the shoulders of his teammates.

At halftime, Ronald Reagan, wearing a cardigan sweater, conducted his national conversation, a segment that Costas preemptively described as a "brief chat" rather than an interview. Any comment on the news could wait. Here was an opportunity for the Gipper to wax nostalgic on national television. And so he told the story, once more, of how he'd gotten his start in broadcasting—the tale of the raspy-voiced Scotsman at the radio station in Iowa, and the revisionist history he'd come up with in the studio, including a key block by a right guard named Reagan. He spoke of the beginning of a career that had led him to Hollywood and to the White House. And then Costas asked the president about his views on keeping sports—and particularly college sports—"in proper perspective."

Said the president: "I think it's awfully easy to get carried away and sort of make players feel that they're hired hands. . . . I hope that it isn't widespread and I don't think it should be. I think the old college try and the college spirit is the thing that makes college football great. . . ."

"Was he kidding?" wrote Howard Rosenberg in the *Los Angeles Times*. "Reagan is warning against overinflating the importance of college sports? He's doing this on a football telecast where he—our president—is part of the halftime break? He's doing this during a game that was made possible only by shifting the Sunkist Fiesta Bowl to prime time and raising the booty per team to $2.4 million? This is not being 'carried away'?"

But this was Ronald Reagan: He was both a nostalgist and a capitalist, and he left us with perhaps the most complex and controversial legacy of any president in modern history; even his own personal biographer, Edmund Morris, admitted to being thoroughly confounded by a man who seemed to be continually playing a role, a man whose approval ratings would rise precipitously as the Cold War ended, as we tumbled headlong into a future shaped by the events of the era. "However historians would judge him," Haynes Johnson wrote, "Reagan had stayed the course, and his presence would be felt long after he was gone."

And so in this moment on national television, our president—deterred neither by these ambiguities nor by the gravity of the scandal swelling around him, ever optimistic about the mythic America of his childhood and about the redemptiveness of history—continued to burnish his legend. In the background, a marching band played a lively tune.

Epilogue

They called it the Reagan Revolution, and I'll accept that,
but for me it always seemed like the Great Rediscovery: a
rediscovery of our values and our common sense.

—RONALD REAGAN

I.

Uncasville, Connecticut

Out of the elevator careens the Punky QB, zigzagging toward daylight, the embodiment of arrested development in motion. Dressed in an abrasive Hawaiian shirt (it is, in fact, part of an extremely casual clothing line he has lent his name to), he is helming a cherry-red motorized scooter through the lobby of a Connecticut casino while trailing a chestnut-colored stream of tobacco juice into a Coca-Cola bottle. Finally, he shrieks to a stop, high and tight against a series of couches, exuding the aura of beer and Copenhagen. It is early evening, and he has just come off the golf course, which is where he spends nearly all of his non-family-related free time, and he is accompanied by a woman whose relationship to him is entirely unclear to me . . . as is, for that matter, the origin of the scooter, which appears to be more a lark than a necessity.

This morning, McMahon left me a polite phone message, blaming alcohol-related outrageousness for his inability to return my call the night before. Then, sometime later, he went outside to wait for the bus that would take him from the casino to the golf course, where he was participating in yet another celebrity-studded tournament, ostensibly for one charity purpose or another. When the bus arrived, the quarterback loaded his clubs on and waited, and the driver told him he was on the wrong bus, that this one was reserved for the members of the Four Tops, who were playing a concert as part of the festivities that evening. But it was all good: The driver was from Chicago, and he gave McMahon his card. *Any time you need a bus,* he said.

It has been more than a decade since his retirement from football, and McMahon, slingshotting past the age of fifty, remains forever true to the portrait of himself in his heyday, that of a jockish Randle McMurphy raging against the asylum of polite society. Since his retirement from football, he has yet to take on what might be termed "a real job"; rarely is he ever forced to buy himself a beer. Occasionally, this has had deleterious effects. In 2003, after swerving across the center line of a highway in Florida at two in the morning, McMahon was pulled over on suspicion of drunk driving. His blood alcohol level was more than three times the legal limit. *I'm too drunk,* he told police. *You got me.* "I think Jim never got out of having a nineteen-year-old's mentality," says his childhood friend Pat Hanley. "I think he identified with his kids in that way."

Somehow, despite a body that never quite held together, the noble savage managed to hang on in the NFL for fifteen seasons; he served as a part-time starter/backup in San Diego (where he was traded in 1989, after he finally drove Bears management over the edge) and then went to Philadelphia and Minnesota and Green Bay, and in 1996, as Brett Favre's backup, he won another Super Bowl ring. When the Packers went to the White House to meet with President Clinton, McMahon wore his Bears jersey, to make up for the

White House visit that had been preempted by the explosion of a space shuttle a decade earlier; he seemed unconcerned (and perhaps even motivated) by the fact that the Bears and Packers are bitter rivals. But it is equally obvious that McMahon's entire athletic identity is now filtered through the lens of a single season, and that he is just fine with this.

Over the years, McMahon and his '85 Bears teammates—especially those, like McMahon himself, who maintain their primary residence in Chicago—have become something of a permanent museum exhibition, their celebrity preserved in amber even for those who never saw them play. Kurt Becker, the lineman who served as McMahon's old roommate, coaches high school football in Aurora, Illinois, and endures constant questions from children who were born years after the Bears swept through the streets of New Orleans. The Fridge, who has struggled with both his weight and his finances, remains an international icon, and "The Super Bowl Shuffle" now serves as a five-minute shorthand for the immoderate absurdities of the era. Those Bears remain a group that, Rick Telander says, was both reflective of the times and ahead of the times.

McMahon doesn't watch much football anymore. He finds the precision and repetition and the careful and conservative marketing of the modern quarterback to be dull and robotic; even the controversies seem contrived, the celebrations lifelessly choreographed. Given the NFL's skillful melding of public relations and marketing in the late 1980s, it could be argued that the Bears were the first and last team to arise as a spontaneously combustive cultural phenomenon, which was what made them seem so much more *real* to us. And perhaps because I am a member of a generation that traffics in nostalgia, there is something comforting about knowing that McMahon is still McMahon—that he is a perpetual adolescent (though he has since made peace with his parents), that he remains true to his values (or lack thereof), that he continues to act out of the self-interest that defined both his career and the age he played in. It makes me feel like I grew up in more authentic times, even if I know that this, too, is nothing more than a nostalgic illusion.

At one point, McMahon visited the troops in Iraq; he felt this was his duty, since these were the men who had earned him the right to cozy up in his Barcalounger with a beer. But beyond that, he doesn't really give a damn if you judge his choices. He is a self-made success, a study in autonomy. And what could be more reflective of the era from which he emerged—what could be more distinctly *American*—than that?

"That's what I'm most proud of in my life," he says. "I've done things my way. Whether they be right or wrong, at least I can sleep at night knowing I don't worry about what other people think. I've raised four great kids, and they know me, and my close friends know me. And the public really has no business in your business. We get to play a *sport* for a living, for Christ's sake."

All those years of cheap shots and late nights and hospital stays, all those years he defied his natural tendencies toward sloth and fragility, all those years spent looking out for his own interests—all were spent in pursuit of Jim McMahon's dream. *Was it worth it?* Hanley asked him a few years ago. And McMahon did not have to reply directly; he merely responded by saying that he'd never had to use the word *job* in his entire post-NFL career. The answer, as always, was self-evident.

II.

Chicago, Illinois

From behind the wheel of an obscenely muscled Dodge pickup, Bo Jackson is reminiscing about the time he took down a three-hundred-pound bear from point-blank range with a .45-caliber pistol. This was over a decade ago in Alaska, a few years after Bo retired from organized sports and a few days before the Princess of Wales died in a car crash, and if you're wondering whether Bo was scared, *hell no*, Bo was not scared. Not even when that bear got so close Bo and his hunting companion could see the hairs bolt upright like pine needles on the back of its neck.

"I wasn't scared," Bo tells me. "I wasn't scared because I knew I could outrun my white buddy. You've got to *think* about these things, man."

The way Bo tells it, he waited as long as he could, then he fired a slug into that bear's skull. The bear kept coming. His buddy yelled, "Shoot him again!" and Bo shot him again, firing another bullet directly into the bear's noggin. Bo 2, Bear 0. And then Bo skinned the bear on the spot and dragged the seventy-pound hide the half mile back to camp. Of course he did.

"Bring yo' little ass on," Bo is saying. He is no longer speaking of the bear, nor to me, cowering in the passenger's seat, but to a small vehicle of foreign descent that has mustered the nerve to pass him on the right on a four-lane road in suburban Chicago. Bo lives not far from here, in a pristine house in a gated community, with a long driveway where he sometimes unpacks his bow and arrows, sits in a metal folding chair, and fires at a deer-shaped target set under a tree in his yard.

At the moment, Bo is on his way to a store called DGY Motorsports, where he is going to pay the balance on a four-wheeled recreational vehicle he plans to use exclusively to plow the snow from his driveway. Ever since a snowplow broke the lights that surround his driveway, Bo prefers to plow his own snow. It is one of those little things that, as he drifts toward the age of fifty, give him a disproportionate amount of pleasure. The others include (not necessarily in order) golfing, cooking, hunting, motorcycle riding, and doting on his wife and three children.

It is a modest life, but in many ways Bo Jackson is a modest man, one who was never particularly impressed by his own achievements. He is still intimidating, thick all over, his head shaved, his stare so pointed at times that it seems as if it could melt glass. But he is also shockingly *normal*, considering that for a short time, he was the most famous athlete in America.

These days, Bo is perceptive enough to see through his own mythology; the "Bo Jackson" he often referred to in the third person was something of a construct, manufactured for public consumption, for marketing purposes, as a way for Bo to separate himself from his own celebrity. That "Bo Jackson" vanishes when he is at home, whether he's with his wife (the only human in the world who refers to him as Vince) or his children (who call him Dad) or his childhood friends back home in Bessemer (who, Bo jokes, refer to him as "asshole").

These days, the real-life Bo Jackson, the Bo Jackson who cooks spaghetti and washes his own dishes and watches reality TV, doesn't even see a need to run around the block anymore. Why bother when a man can play golf instead? Why bother when there is nothing left to prove to anyone?

"But I also know, if I was healthy, with good hips right now, I'd be the fastest [man of my age] in the country or in the world," he tells me. "That much, I know. That much . . . I know."

The myth of Bo Jackson fully crystallized on a Monday night, on the last day of November in 1987—the year ESPN also began televising NFL games, the year the network's reach expanded into more than 50 percent of American households with televisions, and ratings leapt by 33 percent.

Bo was a rookie running back for the Los Angeles Raiders, a two-sport athlete sharing time in the backfield with Marcus Allen. The situation had developed gradually: Al Davis, as was his inclination, took a stab, drafting Bo with a seventh-round pick in the spring, and Bo remained coy for the first half of the summer. And then it happened suddenly: In July, Bo announced that he was working on a deal with the Raiders, and he would join the team at the end of the baseball season. "I'm thinking about adding another 'hobby' to my off-season curriculum," he said, and this aroused the doomsayers once more, a chorus of people who seemed to think that Bo didn't *understand*, that he couldn't possibly realize what he was getting into, that, given the financial payoff, nothing about either game qualified as "hobby" anymore. This was not the era of Jim Thorpe and Frank Merriwell; nobody did something this audacious (not to mention potentially dangerous), as Bo claimed, just for *fun*. For a time, he seemed bothered by the pressure heaped upon him. He struggled for the remainder of the baseball season; he struck out 158 times in total and hit only .188 after the All-Star break. "To be a great baseball player, you need a little humility," wrote Thomas Boswell of *The Washington Post*. "And that, to be blunt, is why Bo Jackson is heading for the door."

This was all Bo needed to hear. As always, skepticism provided him with purpose, a new contour to his legend. During his first practice with the Raiders, on the first pitch he took from behind the line of scrimmage, Bo outran a cornerback attempting to contain him and sped toward the end zone. "All he did was take a pitch," said a teammate, "and all of a sudden a new standard for speed and quickness was set in the NFL."

And if we weren't yet convinced, that Monday night in Seattle, his third start in the National Football League, proved convincing enough. Bo took a handoff, and Bo parted the entire Seattle defense, and then Bo—how does one even *describe* this method of propulsion? glided? propelled? teleported?—ninety-one yards down the sideline, and then Bo kept on running until he disappeared into a tunnel in the bowels of Seattle's Kingdome. The sound of Bo running past him, said Seahawks receiver Steve Largent, was like nothing he had ever heard.

For a moment, Bo was gone, out of the picture entirely, prompting ABC's television analyst, Dan Dierdorf, to proclaim to a TV audience that Bo "might not stop until Tacoma." When Bo emerged from that tunnel, and when he lowered his shoulder and toppled a cocky young linebacker named Brian Bosworth on a short touchdown run later that same evening, nothing was ever the same for either man. As The Boz, plagued by injuries, slowly withered away from football ("Boz and I, we think alike," Bo said afterward. "We'd just like to prove 'em wrong, that's all"), Bo Jackson was on his way to becoming an icon, both physically and commercially, a man who would make a fortune for embodying a two-word catchphrase that helped usher sports into the modern age.

It was a silly idea in the first place, this two-word mantra, proper noun followed by verb, and like most silly ideas, it came to Jim Riswold in the middle of the night. But then, advertising is a silly business, and it was Riswold's sense of irony that had led him here. By the time Bo ran over The Boz on *Monday Night Football,* Jordan was already on his way to becoming an icon, and Nike was in search of another Jordanesque figure to market its cross-training shoes. The company's first choice, Riswold says, was the Raiders' Howie Long. Riswold suggested there was a far better candidate on the same roster, someone who had what in advertising is known as a *unique selling proposition.*

"I'm always surprised by how big something as inconsequential as an advertisement can become," Riswold tells me. "People like their sports heroes, and Bo was something new. A new shiny toy. That was the best example of how big these things can become."

And so Riswold and his colleagues began toying with Bo's maverick image, and Bo willingly played along; in Los Angeles, Nike placed the image of Bo, wearing shoulder pads and wielding a baseball bat, on print pages and billboards and on the sides of tall buildings. For the next couple of years, as the decade neared its end, as the Reagan presidency came to an end, Bo really *was* that huge. What we have now are stories that, with decades of wear, have already begun to feel like tall tales: of the time Bo scaled an outfield wall in pursuit of a fly ball until he was hovering sideways, seven feet off the ground; of the time Bo plowed over an All-Pro safety named Mike Harden "as if [Harden] had been poleaxed," according to one columnist; of the time Bo caught a base hit on a carom off the outfield wall and, while standing flat-footed, threw a ball three hundred feet and cut down Harold Reynolds at home plate; of the time Bo took a handoff against the Cincinnati Bengals, swept around the left side, cut back, and then was gone; of the numerous occasions a frustrated Bo snapped a wooden bat over his knee.

So why not, Riswold thought, in keeping with the ethic of the times, shape Bo as a larger-than-life figure, as a contemporary Paul Bunyan, as a man whose entire life seemed choreographed to near-perfection?

What an unusual name Bo has, Riswold thought, and he began brainstorming ideas with Nike executives—Beau Brummell, Bo Derek, Bo Schembechler, Bo Diddley—until that pronoun-verb combination came to him in his sleep that night.

Bo Knows.

That first iconic television ad, culminating with Bo playing a horrific guitar riff and Diddley himself delivering the line, "Bo, you don't know Diddley," aired during the All-Star game in 1989, which Jackson led off with a colossal home run (he was later named MVP). Riswold was watching at a bar in Portland, with several Nike colleagues. When the spot came on, the entire bar fell silent.

I think God is a Nike fan, Riswold muttered.

It was absurd what happened next, the way the catchphrase caught fire, the way Bo's profile grew and mutated, until, for a short period, he was the most culturally recognizable athlete in the world, above even Michael Jordan himself. By 1990, Nike had surpassed Reebok in market share, and the company's stock price had tripled. Riswold saw pirated T-shirts in Venice Beach: BO KNOWS YOUR MOTHER. In *The New Yorker* magazine, a humor piece entitled "Bo Knows Fiction" imagined Bo's public wrestling with a typewriter: "Then Bo sits back, exhales, and unzips his warm-up jacket, which has 'Smith-Corona' stitched over one pocket and 'JUST TYPE IT' in large letters across his broad back." In *Sports Illustrated,* Leigh Montville began: "I report today on the operation. Bo successfully delivered a seven-pound, three-ounce baby girl this morning at a hospital in a small town in Alabama. . . . 'Bo knows obstetrics,' I tell the home office."

The ads grew more self-referential as Bo got bigger and bigger, as he continued to improve both his baseball and football skills, and as our perception of the outsized era we'd come through slowly dawned on us. The eighties ended, and the nineties commenced, and perhaps we all knew, deep down, that this campaign was unsustainable: On January 13, 1991, during a divisional playoff game against the Bengals, Bo took a pitch and ran right and then, instead of cutting out of bounds, cut back one last time before he was taken down from behind by a linebacker named Kevin Walker, fighting like hell all the way.

In the midst of the push and pull, Bo's hip was yanked out of its socket. Bo's doctor told him if it were anyone else, his leg would have snapped like a dry twig—the irony being that a broken leg would have healed within months. He would make a brief comeback in baseball with the Chicago White Sox, but even after surgery, the hip would never be the same. "The gods of sports decided to punish Bo because he came too close to them, had reached the brink of being a god himself," wrote his biographer, Dick Schaap.

Nike was deeply invested in Bo by then, and America was invested in Bo as the manifestation of its outsized dreams, and Riswold began writing subversive ads that pierced the myth of Bo, and the myth of Nike, and the commercialism and hype and immoderation of the Reagan era (these days, Riswold says, the conglomerate that Nike has become would never permit the same self-referential cheekiness). In one of the last great ads, from the summer of 1991, Bo cuts off a song-and-dance routine, declaring, "I'm an athlete, not an actor." And then, in the midst of a workout, as the music cues once more, Bo breaks through the fourth wall, crying out to the Nike logo, "You *know* I don't have time for this," before George Foreman, huckster and infomercial pitchman sui generis, takes his place.

So it was: Within the span of a decade, Bo's superpowers bloomed and wilted. And yet by then, it was too late. The monster Riswold had created—sports as cult of personality—was slouching out of its cage to be reborn, over and over again.

"All the athletes today grew up with these commercials, and they want them," Riswold tells me. "But the world is more cynical, and with good reason. It's been done before. And the Michaels and Bos of the world don't come around that often."

Bo has always said, and maintains today, that he didn't realize the severity of his injury at the time he suffered it. Perhaps he just *assumed,* with the body he'd been given, that no mortal could rend it. But there is something horrible and wrenching in Bo's expression, captured in a series of photos in the aftermath of that game, of Bo sitting on the bench with his two young sons—photos he keeps, unframed, on the floor behind a filing cabinet in his office, near an autographed picture of Chuck Yaeger, the über–test pilot who is Bo's only real hero. Bo's expression in the photos reflects an emotion he is either unwilling or unable to recognize.

Maybe he could have avoided this hit, and maybe he could have avoided all these what-if questions, if he'd listened to the skeptics and made up his mind and chosen one path or the other. As the myth grew, as Nike depended upon Bo to be ambidextrous, that choice came with more weight; still, Bo says he had all but decided that 1991 would be his last season playing football. By then, he was an athlete *and* an actor—he would later play a prison guard in *The Chamber*, a surprisingly strong performance in an otherwise mediocre John Grisham adaptation. (He caught some of it on cable this morning, in fact.)

Then again, it is his contention that he was acting all along, that he capitalized on the Zeitgeist, on our hunger for the resurrection of old myths.

"I know how to feed guys like you with a long-handled spoon," Bo says while cooking a meal for me at his house, before driving me back to my hotel. "I never let you get too close. I tell you what I want you to know, and I tell you what you want to hear."

In the obscenely muscled pickup, with his hunting equipment squeezed in next to me, Bo flips a wave at the guard, passes through the gates, and then pokes his nose out in the world. He has been telling me stories about his past for several hours now, and although he doesn't seem to mind—he appears to relish the way he has condensed his experiences into parables—he ran away from that Bo Jackson long ago, ran unwittingly out of a sour childhood and into a peculiar life as a demigod, as the last comic book hero we will ever see, as the personification of an era when our national ambitions were outsized and glamorous and entirely unsustainable.

"Sports has never been the main focus in my life," Bo had said to me earlier, while considering those photos of himself. "Dreams of the Hall of Fame never entered my mind when I was playing. The thoughts I had in my mind were of being a businessman. When I did those Nike commercials, I was broadening my horizon, so when the day came, I could get my foot in a lot of doors you probably couldn't."

He would prefer us to believe that his story *was* choreographed: He was, like Ronald Reagan, a boy who ran straight out of a mythical past and into an American dream. And he didn't stop running until he found himself a place behind those gates, shielded from the beasts and monsters of the modern age.

When his wife calls, Bo tells her he'll be home soon enough. He's not staying out here any longer than he has to.

III.

Greenwood, South Carolina

And so the years have passed, and time has been served, and bodies have been buried, and in the face of a cynical world, a mother named Lonise Bias continues to tell the only story she cares to believe. She hears of the continued corruption of college sports and of the Hall of Fame career of Lefty Driesell—she still attends Maryland games with her grandchildren on occasion—but these push-and-pulls over legislation and administration are not her greatest concerns.

Her concerns, and the mission she has been charged with, are more concrete, more personal. She believes that by addressing the way these children see themselves, she can affect the decisions they make. She believes this is her calling, the manifestation of her dreams. She believes her son is exactly the type of transcendent figure who does not come around very often. She believes he died to be a cautionary tale, to be a martyr. And we can fret all we want over the legacy of Len Bias, or the lack thereof, over whether, as one newspaper columnist wrote in the aftermath, ignorance should be a reason for heroism, or whether, as Lonise Bias says, "He went down to give life." Because *she* knows she is right.

"It's not that I'm just some airhead that's just full of faith," she says. "It's just that you have to move on. And through your faith, you believe that things are working out for good, and when you see you're impacting people's lives as a result of this horrific thing that happened, and whether it be a lie or a truth, you continue to move forward in the midst of it."

So she sits here, in a high school classroom in Greenwood, South Carolina, eating a fried-chicken salad, granting an exclusive audience to the members of the boys' and girls' basketball teams before she rides back to the airport.

"*COMPARISON RUINS CONTENTMENT!*" she told them earlier.

"*THERE ARE CONSEQUENCES THAT ARE GOING TO FOLLOW YOU!*" she told them.

Now the girls are cozying up to her, and a boy who is a star player on the football team, a Division I recruit, tells me Lonise Bias reminds him of his mother, a "strong black woman" with a resonant message. Everything this boy says indicates he could not imagine poisoning his career with drugs. Everything he says seems heartfelt and truthful. Everything he says engenders hope for the next generation.

And that's the thing: All of this is so admirable. All that Lonise Bias preaches is backed by a moral certitude you can't help but find compelling. A woman who lost two of her children—a woman who straddled the graves of two of her children—is helping ensuing generations. Where are the flaws in such a story? What isn't redemptive and appealing—what isn't downright *American*—about a narrative like this one?

And you wonder: After a certain amount of time has passed, does the truth even matter anymore?

"Did you know your son was doing drugs?" one of the girls asks.

The mother inhales, exhales, then responds. "It's been said it was his first time," she says.

Acknowledgments

From approximately 1982 until 1990, when I left home for college, I collected every issue of *Sports Illustrated* I received in the mail and filed them away on a shelf in my closet. Even now, I'm not sure I can explain why I did this, except to say that a) it utterly confounded my father, and b) these magazines somehow seemed too valuable to throw away. A few I framed and hung on the walls of my bedroom, but mostly I kind of basked in them, staring at the covers and the photos and reading the articles and then rereading the articles. I realize now that I was fortunate: I grew up in what I imagine will be remembered as the last great heyday of printed journalism, at a time when newspapers like the *Chicago Tribune* were unafraid to publish five-thousand-word features and send a small army of reporters to a Super Bowl, at a time when young columnists like Michael Wilbon and Tony Kornheiser were just finding their voice (and veterans, like Jim Murray and Bob Verdi, were still at their best); at a time when *Sports Illustrated* regularly published the literature of Frank Deford and William Nack and Rick Reilly. I was lucky to experience it the first time around, and I feel privileged that the journalism of the era provided a road map for this idiosyncratic project of mine.

This book is a peculiar hybrid of many different stories, including my own, but it could not have been written without the recollections of those who were there. In addition to reading dozens of books and thousands of articles—and reordering, from eBay, several dozen of the issues of *Sports Illustrated* that my father relegated to a landfill upon my departure for Penn State—I conducted about eighty interviews (most are listed in the notes). A few people went above and beyond the call, including Jim Riswold, who passed along some of his (and Nike's) best work; Don Pierson, who shared many stories about a most interesting time on the Bears beat; and Rick Telander, a writer I've long admired, who may not have realized it but helped to crystallize many of the themes of this book when I spoke to him early in the process. Of course, I'm thankful to the primary subjects who agreed to be interviewed, most notably Lonise Bias, Bo Jackson, and Jim McMahon.

Anne Turkos, the archivist at the University of Maryland, and her staff helped guide me through the considerable amount of material on the life and death of Len Bias. At Auburn, Joyce Hicks, Dwayne Cox, and the staff at the university library provided me with a wealth of material on Bo Jackson, most of which was archived thanks to the efforts of David Rosenblatt—and was originally compiled by Dick Schaap, one of the great journalists of any era (Schaap's interview transcripts, cited in the notes, provided a crucial window into Bo's personality). Brad Gust, Dan Froelich, and Liz Peel helped arrange appointments at Auburn. At Penn State, Lou Prato was (and is) an invaluable resource. Betsy Shepherd helped me to chase down Jim McMahon. Pat Little and Lon Slepicka provided last-minute help with photos.

Monica Pratt and Jennifer Stitt at Families Against Mandatory Minimums talked me through the complexities of the drug laws spurred by Len Bias's death; Mark Hyman provided valuable perspective on the atmosphere at Maryland in the months afterward. Kevin Blackwell of the United States Sentencing Commission pointed me to additional studies.

John Dahl and Paul Melvin at ESPN helped supply videos and other background materials, as did Gentry Kirby, a reader who generously offered his assistance. Nate Mink, a talented young reporter, provided valuable transcription help. Another generous reader, Jay Barrier, made an effort to assist in the research.

Many of my editors and colleagues at ESPN, including Eric Neel, Patrick Hruby, Wright Thompson, Kevin Jackson, Rob King, and David Schoenfield, helped shape (and facilitate) various sections of this book. A number of friends, including Chuck Klosterman, David Giffels, Bob Ethington, Jon Dolan, and Kimon Keramidas, provided critiques of the work in progress, and Ryan Jones, Kevin Gorman, Damian Dobrosielski, B. J. Reyes, Dave Hollingsworth, and Mike Abrams offered the necessary moral support.

Jane Dystel and Miriam Goderich put their faith in me before anyone else did, and for that I am eternally grateful. Daniel Greenberg is simply excellent at what he does.

Gotham Books' Brett Valley purchased this idea, but the ever-reliable Patrick Mulligan (once again) saw it through to its conclusion, with the help of his assistant, Travers Johnson. Bill Shinker was generous enough to believe in the idea even when we weren't quite sure where it might lead.

There are two other people I should mention who played a crucial role in enabling this book to exist. One is Jay Lovinger of ESPN, who essentially built this idea with me, who made me believe I could do it, and who is the smartest and most creatively daring editor I've ever worked with. The other is Cheryl Maday, who is also an excellent editor, and—far more important—is daring enough to have built a life with me.

Notes

Author Interview: AI
The Washington Post: WP
The New York Times: NYT
Sports Illustrated: SI
Chicago Tribune: CT
The Los Angeles Times: LAT
Associated Press: AP
United Press International: UPI

Prologue

My portrait of Brian Bosworth was based on his autobiography, *The Boz: Confessions of a Modern Anti-Hero,* as well as a number of newspaper articles written both during and after his career.

vii "When the legend": Pelecanos, p. 291.

viii "My little clutch bag": "Sooners' Holieway Is Just Doing What Comes Naturally," John Ed Bradley, WP, 12/28/85.

viii "Not unlike the way": "Sooners Put Together Winning Blend on Defense," Malcolm Moran, NYT, 12/30/85.

ix "The Penn State players carry on": "Plain Uniforms Suit the Orange Bowl Underdogs Just Fine," John Ed Bradley, WP, 12/29/85.

x "I got so famous": "The Boz Within," Bill Minutaglio, *Sporting News,*
6/30/97.

x "Not since the turbulent": "1986—A Year of National Shocks," Haynes
Johnson, WP, 12/31/86.

Chapter One

1 "In the myths": Johnson, p. 12-13.

I.

For my portrait of Reagan's life in sports, his presidency and the political
and cultural atmosphere of the mid-1980s, I relied on Bill Boyarsky's *Ronald
Reagan,* Lou Cannon's *President Reagan: The Role of a Lifetime,* Haynes
Johnson's *Sleepwalking Through History,* and Ronald Reagan's own biography *An American Life.* Also particularly helpful was the extraordinary
searchable archives of every public utterance by an American president, at
http://www.presidency.ucsb.edu.

4 "I'll never forget one game": Cannon, p. 187.

5 "sports exploded": Murray, p. 247.

6 "To each sports scandal": Johnson, p. 149.

6 "mythic America": Cannon, p. 435.

6 Most Americans did not see Reagan as a politician: "Is America Really
Back?" Lou Cannon, WP, 11/4/85.

6 "There is a lesson": Cannon, p. 290.

7 The most politicized Olympics: Mills, p. 17.

7 "Oh, what we've done": "Cheer, Cheer, Cheer for the Home Team,"
Frank Deford, SI, 8/13/84.

II.

I interviewed Jim McMahon in the summer of 2008 and spoke with teammates, journalists, and staff members who were around him frequently

during the 1985 and 1986 seasons. I also relied on the reporting of the *Chicago Tribune* (most notably beat writer Don Pierson) and the *Chicago Sun-Times*, as well as a number of books listed in the bibliography, including two written by Mike Ditka, Armen Keteyian's *Ditka,* John Mullin's *The Rise and Self-Destruction of the Greatest Football Team in History*, and McMahon's own autobiography, *McMahon!,* written with Bob Verdi. I was also able to view several games in the NFL Films "Greatest Games Series" DVD collection, featuring twelve of the Bears' games from the 1985–86 season.

10 "I mean, if you don't practice": Ditka/Telander, p. 47.
11 "He didn't have any particular agenda": AI Rick Telander.

III.

This section is based primarily on the *Newsweek* article "Rocky & Rambo," from December 23, 1985, as well as reviews and analyses of *Rocky IV* from a number of major newspapers.

IV.

14 "small life preserver": "McMahon Eager, But Ditka Leans to Fuller," Don Pierson, CT, 9/18/85.
16 "I want to bring out the bright side": "Namath Wants Nice Guy Image, but Zings Cosell," Cooper Rollow, CT, 9/22/85.
16 Doc Blanchard: "Ditka Decides on Fuller," Don Pierson, CT, 9/19/85.
16 "I'm not going to answer any more stupid questions": Ibid.
17 "You told me I'm not playing": AI Jim McMahon, also Ditka/Pierson, p. 202.
18 "ABC could be a little more American": "Bud Flags ABC for Unpatriotic Conduct," Ed Sherman, CT, 9/20/85.
18 "You don't ever want to be upstaged": Ditka/Pierson, p. 207.

18 "Goddammit, Mike": AIs Jim McMahon, Don Pierson, Rick Telander, Chet Coppock; Mullin, p. 58; McMahon/Verdi, pp. 91–92; ABC broadcast.

19 "a kind of noble savage": "Rocky & Rambo," *Newsweek,* 12/23/85.

21 "I always told Dennis": AI Jim McMahon.

22 "It was like one of those old-time": "McMahon's Magic Saves Bears," Don Pierson, CT, 9/20/85.

V.

23 "Reagan said things that everyone knew": Cannon, p. 761.

23 Poll taken before Geneva summit: "President's Popularity Near Peak, Poll Shows," Michael Weisskopf, WP, 11/17/85.

23 "one of the most amazing rallies": "Around the World, Stock Exchanges Mark a Strong Year," John Crudele, NYT, 12/30/85.

23 "What I want to see above all": "President's News Conference on Foreign and Domestic Matters," NYT, 6/29/83.

24 "in a mood for the resurrection": Johnson, pp. 166–67.

Chapter Two

25 "he and a few others": Wolfe, p. 19.

I.

My portrait of Bo Jackson was shaped by an interview with Bo Jackson in the fall of 2007—which led to the publication of an ESPN.com profile, "Bo Knows Best," parts of which are adapted within—as well as interviews with several of his former coaches. Jackson's autobiography, *Bo Knows Bo,* written with Dick Schaap, was a vital resource. David Rosenblatt, an archivist and professor at Auburn University, kept an archive of Schaap's notes and transcripts of his interviews with Jackson at the Auburn University library; Rosenblatt's paper, "Bo Jackson's Image and Impact on Auburn University," was an excellent reference as well.

26 "We had quite a few kids": AI Dick Atchison.

26 Single-parent households: On July 15, 1985, *Newsweek* devoted its cover to a package about "The Single Parent;" according to statistics from the Census Bureau, the number of single-parent families had more than doubled since 1970.

27 "John Gotti of my neighborhood": AI Bo Jackson.

27 "When I was coming up": Schaap interviews.

30 "That janitor": AI Terry Brasseale.

30 "he turned out": AI Dick Atchison.

31 "People who run are stupid": "Hip, Hip, Hooray," Tom Verducci, SI, 4/19/93.

32 "We had an outdoor party": AI Terry Brasseale.

33 "It's almost as if he choreographs": Verducci, SI, 4/19/93.

II.

To study the early days and growth of ESPN, I relied on information and statistics provided by the network's PR department, as well as Michael Freeman's *ESPN: The Uncensored History* and Michael Winship's *Television*. For the brief biographical sketch on Dick Vitale, I referred to Vitale's book *Vitale*, written with Curry Kirkpatrick.

33 "If you're a fan": Replay of first *SportsCenter* broadcast, 9/7/79.

33 "cable television's most ambitious concept": "An All-Sports TV Network," Harry F. Waters with Cynthia H. Wilson, *Newsweek*, 11/12/79.

34 so much Australian Rules Football: "Sports Junkie's Video Heaven," T. R. Reinman, *San Diego Union-Tribune*, 7/2/84.

36 "Everybody's supposed to have a gimmick": "Chris (not Shelly) Berman Cracks Up TV Sports Fans," Nick Canepa, *San Diego Union-Tribune*, 7/4/86.

37 "whereas Howard Cosell can appeal": "Hey, DV, Lower the Volume!" William Taaffe, SI, 5/14/84.

37 "The guy's great!": Canepa, *San Diego Union-Tribune*, 7/4/86.

38   "We had all these ways": AI Mike Caster.

38   To the attention of Charles Dolan: AI Charles Warner.

38   "the largest unregulated monopoly": "Cable TV's Cloudy Skies Could Brighten," Lynda D. McCormick, *Christian Science Monitor*, 12/31/84.

III.

There are several books about the fall and rise of Nike in the 1980s, as well as the advent of the Air Jordan shoe and the iconography of Jordan himself. Most crucial for me were David Halberstam's *Playing for Keeps*, J. B. Strasser and Laurie Becklund's *Swoosh*, and Jim Naughton's *Taking to the Air*. I also interviewed Jim Riswold and Mike Caster, who were both intimately involved with Nike's marketing campaigns.

39   "On September 15": Nike Air Jordan ad, via YouTube.

40   "those are the Devil's colors": Halberstam, p. 145.

40   $2.1 million quarterly loss: Strasser/Becklund, p. 457.

41   "we wouldn't necessarily": "Nike Loses Its Footing on the Fast Track," Eleanor Johnson Tracy, *Fortune*, 11/12/84.

42   "I did think the black and red": AI Mike Caster.

42   "If Michael Jordan": Halberstam, p. 146.

IV.

Information about Auburn's minority enrollment and the lawsuit against the university were drawn from David Rosenblatt's paper on Bo Jackson.

44   "a big strong kid": AI Pat Dye.

44   Auburn boosters bought his mother: Schaap interviews.

45   "couldn't dribble a basketball": Pearlman, *Boys Will Be Boys*, p. 65.

45   4.175 40-yard dash: "Which Way Will You Go, Bo?" Ralph Wiley, SI, 12/14/87.

46   "My approach to it": AI Pat Dye.

46   "Bo, do you realize": Ibid.

47 "I wish I could do both": "Which Way You Gonna Go, Bo?" N. Brooks Clark, SI, 5/13/85.

48 "I'll get 10 pieces of paper": "Running From a Troubled Childhood, Bo Jackson Rushes Toward the Heisman and—Just Maybe—NFL Glory," Jack Friedman, *People,* 12/2/85.

48 "There are some things in life": "Jackson's disappearing act sabotages Tigers' high hopes," Paul Finebaum, *Birmingham Post-Herald,* 11/4/85.

49 "In big games, Bo grabs"—"What the Heck, Why Not Dudek?" Rick Reilly, SI, 12/2/85.

49 "I can't go out": Schaap interviews.

49 "He didn't get a thrill": AI Pat Dye.

50 "He said that Bo Jackson": "Broyle's Secret Play Thrown for Loss," Michael Goodwin, NYT, 12/3/85.

50 X-rays: "X-rays leave no doubt about Bo's ribs," Kevin Scarbinsky, *Birmingham News,* 12/5/85.

50 "submit to the court": Rosenblatt paper on Bo Jackson.

51 Keller . . . came by practice: Strasser/Becklund, p. 492

V.

51 "dunking song": "A Real Downer," Thomas Bonk, LAT, 2/10/85.

52 "I feel like I can trust": "Some Big Players Sure Act Small," Steve Daley, CT, 2/14/85.

53 "It's become our Cabbage Patch": "Michael Jordan Shoe Also Having Big Rookie Season," George Lazarus, CT, 5/14/85.

Interlude

I spent time with Lonise Bias in Greenwood, South Carolina, and in Washington, D.C., in the winter and spring of 2008. This section is based largely on those interviews and is adapted from a story originally written for ESPN .com ("The Day Innocence Died") in the summer of 2008. It also includes the remembrances of several people who contacted me after that article appeared. I also consulted a pair of books written about the Bias tragedy in the 1980s, C. Fraser Smith's *Lenny, Lefty and the Chancellor* and Lewis Cole's *Never Too Young to Die.*

Chapter Three

61   "You are not the kind": McInerney, p. 1.

I.

61   Even as she fought back: AI Lonise Bias; Smith, p. 103.

61   "the surliest, the most uncooperative": Smith, p. 101.

62   despite even the sworn testimony: Cole, p. 229.

II.

For my research into the history and culture of cocaine use in America, I used the reports of the newsweeklies cited in the text, as well as Dominic Streatfeild's *Cocaine: An Unauthorized Biography* and Dan Baum's *Smoke and Mirrors: The War on Drugs and the Politics of Failure.* I also spoke with Dan Baum and Eric Sterling, president of the Criminal Justice Policy Foundation.

63   "blowing life into your": "Tyrannical King Coke," *Time,* 4/16/73.

63   "there's not a great deal": Baum, p. 98.

63   "a supremely beguiling": "Cocaine: Middle Class High," Michael Demarest, *Time,* 7/6/81.

64   "It wasn't just the professional athlete": AI Micheal Ray Richardson.

65   "Absolutely no craving": "Anatomy of the Drug Issue," Peter Kerr, NYT, 11/17/86.

65   "Where should athletes": "Philadelphia Heirlooms, Fame & Fortune on Horseback, Are Pep-Up Pills Cricket?" SI, 11/15/54.

65   "Individuals and teams": "Editorials," SI, 11/21/60.

65 "the excessive and secretive": "Problems in a Turned-On World," Bil Gilbert, SI, 6/23/69.

65 "Pregame medication is": AI Thomas Henderson; Henderson, p. 171.

66 "Early in use": Kerr, NYT, 11/17/86.

III.

Sports Illustrated published its Don Reese cover story on June 14, 1982, with an extensive follow-up on July 5. Michael Oriard's book *Brand NFL* was also a valuable resource for this section. I based my portrait of the Pittsburgh drug trials and their many revelations on newspaper and magazine accounts of the time, as well as retrospectives written by Andrew Conte ("Deja Vu Again," *Pittsburgh Tribune-Review*, 12/19/04) and Chuck Finder ("Trying Times," *Pittsburgh Post-Gazette*, 6/11/95).

67 "Football players who partied": Oriard, p. 107.

67 "If you put him": "Out of Context," John Powers, *Boston Globe*, 6/22/86.

68 "Your idols have": "Issues Remain Unsettled After Strong's Drug Trial," Mark Asher, WP, 9/22/85.

68 "It is these high-priced": Alan Robinson, AP, 9/21/85.

69 his own sixteen-year cocaine: "Seeking Help," NYT, 7/5/86.

69 Dale Berra, Lonnie Smith, Keith Hernandez: "Berra: Cocaine Easy to Get," Sam Smith, CT, 9/10/85. Also "Baseball Drug Trial Has Soap Opera Air," Pohla Smith, UPI, 9/7/85; Finder, *Post-Gazette*, 6/11/95.

70 "have learned the evils": Asher, WP, 9/22/85.

70 "We have abandoned": "Cocaine: Middle Class High," Michael Demarest, *Time*, 7/6/81.

71 Juror quotes: Robinson, AP, 9/21/85.

71 "Just say no": Baum, p. 199.

71 "baseball's drug problem": Alan Robinson, AP, 9/22/86.

72 "A new form": "A New, Purified Form of Cocaine Causes Alarm As Abuse Increases," Jane Gross, NYT, 11/29/85.

72   Coy Bacon: AI Coy Bacon.

73   Thomas Henderson: AI Thomas Henderson; Henderson book.

73   "sounded like a new drug": Streatfeild, p. 296.

IV.

I based my portrait of Micheal Ray Richardson on articles and accounts from that time, as well as a telephone interview I conducted with him.

74   In one essay: "Bittersweet," Bill Brubaker, SI, 2/4/85.

74   "A victim of the times": "The Troubling Career of Micheal Ray Richardson," Sam McManis, LAT, 2/28/86.

75   75 percent of NBA players used cocaine: "N.B.A. Adds Counseling Service," Sam Goldaper, NYT, 3/17/81.

76   "It was what he wanted": "A Party, A Binge, A Void," Gerald Eskenazi, NYT, 6/25/90.

78   "Here's a kid": McManis, LAT, 2/28/86.

V.

Most of the details about the lead-up to Len Bias's senior season were drawn from news accounts in the wake of Bias's death, the Lewis Cole and Fraser Smith books and interviews with Lonise Bias and several reporters who covered the Bias story, plus the ESPN SportsCentury documentary on Taylor and Kirk Fraser's 2009 documentary "Without Bias." For my portrait of Lawrence Taylor, I relied on copious news accounts—most notably Bill Brubaker's "Taylor: A Troubled Giant" (WP, April 6, 1986), as well as Taylor's two autobiographies, *LT: Living on the Edge* and *LT: Over the Edge,* Michael Lewis's *The Blind Side,* and ESPN's SportsCentury documentary on Taylor.

79   "Len Bias has a chance": "Peak of Bias," John Feinstein, WP, 3/7/85.

80   "Sometimes I couldn't control": Taylor/Serby, p. 63.

81   "What I remember": Taylor/Serby, p. 89.

81   "When somebody calls me": Taylor/Falkner, p. 5.

82   "Cocaine was illegal": Taylor/Falkner, p. 155.

83   Maryland drug testing: Smith, p. 105.

83   "Sometimes you do things": Smith, p. 107.

Chapter Four

84   "You know what": http://www.ultimatedynasty.net/quotes.html.

I.

86   "His belly did not": Nack, p. 264.

86   "I was big, even when": "Bears Swallow Hard, Pick Perry," Bill Jauss, CT, 5/1/85.

86   "I'm very excited": Ibid.

86   "Buddy liked playing": AI Chet Coppock.

87   "a wasted draft choice": "Warming Up the Fridge," Roger Wolmuth, *People*, 9/9/85.

87   Gimme da ball: Mullin, p. 75.

88   "If a lot is two bottles": Ditka/Pierson, p. 182. Also Keteyian, p. 13.

90   "Through a guy like": "Refrigerator Turns on Hungry Public," Michael Janofsky, CT, 11/10/85.

91   "The reason Fridge": Mullin, p. 83.

91   "He was American excess": "American Sports, American Excess. No Thanks," Mark Hodgkinson, NYT, 10/28/07.

II.

91   "a full-blown expression": MacCambridge, *America's Game*, p. 245.

93   "At no time during": Ibid, p. 341.

93   "Turmoil Page": "Pete, the Way They Play Today Stinks," Paul Zimmerman, SI, 12/12/83.

93   "I think there was some truth": AI Don Pierson.

94   "We were children": AI Hub Arkush.

95   "I like to think": "McMahon Enjoys Head-Case Image," Bob Verdi, CT, 1/13/86.

95   "from that first generation": "Born to Be Wild," David Breskin, *Rolling Stone*, 3/13/86.

III.

For insight into Jim McMahon's childhood and college career, I relied on several articles, as well as McMahon's autobiography, the ESPN SportsCentury documentary on McMahon, and interviews with McMahon; his high school teacher Eleanor Olson; his high school coaches Fred Thompson and Ted Smith; and his friends Pat Hanley and Fred Fernandes.

96   "If you don't feel": "Winning Mystique," Phil Hersh, CT, 1/5/86.

96   "She slapped me": "McMahon Doesn't Fit the Mold But He Passes Test," Alan Greenberg, LAT, 12/14/80.

97   "We've a got a new starting": AI Fred Thompson.

98   "At BYU": AI Pat Hanley.

99   BYU honor code: http://honorcode.byu.edu.

100   "You couldn't even": "Born to Be Wild," David Breskin, *Rolling Stone*, 3/13/86.

101   "Every Monday": AI Jim McMahon.

101   "Mormon superman": McMahon/Verdi, p. 191.

102   "Until recently, football": "Suddenly, College Coaches Have Made an Amazing Discovery," LAT, 11/13/80.

104   "You're crazy": McMahon/Verdi, p. 197.

105   "The school got": "College Teaches Athletes a Lesson," Steve Daley, CT, 2/12/82.

105   "I would like to be": "Jim McMahon Can Hardly Wait to Escape BYU," Chris Cobbs, LAT, 12/4/81.

106   "Jim is a taker": AI Eleanor Olson; "Winning Mystique," Phil Hersh, CT, 1/5/86.

IV.

106 "You might even say": AI Ken Valdiserri.

106 "creative dissonance": AI Rick Telander.

106 "There were daily": AI Kurt Becker.

107 "with an ego as big": AI Chet Coppock.

107 "Jim's a smart guy": AI Kurt Becker.

108 "The public must": "Bears Discover Meaning of 8–0," Bob Verdi, CT, 10/31/85.

108 "If bland Boys": "A Bear Called McMahon," *Newsweek*, 10/21/85.

109 "He shit all over": AI Hub Arkush.

109 "A psychobabbling": AI Chet Coppock.

V.

110 "I'd seen it": AI Chet Coppock.

111 "might have made Boy": "Ditka Sees Himself in Rebels," Ray Sons, *Chicago Sun-Times*, January 21, 1986.

111 "I missed one day": AI Jim McMahon.

112 "We're not going to have": Ibid.

112 Soon after: "'Shuffle' Sires Mess of Mimics," Paul Sullivan, CT, 11/30/86.

Interlude

I interviewed John Shaffer at his home in late 2006.

114 "I do think he would have a hard time": AI Don Meyers.

114 "Their quarterback?": AI Winston Moss.

115 dislocate his shoulder: "Penn State Player Hit By a High 5," NYT, 10/23/84.

116 "I really trusted": AI John Shaffer.

116 "In the fifties": "One Champion After All," Tom Callahan, *Time*, 1/13/86.

117 "It's just too bad": Ibid.

Chapter Five

118 "So what if": "The Bear in Mind," Curry Kirkpatrick, SI, 2/3/86.

I.

119 "We have a hundred and ten": Presidential News Conference, 1/7/86.

119 "I might have a beer": Nicholas K. Geranios, AP, 12/31/85.

120 "I'm thinking in terms of": Paterno/Asbell, p. 118.

120 "Joe Paterno assaulted": O'Brien, p. 126.

120 "a bunch of babies": "For Joe Paterno, Tough Climb Back," Malcolm Moran, NYT, 11/17/85.

121 "In the dark days": AI John Shaffer.

121 "Barry and I": Switzer/Shrake, Foreword.

122 the SEC filed: March 22, 1984.

122 "struck up feuds": "No Doubt About It: Oklahoma's No. 1," Rick Reilly, SI, 1/13/86.

122 "As a winner": "New Philadelphia Story," Douglas Looney, SI, 6/20/83.

II.

Several stories about Bosworth's post-football career proved helpful in writing about him, including Steve Weinstein's "The New Land of Boz" (LAT, 3/3/91) and Steve Minutaglio's "The Boz Within" (*Sporting News*, 6/30/97).

123 "the most boring decade": Bosworth/Reilly, p. 61.

124 "balance on that line": "Bosworth: Getting Better Means Getting Tougher," Malcolm Moran, NYT, 8/24/86.

124 He admitted to *Sports Illustrated*: "Have a Rattle in Your GM Auto? Check with Oklahoma University," Jacob M. Schlesinger, *Wall Street Journal*, 10/17/86.

125 "Somewhere in there": Bosworth/Reilly, p. 121.

127 Jerome Brown wrote: "Oklahoma Could Tell Miami Was in for a Fall," Randy Harvey, LAT, 1/3/86.

III.

127 "dancing and jiving": "Bears Don't Plan to Let Chicago Down," Don Pierson, CT, 1/3/86.

127 "First we have to": Ibid.

128 "Lawrence, Lawrence something": "Big, Bad Bears Meet Old What's-His-Name and Giants Today," Mike Downey, LAT, 1/5/86.

128 "like a little kid": "Bears Knock Giants Cold," Don Pierson, CT, 1/6/86.

129 "What kind of": "Morning Briefing," LAT, 1/7/86.

129 "Sophisticated, pearl-clad": "Fans Tempo Builds to Crescendo," Andy Knott, CT, 1/20/86.

130 "Ryan and Ditka": AI Don Pierson.

130 "I don't think": "Grabowski Town," Paul Galloway, CT, 1/19/86.

130 "My offensive linemen": "Jim McMahon Is No Passing Fancy," Jack Friedman, *People*, 1/6/86.

131 "That's publicity": "McHeadband Is 'Different,'" Dave Anderson, NYT, 1/13/86; "To the NFL, McMahon's Headband Spells Trouble," Christine Brennan, WP, 1/12/86.

131 "He was a crazy": "Slam! Bam! Goodby Rams!" Rick Telander, SI, 1/20/86.

IV.

My portrait of Super Bowl week in 1986 was drawn from articles in the *Chicago Tribune*, the *Sun-Times*, and other national papers, as well as interviews with several journalists who covered the game. Many of the details of McMahon's debauchery in New Orleans are taken from David Breskin's *Rolling Stone* cover story, as well as interviews with McMahon and Kurt Becker.

132 "it was still jarring": *America's Game*, p. 254.

133 "It was the beginning": AI Thomas Henderson.

134 "If Jim can go down there": Skip Myslenski and Linda Kay, CT, 1/14/86.

V.

135 "fame broker": "Sore McMahon Irritates Media," Bernie Lincicome, CT, 1/22/86.

136 "If it works": "Sticking Point," Don Pierson, CT, 1/21/86.

136 "I don't want no job": Lincicome, CT, 1/22/86.

137 "walking testimonial": Ira Kaufman, UPI, 1/23/86.

137 "This is a noncontroversy": "McMahon Punctures Bears Peace," Clark Judge, *San Diego Union-Tribune*, 1/21/86.

137 "I stick pins": "McMahon's Point Man Is on Hand," NYT, 1/23/86; "Bottom Line: It Works," Bob Verdi, CT, 1/23/86.

138 "I felt sorry": AI Kurt Becker.

139 "He's my friend": Ibid.

140 "You rotten son": AI Jim McMahon; Mullin, p. 144; McMahon/Verdi, p. 27.

142 "He did [say it]": Mullin, p. 168.

142 Y'all bettuh: Mullin, p. 147.

142 "There's no way": AI Jim McMahon; McMahon/Verdi, p. 31.

143 "It was fucking hell": AI Jim McMahon.

143 "I can't go anywhere": Breskin, *Rolling Stone*, 3/13/86.

144 otherwise, they're going: Mullin, p. 144.

144 locked himself in a storage closet: Mullin, p. 160.

145 "loudmouths and cheap-shot": AI Chet Coppock; "Ditka Rips Pat 'Loudmouths,'" Dan Pompei, *Chicago Sun-Times*, 1/26/86.

146 "I thought the entire system": "Shocking News Staggers City," CT, 1/29/86

Chapter Six

147 "At a news conference": "Reagan Supports 4th Orbiter for Space Shuttle Program," David Sanger, NYT, 6/12/86.

I.

147 "the fellow on welfare": Cannon, p. 440; Slansky, p. 153.

148 "And I want to say": Presidential Address, 1/28/86.

149 THE DAY GEN X: Kevin Smokler, *Baltimore Sun*, 2/3/06.

II.

For my portrait of Lefty Driesell, I relied on news reports and in-depth features from several local papers, including, most notably, the *Washington Post* and the *Baltimore Sun*. Also, C. Fraser Smith's book provided excellent insight into Driesell's background and character. I also conducted a phone interview with Driesell in March 2008, and spoke to several reporters who covered his teams.

150 "You're still in seventh": "Terrapins Post First ACC Victory," Sally Jenkins, WP, 1/29/86.

150 "the hybrid of a": Smith, p. 115.

151 after a particularly harsh column: AI Ken Denlinger.

152 "I've had (high-school) coaches": "Driesell Lambasts NCAA," Michael Wilbon, WP, 10/15/85.

152 "Coach Driesell is": "Driesell, As Recruiter, Is Deaf to Word No," Bill Brubaker, WP, 7/9/86.

152 "I like talking": "Driesell: The Subject of Some Debate," Sally Jenkins, WP, 2/20/86.

154 "I'm the men's center": Smith, p. 128.

154 "Lefty didn't buy": AI Mark Hyman.

155 "I understand coach": Jenkins, WP, 2/20/86.

III.

My account of the Jan Kemp trial was drawn from newspaper and magazine articles, including Art Harris's "Jan Kemp and the Georgia Judgment" (WP, 2/14/86), Michael Goodwin's "Jan Kemp's Agony in Beating a System" (NYT, 2/16/86), and Randy Harvey's "Fighting the System" (LAT, 2/3/86), as well as daily coverage of the trial from the AP and UPI.

156 "Who do you think": "On Trial in Georgia: Academic Integrity," SI, 1/27/86.

157 "amateurism was just the lie": Telander, p. 54.

157 CBS had paid: "The College Sports Industry," Michael Goodwin, NYT, 6/8/86.

158 school "self-reporting": AI Chuck Smrt.

159 "These wealthy-businessmen": "Football and Cheap Ego-Gratification," David Broder, WP, 3/11/87.

160 "reanalyze their own policies": "Kemp Case Seen Having Major Impact," Michael Wilbon and Ed Nicklas, WP, 2/14/86.

160 "The nerds were right": "The Nerds Were Right," Richard Cohen, WP, 2/19/86.

160 Meanwhile, Len Bias: "Aftermath of Bias' Death: Questions About His Life," Sally Jenkins and Michael Wilbon, WP, 8/18/86.

IV.

161 "Basic Bias": "Bias: A Master of His Craft," Thomas Boswell, WP, 2/22/86.

161 "WHAT HAPPENED": "Terrapins Savor Taste of Triumph," Sally Jenkins, WP, 2/22/86.

162 "No comment": "Bias, Berry Are No. 2 and No. 1, Perhaps Not Respectively," Mark Heisler, LAT, 3/16/86.

163 "I agree with Reagan's": "Reagan Tuned Out in Full-Court Press," Jon Margolis, CT, 3/18/86.

Chapter Seven

164 "the code of the": Lewis, *Liar's Poker*, p. 17.

I.

For insight into Bo Jackson's thought process as he turned professional, I spoke to his former lawyer Tommy Zieman, as well as his college football coach, Pat Dye, and college baseball coach, Hal Baird. I also relied on my own interview with Bo and the transcripts of Dick Schaap's interviews with him twenty years earlier.

164 Dunlop Pro-Am: "Heisman Winner Won't Say Whether It's Football or Baseball," John F. Bonfatti, AP, 2/10/86.

167 "cut the base in half": AI Hal Baird.

167 *If that big donkey:* AI Hal Baird.

168 "a perfect redneck": "Time Doesn't Heal Wounds for Williams," Gary Shelton, *St. Petersburg Times,* 7/11/90.

168 being counseled: AI Bo Jackson; Schaap interviews.

168 "I'd like to pull him": "Culverhouse: The Old Schemer's Legacy," Mike McLeod and Mike Thomas, *Orlando Sentinel,* 3/2/97.

169 "Young black guys": Schaap interviews.

169 "Bo still has": "Tampa Bay Thought It Had All the Bases Covered," Gordon Forbes, *USA Today,* 4/1/86.

170 "The culpability": AI Hal Baird.

170 "I refuse to be": Sporting News, *Bo Stories,* p. 74.

II.

To gain perspective on Michael Jordan's foot injury and his sixty-three-point game against the Celtics, I relied on David Halberstam's *Playing for Keeps*—the seminal book on Jordan's career and cultural impact—as well as Peter May's *The Last Banner,* J. B. Strasser and Laurie Becklund's *Swoosh,* articles from the *Chicago Tribune* and *Sports Illustrated,* and a conversation with former Nike executive Mike Caster.

171 He missed basketball: "Players," Roy S. Johnson, SI, 3/11/86.

171 "What Michael is doing": "Air Jordan Has No Fear of Flying," SI, 3/24/86.

172 "While you can't question": Ibid.

III.

Tommy Zieman, one of Bo Jackson's former managers, filled me in on the negotiations and Bo Jackson's mind-set as he chose between football and baseball, as well as the state of the agenting industry at that seminal moment. Michael Florence's "The Kansas City Deal," which appeared in the October 1986 issue of *Business Alabama* magazine, was also a key resource.

175 the highest-paid: Hal Bock, AP, 4/30/86.
175 "Few persons": "Jackson 1st Choice in Draft," Cooper Rollow, CT, 4/30/86.
176 "The sad fact": Strasser/Becklund, p. 472. This section was also informed by Naomi Klein's book *No Logo*.
178 "plantation stepchild": Strasser/Becklund, p. 494; AI Tommy Zieman.
179 "Was it for love": Jonathan Vitti, AP, 6/22/86.
179 "Let me state": "Bo's Blast: 450 Feet Plus," Dave Anderson, NYT, 6/23/86.

IV.

For information on Ivan Boesky and his speech, I relied on James B. Stewart's book *Den of Thieves*.

Interlude

183 "What can I do": AI Lonise Bias.
183 "The current generation": "Desperate Over Drugs at Home, Kids Are Turning In Mom and Dad," Montgomery Brower, *People*, 9/29/86.
184 "All of us": AI Eric Sterling.

Chapter Eight

I.

My account of Len Bias's final days is drawn from countless television reports—as archived at the University of Maryland—as well as articles in the *Washington Post* and *Baltimore Sun*, books by C. Fraser Smith and Lewis Cole, and a number of interviews with reporters and other observers. Sections of this chapter are adapted from my ESPN.com article "The Day Innocence Died."

186　these sounds compared: FBI file on Leonard Bias.

187　The 911 call was released to the public and replayed on numerous television reports.

188　he was "a horse": Smith, p. 13.

189　"I think it's very fair": "Rich 76ers and Celtics Get Richer In Lottery," Sam McManis, LAT, 5/12/86.

189　"We're an old team": "No Stopping 'Em," Jack McCallum, SI, 6/16/86.

190　flustered by a nightmare: TV news reports; Smith, p. 1.

190　"young, bare-chested": "Crack Explodes on U.S. Drug Scene," Jane Rosen, *Guardian*, 6/16/86.

190　"almost instantaneous": Baum, p. 219.

191　"The typical crack murder": Levitt/Dubner, p. 134.

191　"made me feel like": "Battling the Enemy Within," Janice Castro, *Time*, 3/17/86.

191　"not living with blacks": Baum, p. 223.

192　"It's everywhere": "An Inferno of Craving, Dealing and Despair," Peter McKillop, *Newsweek*, 6/16/86.

192　"six inches of paperwork": "Draft Daze," Paul Forrester, SI.com, 6/23/06.

193　"I'm suspicious": TBS Broadcast of 1986 NBA draft, via NBA TV.

193　"Time goes": Ibid.

194　"Even your fingernails": Smith, p. 6.

194　in constant search of a paycheck: Cole, p. 245.

194 at Chapter III: "Aftermath of Bias' Death: Questions About His Life," Sally Jenkins and Michael Wilbon, WP, 8/18/86.

II.

196 Tribble declined: Brian Tribble, in an appearance on ESPN's Scott Van Pelt radio show on November 3, 2009, was asked whether he or Bias had provided the drugs that evening. "That right there is a question that is really never going to get answered," he said, "because of, the fact is, Leonard's not here to defend himself, and I can't, you know, do it, and it's just you need both people here to be fair about that."

196 "Brian was a drug dealer": AI Derrick Curry.

197 WAKE THE FUCK UP: Smith, p. 11.

197 Statter phoned a woman: AI Dave Statter.

198 "one of the cruelest things": "The Mystery of a Star's Death," *Newsweek*, 6/30/86.

198 "He's already gone": AI Lonise Bias.

III.

Much of this section is drawn from the archives of news broadcasts centered on the coverage of Bias's death, which are housed at the University of Maryland.

199 "I think today": AI Dave Statter.

200 "Lenny elevated": "They Went to Cole to Light a Candle," Tony Kornheiser, WP, 6/20/86.

202 "It was awful": AI Frank Herzog.

202 "God sometimes uses": Smith, p. 35.

203 "interrupted the normal": Bias autopsy report, provided by the State of Maryland.

203 "I can't tell you": "'It Could Have Been Seconds . . . ,'" WP, 6/25/86.

205 "There was no covering": AI Lonise Bias.

206 "We must have a war": Will Dunham, UPI, 6/25/86.

IV.

Sean Harvey's *One Moment Changes Everything* provides a thorough account of the life and death of Don Rogers.

206 a young lawyer: AI Eric Sterling.

207 "People were generally fat": "Bias' Death Fueled Anti-Drug Fervor," Edward Walsh, WP, 9/14/86.

208 "the kind of sound": Harvey, p. 122.

Chapter Nine

209 "Bigness apparently": Stewart, p. 97.

I.

For perspective on Bo Jackson's days in Memphis, I relied on my own interviews with Jackson as well as Dick Schaap's, an interview with the Chicks' general manager, George Lapides, and a number of newspaper and magazine articles.

209 "last observed approaching": "A Minor Event Becomes Major," Ross Newhan, LAT, 7/1/86.

210 "the best pure athlete": "Bo's Not One to Go with the Flow," Douglas Looney, SI, 7/14/86.

211 "my trophy case": Newhan, LAT, 7/1/86.

211 "I can't come up": Hoyt Harwell, AP, 8/5/86.

211 Lapides took a midnight: AI George Lapides.

213 "His talent combined": Strasser/Becklund, p. 497.

II.

214 "I mean, ESPN": AI Jim Riswold.

215 "In the modern": Halberstam, p. 186.

III.

Michael MacCambridge's *America's Game* provided a solid background on the rise and fall of the USFL. Several newspapers, and *Sports Illustrated*, provided comprehensive coverage of the antitrust trial.

216 "That's what I'd done": AI Bo Jackson.

216 "monster salary demands": "It's 4th and 10—The NFL Needs a Long Bomb," Thomas Moore, *Fortune*, 8/4/86.

217 "What a performance!": "Give the First Round to the USFL," William Nack, SI, 7/7/86.

218 "long shot, a lark": Trump/Schwartz, p. 181.

218 "Doug Flutie had": Trump/Schwartz, p. 189.

218 "some stiff": "Rozelle Contradicts Trump," Michael Janofsky, NYT, 7/18/86.

219 "Nail 'em!": "Final Points Made in USFL Suit," Gary Pomerantz, WP, 7/24/86.

220 "cheat myself out of": Jackson/Schaap, p. 148.

Chapter Ten

221 "You don't understand": "A Jolt for Wall St.'s Whiz Kids," Bill Powell and Carolyn Friday, *Newsweek*, 10/26/87.

I.

221 "weirdest sports duet": "Go Downpitch and Buttonhook Smartly, Mate," Rick Telander, SI, 8/11/86.

222 "Jim McMahon must've": Skip Myslenski and Linda Kay, CT, 3/25/86.

223 And then Zucker called: McMahon/Verdi, p. 106; AI Jim McMahon.

223 "shades-and-swagger": "Ad Outlook Mixed for Super Bowl Bears," Robert Raissman, *Advertising Age*, 2/3/86.

223 "I made more": AI Jim McMahon.

224 he hoisted a pair of women: "NFL Gives Folks a Lift in London," Karen DeYoung, WP, 8/3/86.

225 "that the fans knew": "A New Sight in London," Karen DeYoung, WP, 8/3/86.

II.

226 "money days": Keteyian, p. 201.

226 "Our cause": AI Kurt Becker.

226 On an off-season Caribbean: AI Chet Coppock.

226 "It was like *Wheel*": Keteyian, p. 202.

227 groupies atop pool tables: Mullin, p. 180.

228 "More weight is more": AP, 8/13/86.

228 "The inability of teams": "Landry May Be Riding Last Trail," Jerry Magee, *San Diego Union-Tribune*, 7/13/86.

229 "Can you imagine": AP, 9/3/86.

229 "I think we're getting": "No Holds Beared in Chicago," Gene Wojciechowski, LAT, 11/1/86.

III.

230 "a bunch of vile": *The Bad Guys Won*, p. 5.

231 "God-given machines": "Deja Vu Again," Andrew Conte, *Pittsburgh Tribune-Review*, 12/19/04.

IV.

232 "He never had": AI Don Pierson.

233 "What we are seeing here": "Flutie Is Ditka's Shortest Whim," Bernie Lincicome, CT, 10/17/86.

233 What's this fucking Flutie: Keteyian, p. 206.

233 "courtesy of Jim": "Vikes Repay Bears in Full," Don Pierson, CT, 10/21/86.

234 what made McMahon unique: AI Rick Telander.

234 "I shouldn't have played": AI Jim McMahon.

234 "Remember the Oakland": "Morning Briefing," LAT, 11/23/86.

235 columnist Dave Anderson: "X Factor in N.F.L. Violence," Dave Anderson, NYT, 11/30/86.

236 Martin would come to terms: "The Man Behind the Mean," David Haugh, CT, 2/1/05.

236 "As soon as Frank": AI Jim McMahon.

V.

236 "It was new": AI Rick Telander.

237 Dan Hampton insisted: "Hampton Breaks 'Gatorade Dunk' Silence," Barry Rozner, *Chicago Daily Herald*, 11/21/97.

237 "What happened during": AI Ken Valdiserri.

Chapter Eleven

238 "It was the epitome of": "Antidrug Plan Loses Spotlight," Bill Peterson, WP, 1/14/87.

I.

239 "So many different turns": AI Derrick Curry.

II.

239 "Like everyone else": "The Need for Intolerance," Nancy Reagan, WP, 7/7/86.

240 decrease 37 percent: Streatfeild, p. 309.

240 "legislative frenzy": AI Eric Sterling.

240 "The chemistry to create": "Bias' Death Fueled Anti-Drug Fervor," Edward Walsh, WP, 9/14/86.

241 "out of control": Baum, p. 231. This section was also informed by Craig Reinerman and Harry Levine's book, *Crack in America*.

241 "America has accomplished": President's Address to the Nation on the Campaign Against Drug Abuse, 9/14/86.

III.

243 Wendy Whittemore resigned: "Players Counselor Resigns," Mark Asher and Sally Jenkins, WP, 6/25/86.

243 "What the crap?": "Placing the Blame Is Not So Easy," Ken Denlinger, WP, 6/26/86.

243 "M-o-n-e-y": "Driesell Was 'Negligent,' Bias 'Used,' Dad Charges," CT, 8/30/86.

244 "I wasn't going": Cole, p. 249.

244 "trying to save her butt", "jerk": AI Lefty Driesell.

244 "Some guy was doing cocaine": AI Lefty Driesell.

244 "a caricature": "'Win-Or-Else' Puts Lefty In No-Win Spot," Tom Knott, *Washington Times*, 10/30/86.

244 "the scapegoat": "Lefty, They Done You Wrong," Robert D. Novak, WP, 11/2/86.

244 "Lefty is some sort": "Driesell Defends Academics, Vows to Keep His Job," Don Markus, *Baltimore Sun*, 10/1/86.

245 "We recommend": From the Report of the Task Force on Academic Achievement of Student-Athletes, courtesy of the University of Maryland archives.

245 "It's a little hard": AI J. Robert Dorfman.

246 "There was nothing I did wrong": AI Lefty Driesell.

246 "Maybe we should": "One Shock Wave After Another," Craig Neff and Bruce Selcraig, SI, 11/10/86.

247 "Leonard Bias didn't": AI Lefty Driesell.

247 He had abruptly shed: Cannon, p. 599

247 "Sir, if I may": Presidential News Conference, 11/19/86.

248 "here was a man": Cannon, p. 639.

248 "He was no longer": Cannon, p. 657.

248 "Don't worry about laws": Johnson, p. 371.

IV.

248 "from the bottom": "Driesell: Told of Bias Drug Use," Keith Harriston, WP, 5/29/87.

249 "courtesy middleman": "Len Bias' Life Takes on New Meaning a Year After His Death," Keith Harriston, WP, 5/31/87.

249 "I have no doubt": AI Derrick Curry.

249 "I loved Lenny": "Tribble Acquitted of Charges," Keith Harriston, WP, 6/4/87.

250 "After Lenny died": AI Derrick Curry.

250 he went to Miami: "Bias Case Enhanced Tribble's Drug Career," Fern Shen, WP/LAT, 11/25/90.

251 "I think what happened": AI Derrick Curry.

252 "He had ballplayers": AI Derrick Curry.

253 "casual acceptance": The plight of Derrick Curry is expertly chronicled in "A Crack in the System," Richard Leiby, WP, 2/20/94.

Chapter Twelve

256 "*Miami Vice* typically": Reeves/Campbell, p. 257.

I.

For background on the Penn State–Miami game, I relied on more than a dozen interviews with players and coaches, newspaper and magazine articles, as well as several books, including Joe Paterno's autobiography, *Paterno: By the Book*; Michael O'Brien's biography, *No Ordinary Joe*, Lou Prato's *The Penn State Football Encyclopedia*; and Bruce Feldman's *'Cane Mutiny*.

256 78 percent: Slansky, p. 180.

256 "great irresponsibility": "'I'm Not Going to Back Off,'" David Hoffman and Lou Cannon, WP, 12/1/86.

256 "The image of Mr.": "Lordy Me," *Economist*, 12/13/86.

257 "Oh, now and then": "White House Refusing to Clear Up Conflicting Claims on Arms Deal," Terrence Hunt, AP, 12/10/86.

257 Miami, where one linebacker: Feldman, pp. 72–74.

257 "minor incidents": "Off the Field, Testaverde Gets Second Billing," WP, 9/25/86.

257 "to mask nervousness": Feldman, p. 64.

258 "If you asked": AI Alonzo Highsmith.

258 "They made us out": AI Trey Bauer.

II.

259 Such hyperbole: AI Don Meyers.

261 Skinner had generated the notion: AI Bruce Skinner.

262 "The Game That": "Penn State Survives Miami, Hype," Matt Herb, *Daily Collegian*, 1/12/87.

III.

262 In December: "Steroids: 'Scary' Student Body Fad," *Miami Herald*, 12/21/86.

262 "Anybody could tell": Switzer/Shrake, p. 239.

263 fifty-nine-page list: "NCAA Is Hoping for Positive Outcome in Area of Deterrence," Richard Hoffer, LAT, 12/26/86.

263 "aren't destroying": "Bosworth Faces the Music," Craig Neff, SI, 1/5/87.

264 "a bunch of": Bosworth/Reilly, p. 184.

264 "took a shotgun": "As Always, 'Boz' Was Boggling," John Freeman, *San Diego Union-Tribune*, 1/2/87.

IV.

265 "Four o'clock": AIs Don Meyers, Sam Jankovich.

266 "We're one big": Herschel Nissenson, AP, 12/29/86.

267 "They were a bunch": AI Trey Bauer.

V.

268 What am I doing here?: AI John Shaffer.

268 "When you look at it": AI Bruce Skinner.

283 the most blatant confrontation: O'Brien, p. 136.

268 "I think they're nothing": "Guts, Brains and Glory," Rick Reilly, SI, 1/12/87.

268 "To this day": AI Alonzo Highsmith.

270 "I think it's awfully easy": From NBC broadcast, 1/2/87.

270 "Was he kidding?": "Gipper Tries to Win One for Himself at Halftime," Howard Rosenberg, LAT, 1/5/87.

271 "However historians would judge him": Johnson, p. 459.

Epilogue

The bulk of this chapter is formed from personal encounters I had with Jim McMahon, Bo Jackson, and Lonise Bias.

272 "They called it": Ronald Reagan, Farewell Address to the Nation, 1/11/89.

I.

273 "I'm too drunk": "Former Bears QB McMahon Charged with DUI in Florida," AP, 11/9/03.

273 "I think Jim never": AI Pat Hanley.

274 Bears . . . reflective of the times: AI Rick Telander.

275 "That's what I'm most proud of": AI Jim McMahon.

II.

276 "I wasn't scared": AI Bo Jackson.

278 "I'm thinking about": "Bo Jackson's New Hobby: Football," AP/NYT, 7/12/87.

278 "To be a great": "Royally Bruised Ego Looks for Way Out," Thomas Boswell, WP, 7/14/87.

278 "All he did": *Sporting News Bo Stories*, p. 137.

279 "Boz and I": "Just Which Game Are You Playing, Bo?" Mark Heisler, LAT, 12/2/87.

279 "I'm always surprised": AI Jim Riswold.

281 "I report today": "Yes, Bo Even Knows . . ." Leigh Montville, SI, 2/12/90.

281 "the gods of sports": Jackson/Schaap, pp. 265–66.

282 "All the athletes today": AI Jim Riswold.

283 "I know how to feed": AI Bo Jackson.

III.

284 "It's not that I'm just": AI Lonise Bias.

Bibliography

Arledge, Roone. *Roone: A Memoir*. New York: HarperCollins, 2003.

Baum, Dan. *Smoke and Mirrors: The War on Drugs and the Politics of Failure*. New York: Little, Brown and Company, 1997.

Bosworth, Brian, with Rick Reilly. *The Boz: Confessions of a Modern Anti-Hero*. New York: Doubleday, 1988.

Boyarsky, Bill. *Ronald Reagan: His Life & Rise to the Presidency*. New York: Random House, 1981.

Brown, Scott, and Will Collier. *The Uncivil War: Alabama vs. Auburn, 1981–1994*. Nashville: Rutledge Hill Press, 1995.

Cannon, Lou. *President Reagan: The Role of a Lifetime*. New York: PublicAffairs, 2000.

Chicago Tribune (eds.), *The '85 Bears: Still Chicago's Team*. Chicago: Triumph Books, 2005.

Cole, Lewis. *Never Too Young to Die: The Death of Len Bias*. New York: Pantheon Books, 1989.

Ditka, Mike, with Don Pierson. *Ditka: An Autobiography*. Chicago: Bonus Books, 1987.

Ditka, Mike, with Rick Telander. *In Life, First You Kick Ass: Reflections on the 1985 Bears and Wisdom from Da Coach*. Champaign, Ill.: Sports Publishing LLC, 2005.

Feldman, Bruce. *'Cane Mutiny: How the Miami Hurricanes Overturned the Football Establishment.* New York: New American Library, 2004.

Freeman, Michael. *ESPN: The Uncensored History.* Dallas: Taylor Publishing Company, 2000.

Halberstam, David. *Playing for Keeps: Michael Jordan and the World He Made.* New York: Broadway Books, 2000.

Harvey, Sean D. *One Moment Changes Everything: The All-America Tragedy of Don Rogers.* Champaign, Ill.: Sports Publishing LLC, 2007.

Henderson, Thomas, with Peter Knobler. *Out of Control: Confessions of an NFL Casualty.* New York: Pocket Books, 1987.

Henderson, Thomas, with Frank Luksa. *In Control: The Rebirth of an NFL Legend.* Austin, Texas: Thomas Henderson Publishing, 2004.

Jackson, Bo, and Dick Schaap. *Bo Knows Bo.* New York: Jove Books, 1991.

Johnson, Haynes. *Sleepwalking Through History: America in the Reagan Years.* New York: W. W. Norton & Company, 2003.

Kanner, Bernice. *The Super Bowl of Advertising.* Princeton: Bloomberg Press, 2004.

Keteyian, Armen. *Ditka: Monster of the Midway.* New York: Pocket Books, 1992.

Klein, Naomi. *No Logo.* New York: Picador, 2002.

Kriegel, Mark. *Namath: A Biography.* New York: Penguin Books, 2005.

Levitt, Steven D., and Stephen J. Dubner. *Freakonomics: A Rogue Economist Explores the Hidden Side of Everything.* New York: William Morrow, 2005.

Lewis, Michael. *The Blind Side: Evolution of a Game.* New York: W. W. Norton & Company, 2006.

Lewis, Michael. *Liar's Poker: Rising Through the Wreckage on Wall Street.* New York: W. W. Norton & Company, 1989.

Bibliography

MacCambridge, Michael. *America's Game: The Epic Story of How Pro Football Captured a Nation.* New York: Anchor Books, 2005.

MacCambridge, Michael. *The Franchise: A History of Sports Illustrated Magazine.* New York: Hyperion, 1997.

Maisel, Ivan, and Kelly Whiteside. *A War in Dixie.* New York: Harper-Collins, 2001.

May, Peter. *The Last Banner: The Story of the 1985–86 Celtics, the NBA's Greatest Team of All Time.* Holbrook, Mass.: Adams Media Corporation, 1996.

McInerney, Jay. *Bright Lights, Big City.* New York: Vintage Books, 1984.

McMahon, Jim, with Bob Verdi. *McMahon!* New York: Warner Books, 1987.

McMichael, Steve, with Phil Arvia. *Steve McMichael's Tales from the Bears Sideline.* Champaign, Ill.: Sports Publishing LLC, 2004.

Mills, Nicolaus (ed.). *Culture in an Age of Money: The Legacy of the 1980s in America.* Chicago: Ivan R. Dee, 1990.

Missianelli, M. G. *The Perfect Season: How Penn State Came to Stop a Hurricane and Win a Championship.* University Park: The Pennsylvania State University Press, 2007.

Mullin, John. *The Rise and Self-Destruction of the Greatest Football Team in History: The Chicago Bears and Super Bowl XX.* Chicago: Triumph Books, 2005.

Murray, Jim. *Jim Murray: An Autobiography.* New York: Macmillan, 1993.

Nack, William. *My Turf: Horses, Boxers, Blood Money, and the Sporting Life.* Cambridge, Mass.: Da Capo Press, 2003.

Naughton, Jim. *Taking to the Air: The Rise of Michael Jordan.* New York: Warner Books, 1992.

O'Brien, Michael. *No Ordinary Joe: The Biography of Joe Paterno.* Nashville: Rutledge Hill Press, 1999.

Oriard, Michael. *Brand NFL: Making & Selling America's Favorite Sport.* Chapel Hill: The University of North Carolina Press, 2007.

Paterno, Joe, with Bernard Asbell. *Paterno: By the Book.* New York: Random House, 1989.

Pearlman, Jeff. *The Bad Guys Won.* New York: HarperCollins, 2004.

Pearlman, Jeff. *Boys Will Be Boys: The Glory Days and Party Nights of the Dallas Cowboys Dynasty.* New York: HarperCollins, 2008.

Pelecanos, George P. *The Sweet Forever.* New York: Little, Brown and Company, 1998.

Prato, Louis. *The Penn State Football Encyclopedia.* Champaign, Ill.: Sports Publishing, Inc., 1998.

Reagan, Ronald. *An American Life.* New York: Pocket Books, 1990.

Reeves, Jimmie L., and Richard Campbell. *Cracked Coverage: Television News, the Anti-Cocaine Crusade and the Reagan Legacy.* Durham, N.C.: Duke University Press, 1994.

Reinarman, Craig, and Harry G. Levine (eds.). *Crack in America: Demon Drugs and Social Justice.* Berkeley: University of California Press, 1997.

Sewall, Gilbert T. (ed.). *The Eighties: A Reader.* Reading, Mass: Addison-Wesley, 1997.

Slansky, Paul. *The Clothes Have No Emperor: A Chronicle of the American '80s.* New York: Fireside/Simon & Schuster, 1989.

Smith, C. Fraser. *Lenny, Lefty and the Chancellor.* Baltimore: The Bancroft Press, 1992.

Sporting News (eds.). *Bo Stories.* St. Louis: The Sporting News Publishing Co., 1990.

Stewart, James B. *Den of Thieves.* New York: Touchstone/Simon & Schuster, 1992.

Bibliography

Strasser, J. B., and Laurie Becklund. *Swoosh: The Unauthorized Story of Nike and the Men Who Played There.* New York: HarperBusiness, 1993.

Streatfeild, Dominic. *Cocaine: An Unauthorized Biography.* New York: Picador, 2001.

Switzer, Barry, with Bud Shrake. *Bootlegger's Boy.* New York: William Morrow and Company, 1990.

Taylor, Lawrence, with David Falkner. *LT: Living on the Edge.* New York: Times Books, 1987.

Taylor, Lawrence, with Steve Serby. *LT: Over the Edge.* New York: Harper-Collins, 2003.

Telander, Rick. *The Hundred Yard Lie: The Corruption of College Football and What We Can Do to Stop It.* New York: Fireside/Simon & Schuster, 1989.

Trump, Donald J., with Tony Schwartz. *Trump: The Art of the Deal.* New York: Random House, 1987.

Vitale, Dick, with Curry Kirkpatrick. *Vitale.* New York: Simon & Schuster, 1988.

Winship, Michael. *Television.* New York: Random House, 1988.

Wolfe, Tom. *The Bonfire of the Vanities.* London: Picador, 1990.

Video

1985 Chicago Bears: 12 Classic Games. NFL Productions LLC, 2007.

America's Game: 1985 Chicago Bears. NFL Productions LLC, 2007.

Classic Nike commercial DVD, courtesy of Jim Riswold, Wieden and Kennedy.

ESPN SportsCenter Flashback: Len Bias.

ESPN SportsCentury: 1986.

Bibliography

ESPN SportsCentury: Bo Jackson.

ESPN SportsCentury: Jim McMahon.

ESPN SportsCentury: Lawrence Taylor.

Len Bias Death Investigation: July 1986–June 1987 (news reports), courtesy University of Maryland.

NBA's Top 10 Greatest Games. NBA Entertainment, 2005.

News Reports Surrounding the Death of Len Bias: June 19, 1986, through July 25, 1986, courtesy University of Maryland.

U, The, dir. Billy Corben. Rakontur/ESPN Films, 2009.

Without Bias, dir. Kirk Fraser. May 3rd Films/ESPN Films, 2009.

Index

Note: Page numbers followed by an *n* refer to notes.

Index

Index

Index

Index